James H. Graff, Frederick Gilbert, Miriam Ross

Against Tide

A Story of a Poor Street Arab

James H. Graff, Frederick Gilbert, Miriam Ross

Against Tide
A Story of a Poor Street Arab

ISBN/EAN: 9783744760003

Printed in Europe, USA, Canada, Australia, Japan

Cover: Foto ©ninafisch / pixelio.de

More available books at **www.hansebooks.com**

THE FAVOURITE ILLUSTRATED MAGAZINE OF THE DAY,
AND CHEAPEST IN THE WORLD,

BOW BELLS,

Is Published Every Wednesday. Each Number Contains
Twenty-four Large Folio Pages of Original Matter, and about Twelve
Illustrations by Eminent Artists.

The General Contents consist of
TWO OR THREE CONTINUOUS NOVELS, COMPLETE STORIES, PICTURESQUE SKETCHES; Adventures, National Customs, and Curious Facts; Biographical Memoi... ...ld to the Ladies; New and Original Music; Poetry; The Work-Table; The Toilette... ...yings and Doings; Fine Arts and other Engravings, by Eminent Artists; Our O... ...ts, &c.

⁎ As a FAMI... ...DS UNRIVALLED.
Weekly, One Penny" Monthly Pa... ...for Specimen Copy.

This Periodical, cont... ...Inesday with Bow BELLS,
PRICE ONE HAL... an Illustrated Wrapper.

A V(... ..., CALLED

V... NEXT,

Being th... n the Press.

Co... ...nd, W.C.
NO\V L WORK,

DICKS ## TUTOR.

Edited y understood.
ued.

Caven... e, London, W.
C... and, W.C.

THE ## BOOK.
Cloth,

A GUII... ...IERAL USE.
"Few books of... ...ssued from the press for
many years past.... condensed the main pro-
visions of the law... er, or thing incidental to
the relations between one individual...

⁎ This new edition contains all the new or altered laws of recent enactment, especially the new Bankruptcy Act.

STEVENS & SONS, 119, Chancery-lane, Fleet-street.

THE
DULCIANA PIANOFORTE.

This splendid Instrument is of full compass, with full metal string plate, and is altogether built on the soundest scientific theories, and approved by the most severe trials. It possesses a tone at once dulcet, firm, and powerful, and a touch answering to the most delicate as well as the strongest finger of the performer. It has a rich walnut-wood case, of elegant design, heavy fret, with artistic design in centre, and stands on handsome trusses.

PRICE TWENTY-SIX GUINEAS.

London: The Cavendish Music Depôt, 70, Mortimer Street, Cavendish Square, W.

NOW READY.
BOW BELLS HANDY BOOKS.

A Series of Little Books under the above title, got up in the most elegant style, gilt lettered, are now publishing. Each book contains 64 pages, beautifully printed in clear type and on fine paper.
1.—ETIQUETTE FOR LADIES.
2.—ETIQUETTE FOR GENTLEMEN.
3.—LANGUAGE OF FLOWERS.
4.—GUIDE TO THE BALL ROOM.
5.—ETIQUETTE OF COURTSHIP AND MARRIAGE.

Price Fourpence; per Post, One Halfpenny extra.
⁎ Every family should possess the BOW BELLS HANDY BOOKS.

London: J. DICKS, 313, Strand; all Booksellers.

AGAINST TIDE.

A NOVEL.

PAUL BECOMES AN INTERESTED SPECTATOR. (See page 18.)

AGAINST TIDE:

A STORY OF A POOR STREET ARAB.

BY

MIRIAM ROSS.

WITH THIRTEEN ILLUSTRATIONS

BY F. GILBERT.

LONDON:
JOHN DICKS, OFFICE OF "BOW BELLS," 313, STRAND.

1871.

AGAINST TIDE:

A STORY OF A POOR STREET ARAB.

PRELUDE.

It was an annual fair, and the litttle market-town of ——, in the county of Surrey, where it was held, was filled with rustic visitors.

They crowded the inns and streets, waking the humdrum place with the clatter of their voices and laughter; while the bright dresses of the fair portion of the revellers made an ever shifting kaleidoscope of gay colours. The market-place was, however, the great central point of attraction.

There stood the lads and lasses who were waiting to be hired; there, side by side, were ranged stalls, heaped with tempting fairings, of fruit, gingerbread, nuts, and fancy ware; the latter consisting chiefly of ribbons, china dogs of preposterous breeds, knives, and wooden dolls of strange and marvellous shapes. There, too, were the great glories of the day—swings, roundabouts, shooting galleries in miniature; and crowning even these, a wild beast show, with a gorgeously painted canvass front, on which was depicted a particularly ferocious lion, engaged in a savage fight with a very striped and spotted tiger; while, in the same Indian jungle where the encounter was represented, a polar bear stood erect, with wide open jaws, and, probably, playing umpire.

In addition to these wonders, it was also notified that within could be seen a giant, a dwarf, a living skeleton, a fat girl, and a learned pig; all of which could be inspected for the small sum of twopence. The whole was wound up to the highest pinnacle of perfection by the stirring strains of a band pertaining thereto, which band consisted chiefly of a big drum of martial and sonorous tone, mingled with the spasmodic groans of a superannuated cornet.

The whole morning long this establishment had waged a fierce war with a rival booth, immediately opposite—a temporary theatre, decorated with a portrait of Shakspere, much distorted in the forehead, and on either side the full-length pictures of a columbine and clown, who seemed to be throwing up their feet in an ambitious attempt to kick over the bust of the "immortal bard of Avon."

On the platform outside this Thespian temple a lady and gentleman were engaged in a lively dance, and footed it merrily to the sweet strains of a fife and a cracked fiddle; while a person in a turban and long flowing cloak, which at times revealed glimpses of a pair of red hose, surmounted with yellow shorts, put in an appearance, and announced that the great tragedy of "Othello," to be followed by a ballet and a screaming farce, the whole to occupy half an hour, was about to commence, and invited the lookers-on to patronise the entertainment.

That this man was the delineator of the jealous Moor there is little doubt, for his face exhibited a general appearance of burnt corkiness, save where it was surrounded by a white ring, which had escaped the blackening process.

The wild beast-show, however, carried off the palm in point of success, and the coppers jingled into the hat of the money-taker in a continuous shower, while the "mean-spirited" proprietor jingled his full pockets triumphantly in his rival's face, and shouted persistently to the public "to come up, and see the only show in the fair worth looking at;" which conduct called upon him the universal contempt of the theatrical company. Matters were indeed looking serious for these poor "play actors;" Othello had bawled himself hoarse, and had even taken his Desdemona for a stroll on the platform, in the forlorn hope that the sight of her dishevelled tresses, and the bridal costume, would attract the multitude; but it had, alas! proved a vain attempt, and the pair had retired in dismay, while the other lady and gentleman ceased their dance, and leant despondently over the rails, watching the crowd surge into the opposite show.

Suddenly Othello once more appeared, with a smile of hope, and whispered to the disconsolate pair, who also brightened, and retired each to an end of the platform, where they assumed picturesque attitudes.

Then through the door of the theatre there bounded forth a girl of about seven years of age, who ran lightly forwards, shaking her spangled skirts, and curtseying to the lookers on.

This made a sensation.

The people turned from the wild-beast show to look at and admire the slender little creature, with starry blue eyes, and a wealth of golden brown curls, crowned with roses.

In their unsophisticated gaze, she looked like an angel; and they forgot to notice that her garland was faded, and her dress tarnished and soiled, as they gazed into her arch, winning face. At last, shaking a tambourine, which she held in her hand, the child dashed off into a wild, untutored dance, flitting hither and thither, with graceful movements, and saucy glances at the spectators, who were every moment thickening around the booth.

The opposition show looked blue; and the proprietor, fearing that the tide of public opinion was on the turn, came forward, and jibed and sneered at the tiny dancer, while he lauded the lion and tiger to the skies.

The crowd derided him, and turned resolutely to the Thespian temple.

The child ceased her dance, and again rattling her tambourine, accompanied herself with its jingling while she sang.

It was but a common street air; but she trilled it with all the strength of her clear, sweet voice.

Her conquest was complete.

The listeners accorded her a rapturous encore, and the man in the neighbouring show, who had brought out his big drum in the hope of drowning her notes, was stoned back into retirement.

Then, once more, Othello came back, his face black as ever, but with the turban and cloak discarded. He now wore a sailor's hat, while a blue jacket overtopped the yellow shorts and red hose, and he announced that the play would be "The Black Pirate of the Blue Sea," in which the infant wonder, now before them, would personate the good fairy of the coral cave, and, in her part, sing a comic song, and dance a Highland fling.

It was all over with the wild-beast show.

The people rushed to the play, and the enterprising proprietor of the formerly triumphant booth found himself deserted. It was all in vain that he brought out one of the giant's boots and the dwarf's pantaloons, as inducements to the recreants to return; in vain that he commanded the lion's tail to be pinched to make him roar; his sun of prosperity had set in sorrow, and the shower of coppers floated over to the other side of the way, where the tragical drama of "The Black Pirate, and the Fairy of the Coral Cave," had an enormous run until midnight, and was acknowledged the "great sensation" of the festive season.

CHAPTER I.

"Homeless, ragged, and tanned,
Under the changeful sky."

THE fair was over, the booths and stalls had disappeared, and the theatrical company, having packed their properties into the smallest possible compass, were assembled in the market-place, ready to take their departure.

An old farm-waggon, destined both as a conveyance of the luggage and the fair portion of the community, had been wheeled into the open space, while a tall, big-boned horse, which was evidently discontented with his station in life, was being harnessed to the shafts, much to his own discomfiture and the glee of the child, who, sitting on an old block of stone, was watching the operation with the utmost interest.

It was the little girl who had wrought so great a change in the fortunes of the actors on the previous evening.

She was dressed in tattered, soiled clothes, but her face peeped forth from them archly and prettily as ever, while her hair caught the early rays of the morning sun, and glistened in them like burnished gold.

At a little distance, pacing the narrow path, under a row of sheds, were the proprietor of the show and a boy of about twelve years of age—a ragged, sturdy lad, with bare, dusty feet, and a bare head, covered only with a thick crop of short black curls.

They were engaged in earnest conversation, every now and then making a slight pause, and turning to glance at the unconscious child and the laden waggon.

"I say it, and I mean it," observed the man, after one of these pauses. "Only trust that child to me, and I'll bring her up to be an ornament to the profession."

"'Tain't no use of your talkin'," said the boy; "I ain't a-going to part with Rachel. I'd like to know what I'd do without her, I would."

"I am not a hard man, nor a proud one either," said the theatrical manager, looking as though he expected to be admired for his excessive humility. "I say I'm not constitutionally a proud man; and, I tell you what, I don't mind taking you into the bargain. You can learn the double shuffles, and two or three other steps, and you could come out as a sailor or harlequin next Christmas. We'd have bills printed—real bills, my boy—a thing I've never done before—and we'd advertise you and the infant wonder. I dare say, in time, you'd earn five shillings a-week and your keep," he added, growing speculative and generous at the same time.

The boy shook his head.

The action petrified the manager.

"Are you blind?" he questioned solemnly of the boy.

"Can't yer see I ain't?" he answered, irreverently.

"I mean mentally blind," explained the man. "Can't you see you are throwing away your only chance to rise in the world? Believe me, I know what I'm about. I know what people are, the very minute I set eyes on them. Think of yesterday. I walked out into the fair, and I saw your sister singing and dancing to a parcel of country louts."

"And a bringin' in coppers as fast as I could pick 'em up," interposed the lad, with a knowing look.

"*Singing and dancing!*" repeated the manager, utterly ignoring the fact of the coppers; "and said I, 'That's genius, Morrison, my boy. There's one who will suit you, and whom you will suit. What's your mission in the world? To bring out rising talent?' I offered to let the child, your sister, dance on my platform. She did. The result was success. Last night she played a fairy; some night she will play 'The Lady of Lyons,' and 'Lady Macbeth,' and all the world will hear of her."

He paused to note the effect of this burst of eloquence on the lad at his side, then went on, I say the same of you. Trust yourself in my hands, and you'll have cause to remember and bless the name of Morrison."

There was a moment of silence, during which the boy looked wistfully, first at the benevolent Morrison, then at the little figure still crouching on the stone. His conclusion was adverse to the theatrical interest, it seemed, for he shook his head, and muttered in an under-tone, "I'd rather not."

"Boy," said the stage-manager, solemnly, "where's your father and mother?"

"That's it!" he answered. "I never had none, as I knows of; and as for Rachel, hers is dead, and buried by the parish, nearly three years ago. We ain't got nobody in the world but ourselves; but we does very well as we is. We don't want nare a marster, Rachel and me."

"Then she's not your sister?" said Morrison.

"No," returned the lad. "But she's as good as one. Her own mother give her to me, three years ago, when she were only a little thing, so high. I lived along with Jacob Prew then, and Rachel and her mother, they lived in the room above ourn."

"Well?" questioned Morrison, eagerly.

"Well, Ray and I, we used to play together, and I cared more for her than anythink else in the world. Well, by-an'-by, Jacob Prew, he got sent to furrin lands. for breakin open a shop; and Ray's mother, she let me live in her room, and give me vittals, when she had any, and I got fonder than ever of Ray."

"Go on, boy!" said Morrison. evincing great interest in the story.

"At last, the summer come, and it brought the fever. The people in our court died awful, and Ray's mother was took."

He turned round, and furtively wiped the tears from his eyes.

"I left her at home in the day, and went and begged for vittals for me and the little one and the poor 'oman in bed; and I allers made haste back when I got anythink."

Mr. Morrison interrupted him here with a blow on the shoulder.

"I'm not a proud man," he ejaculated. "Boy, shake hands."

"What for?" questioned the urchin. "I ain't a done nothink to you."

"Never mind!" said Morrison, waving the subject. "Go on!"

"We had the doctor from the work'us', but she didn't get no better; and one night, when I come in, she called me, and she says, 'Paul, I'm a-goin'.' 'Where?' says I, for I thought as she was talkin' some of the mad rubbidge she used to when the fever was strong. But she wasn't—she was as sensible as you; and she tells me ag'in, 'Paul, I'm a-goin'.'"

Mr. Morrison heaved a sigh, and turned to look at little Rachel, who was feeding the tall horse with cabbage-leaves, and laughing merrily.

"I didn't arsk her where then," said Paul. "I knowed she was a-going to die, and I put my head on the pillow, and cried for the first time since she was took; and Ray cried, too; and we was a miserable lot on us in that 'ere attic."

"Poor children!" said the stage-manager, with a suspicious huskiness in his voice.

"Arter a bit, I was quiet, and I picked out my best bit of bread and meat, and tried to feed her; but it warn't of no good—she was going with the fever, out of the world; so she says, 'It ain't no use, Paul; I'm a-goin' fast. Promise, when I'm dead, as you'll look arter little Rachel; she ain't got a friend in the world but her poor dying mother and you.'

"Only fancy," whimpered Morrison; "it beats Shakspere hollow."

"'I will,' I says; 'I'll stick to Ray like bricks and mortar.' 'Paul,' she went on, 'you won't let her steal?' 'Never!' I said; 'I'll look arter her as good as you do; I will.' She was a bit pleased at that, and we was all quiet. It was gettin' darkish, and her face looked whiter and whiter; and Ray had gone to sleep, and I and her mother was awake, waitin', like, for the end of it."

"Gracious!" whispered Morrison. "It makes my nerves quiver. Go on, Paul."

"All at once she called out, and took my hand. 'Paul,' says she, 'say "Our Father."' I didn't know what she meant, but I looked up where she was a-pointing to a star through the winder, and I kep' on a sayin' it, 'Our Father, our Father, our Father,' and wonderin' where he was; and when I looked round she was gone."

"Poor Paul!" said Morrison, gently patting his head. "Well?"

"Well, she was buried, in course—the parish, you know; and I took little Ray, and we've bin together ever since."

"Three years!" mused Mr. Morrison. "I say, how did you manage to live all that time?"

"An old 'oman as kep' a apple-stall, and lived in our court, give me a broom, and I set up as a crossin'-sweeper, and Ray took the coppers; an' a very good trade it was sometimes."

"Well, well!" ejaculated Mr. Morrison. "Such is life! Some of us are born to lowly estates; some of us are theatrical managers. It's Providence, Paul, Providence!"

"Is that anythink to do with the parish?" questioned the boy, with a wondering stare.

"Bless you, no!" said the manager, hastily.

"But how did you come to leave London, eh?"

"Why, one day, when there was sich a crowd of carridges that the people couldn't get across, there was a lady and gent a-talkin' jest behind me and Ray. 'And,' says the lady, 'we must soon be thinkin' of goin' in the country, now the summer's a-comin' on.' And Ray wanted to know what the country was, so we asked the old apple-'oman, and she told us. Says I, 'Do they get the fever there?' 'Lor', no!' says she. So I makes up my mind that as it was nearly time for it to be in the court, and I couldn't abear to lose Ray, and she couldn't abear to lose me, we'd go inter the country till it was over. So I give the old 'oman my broom to mind, and one day we set off, and here we is. When we wants money, we sings, and Ray dances; and we gets along somehow. We likes the country; but when the winter comes, we must go back to the crossin' in London and the old court."

"Consider, Paul," said the manager—"is that a fit life for a girl like that? London's a bad place for a pretty little thing like Rachel. Better learn a honest profession. She can't sweep a crossing all her life long. You promised her mother to take care on her. She'll be safe here—she won't in London."

The boy looked up, with sudden pain in his eyes, and turned hastily towards the place where Ray still stood, lost in admiration of the theatrical turn-out.

"They're ready to go," he said, pointing to the waggon, from which the faces of the females were peeping impatiently.

"Ride along with us a little way, and think it over," said Mr. Morrison, persuasively.

Paul nodded an assent, and slowly followed the manager to the waggon.

Five minutes later they were rattling merrily through the town, Paul and Rachel sitting beside the driver, who was no less a personage than the "Black Pirate" in his private dress of dingy plaid. The boy's arm was wound caressingly round her, his eyes fixed mournfully on her pretty face; little Ray, shouting with glee, and laughing like a peal of silver bells, as she revelled in the glories of her first ride.

CHAPTER II.

An hour later, the waggon was trundling slowly down a broad country road, bordered on either side with rich pasture and wheat-fields. The professional ladies here alighted from

PAUL TAKES LEAVE OF LITTLE RAY. (See page 6.)

the vehicle, and rambled on, organizing coquettish flirtations with their brethren in the histrionic art.

Ray and Paul likewise descended from their elevated perch, the former skipping along by the horse's side, the latter once more joining the expectant manager.

"I've been a-thinkin' it over," he said, plunging abruptly into the subject; "and I've made up my mind you shall have little Ray."

"You don't mean it?" cried Morrison, in delight.

"I do; on'y you must promise to be kind to her. She'll have nobody to look arter her when I'm gone."

"What! ain't you coming, too?" said Morrison, persuasively. "I tell you, Paul, I've taken a fancy to you; and I'll do the right thing by you if you'll join us."

"No; I'm going back to London," said the boy, sadly. "Afore we started to come into this yer country, Nance—that's the old apple-'oman—lent me five shillins, and I promised I'd go back and pay her. I can't come; she'd think me a thief."

"Now, only listen!" said the manager, in parenthesis. "But you give me Rachel of your own free will?"

"Not of my own free will," said Paul, "Years ago, when I was a bit of a chap, and lived with Jacob Prew, I had a dorg as follered me everywhere, slep' with me at night, and allers had half of my vittals. But when Jacob got drunk, he used to kick it and abuse it, and that happened near every night, and Boxer's life was a tormint to him."

"I should think so," said Morrison.

"I stood it a long time, but at last I makes up my mind one night, when he'd beat Boxer worser than ever. I waited till he was asleep, and then I took the dorg in my arms, and out of the house, down to the river. The tide was runnin' in, and the water was high, and I slips down the steps to the edge on it, and ' Boxer,' says I, 'good-bye; I'm a-goin' to chuck you in, for you sharn't be tormented no longer.' And Boxer, he looked up, so 'feckshunate, like, I busted out cryin'; but I tied a brick round his neck, and I shied him in. I watched him go down, and went home ag'in, feelin' as lonely as anybody could feel; but I was glad Boxer couldn't be beat any more."

"Gracious!" said Morrison, "you have got a spirit."

"So," said Paul, not noticing the compliment, "when you spoke in that way, about Ray not bein' safe in London, I thort it over

I remembered it was precious hard in London in winter time, when the cold, and the snow, and the rain, and slush, and wind nips yer all over, and makes me shiver, and Ray cry; and I thort, too, of the times when we takes scarcely anythink, when folks is too busy to put their hands in their pockets and chuck us a ha'-penny, and when we goes home tired, and cold, and hungry, and creeps to bed in the dark, athout a fire, and on'y a crust to eat, and I makes up my mind its a tormentin' life for little Ray, jest as Boxer's was to him!"

"There's a head for you!" said Morrison, admiringly.

"Where?" asked Paul, not comprehending the compliment.

"Never mind." said Morrison; "go on."

"So, seein' a chance for her to get out on it, I've made up my mind to let her go, jest as I made up my mind to drown'd Boxer; so it's all settled—you can take little Ray."

He smothered a sob, and drew the sleeve of his ragged jacket across his eyes.

"You are one of Nature's own nobility," said Morrison, impulsively; then, with a shake of the head, he added, "What's the good of applauding him?—he's no idea of what one means by it."

"One thing more," said Paul. "Ray's mother never whopped her, and I never hit her all the time I've had her."

"And I'll promise you, honour bright, that I never will, nor shall a soul in my company treat her ill. And I'll buy her new clothes, Paul; boots with shiny toes, and a red frock, and a hat trimmed with yellow; and I'll feed her on the fat of the land—beef-steaks and onions every night, and pudding on a Sunday. She'll live like a queen, and me and my wife will love her as if she was the child we have always wished for, and never had."

He paused to take breath.

"I am sorry you can't come," he continued. "But honour's honour, in a crossin'-sweeper as well as a theatrical proprietor and manager, and that five shillings you borrowed from the apple-woman would lie heavy on your conscience, I'm sure, if you didn't go back, and do the thing that's right. But when you have paid it, if you like to join, why come; and if you let me know first, I'll forward you the cash to do it, so that you will not have to tramp."

"But you won't be here; I sharn't know where to let yer know," said Paul.

"Why, look here; I'll write to you at the end of a month, and direct the letter to the General Post Office, London; and you can fetch it when you get back. And, after that, I'll write every now and then, and you'll know where I am, and, better than that, all about little Ray."

"Thank yer," said Paul gratefully. 'The Ginral Post Orfice, you said. But how'm I to get the letter?"

"Why, go in and ask a clerk for it—one of the men you'll see behind the counter, You must say, 'Have you a letter for Mr. Paul—Paul'—I say, what's your name, boy, besides Paul? I must know, to put on the outside of the letter."

"I don't know; I never had another," he answered.

"Was that Jacob Prew your father?" asked Morrison.

"No," said Paul. "He was no relation to me; he told me that over and over and over again."

"Then your name is not Prew, that's certain," said Morrison. "What did he use to call you?"

"Paul, when he wasn't cross, or drunk; but mostly, Vagabond."

"Paul the Vagabond," mused Morrison; "what a title for a tragedy! But we can't put that on a letter; suppose we put Mr. Paul. I think that'll suit. You go to the General Post Office, and you ask for a letter for Mister Paul."

"I goes to the Ginral Post Orfice, and I arsks for a letter for Mister Paul," repeated the lad. "I sharn't forgit. It'll be summut to hear about Ray: I never heard nothink about Boxer; but I carn't read, 'speshully 'ritin'."

"Here's a go!" said Morrison, whistling. "What will you do?"

"I'll ask the old apple-'oman to; I see her a 'ritin' a letter once," mused Paul, hopefully.

Just then, little Ray came bounding up, and clasped her hands round Paul's arm.

The boy caught her to him, and sitting on the ground by the wayside, leant his head on her shoulder, and sobbed aloud.

"What is it, Paul?" she asked. "You ain't hungry?"

"No!"

"He ain't cross?" she pursued, pointing to Morrison.

"No!"

"Then don't cry," she said, positively, "but run on along of me, and catch the waggin. They're all of 'em gettin' in ag'in, and I want to ride as much as ever I can. Come along Paul."

She tried to pull him from his seat, but the boy resisted.

"Kiss me, Ray, and then go along of him. He'll put you into the waggon," he said.

"Why won't you?" persisted Ray.

"Because I'm a-goin' to stop here," said Paul, biting his lip to keep back his tears. "I ain't a-comin' any further. I'm a-goin' back to London, to the crossin'; you're a-goin' along of him, and you'll be a little lady; you'll never be cold ag'in, and you'll have beefsteak and inguns every day."

He sobbed again, while Ray cried aloud, and flung her arms round his neck.

Morrison approached, and taking her in his arms, drew her away.

"Good-bye, Paul," he said; "there's half-a-crown on the ground by you. I'll get her away at once. Keep up your sperits, and look out for a letter."

He carried the crying child away, and placing her in the waggon, it rumbled off, and he saw it disappear round a turn in the road.

"It's a precious sight worse than drowndin' poor Boxer," he said; and bowing his head to his knees, Paul the vagabond wept on, oblivious of the bright half-crown which lay in the dust at his feet.

CHAPTER III.

It was a sultry afternoon, and the sun shone through the office windows of Beverley Bogg, Esq., lighting up the whitewashed walls into hard, glaring brilliancy. It was, in fact, astonishing to note how the sun, glancing into the room, conveyed to one's mind the idea of hardness, and forced upon it the reflection of what a hard man its master must be. In its palmy days, it had been evidently a family sitting-room: if so, the ghost of the past, looking upon the present, must have been filled with indignation and dismay.

It was, in fact, one of the most uncomfortable apartments in existence.

The chairs were of the stiffest possible shapes, cushioned with the hardest, most slippery cushions ever invented; at least, all save one, and that was the seat sacred to Beverley Bogg.

The table, with its uncompromising brown leather top, and square brown legs, looked stern and grim enough to scare a timid client; so did the pewter inkstand, and the packets of papers and letters lying around it.

The very pattern of the carpet seemed a maze of angular lines and staring colours.

starting prominently forth, as though they were at variance with each other.

Nay, everything in the room seemed to proclaim the fact that its master was emphatically a "hard man."

Certainly, Beverley Bogg's appearance did not contradict the idea, as he sat in his easy-chair, enjoying its luxurious proportions and soft padding, and looking with a smile at the miserable specimens of the chair tribe ranged around him, as though he appreciated his own comfort more, when contrasted with what must inevitably be the discomfort in any person compelled to sit on those leather cushions, with a crick in the small of their backs, and an ache in the nape of their necks, caused by the extreme slipperiness of their seats.

He was a man verging on middle age, with a long face, topped by a high, narrow forehead, and ending in a heavy, square chin—a chin that looked like the section of a steel trap, the jaws being the remaining portion, which could shut down with a snap, cruelly, relentlessly, on anything that came into their vicinity. His eyes were small, of a pale blue; his hair, whiskers, and moustache a pale brown; the whole contour of his features cold, morose, and hard as any features well could be.

His very smile partook of the same character; there was no kindly sympathy in it, and the impression it conveyed was that it never played around his lips unless it was as a congratulatory oblation to himself.

In fact, Beverley Bogg never looked harder or more repulsive than he did on this summer afternoon, when he sat in his office, watching the motes float in the golden sunbeams.

His reflections were probably of a pleasing nature, for he stroked his chin contentedly, as he every now and then bestowed a portion of his attention upon a long bill of costs which lay before him.

"One of the best cases I ever had to deal with," he observed to himself. "If I had a few more such, they would considerably increase the balance at my banker's, but law is becoming as dead and dull as everything else in this money-making world. Not a single new case, worth more than fifty pounds, for a month past! If something novel would only turn up—novel and lucrative, I mean." He was interrupted here by a sharp rap at the door.

"Who's there?" he growled, in a manner which was quite as indicative of his tendency to snap, as was the mouth from which it issued.

"It's me, sir! Simkins, sir!" said a conciliatory voice, without.

"Come in," he replied, not in the slightest degree softened by Mr. Simkins's evident humility.

"If you please, sir, it's Judge Vincent," said the man.

"Oh, very well; I'll see him, of course." returned Mr. Bogg, while a sinister smile flickered across his lips.

"Yes, sir," replied Simkins, who seemed glad to beat a retreat.

He had nearly accomplished it, when he was once more summoned into the room.

"Simkins," said his master, "you remember the affair of old David Platt?"

Simkins coloured uneasily.

"When, going hastily from this room, I detected you—yes, surprised you, listening at yonder keyhole!"

Simkins made no reply, but shifted uneasily about from one foot to the other, and looked longingly towards the door.

"You'll bear that in mind to-day," continued Beverley Bogg, fixing him with his little, cold eyes. "If I should happen to stumble on you 'anywhere in the region of this door, while I am holding an interview with a client or friend, I shall discharge you from my service, with such a character as would prevent any one in London from employing you."

Simkins backed away, as though he was again contemplating an exit, and muttered a confused "Thank you, sir."

"Stop a moment; I've a word more to say," continued his master. "You know the consequences of that dismissal? Misery and starvation, in that happy little home of yours, to your merry wife, and those fine boys you think so much of. You wouldn't look so red and stout as you do now, after a month's trial of it. Now you can go."

Simkins looked unutterably wretched, and shuffled from the room; and it was noticeable that when he ushered the Judge into the presence of his employer, he never for a moment put so much as the toes of his boots into the chamber, but seemed to back away in indescribable terror from the withering vicinity of Beverley Bogg.

But once having retired into his own particular den, and his seat behind a tall desk on a high stool, his face changed, and a look of glee and triumphant malice passed over it.

After a moment or two of careful listening, he turned to the wall, which alone divided him from his master's private room, and with skilful fingers extracted a kind of plug, or stopper, so carefully fitted and coloured, that it was scarcely discernible when fixed into its place in the dingy wall.

When this feat was accomplished, a funnel-like hole could be seen neatly bored through to the next room, where it terminated in what looked like a natural crevice in the opposite surface of the wall.

"Ha, ha!" chuckled the little, round clerk, rubbing his hands. "Dinner-hour work." Here he pointed down the funnel. "Independent of the keyhole, Mr. Beverley Bogg." So saying, he applied his ear to this new specimen of acoustic tube, and listened diligently.

In the meanwhile the lawyer had arisen with a smiling face, and stretched out his hand in cordial greeting to his visitor.

"Ah, my dear William, I am delighted to see you!"

The Judge took the proffered hand, and pressed it warmly; then, sinking down in the chair drawn out for him, sighed wearily as he glanced round the bare office.

"Warm, isn't it?" said Beverley, by way of opening the conversation.

"Yes, yes!" said the Judge.

"Almost time to be thinking of a change," resumed the lawyer, watching his guest with a look of intense amusement. "Mrs. Bogg and myself have made up our minds to go to Italy."

"For heaven's sake, stop!" cried the Judge, springing from his chair. "What interest have I in the movements of you and your wife? What interest have I in anything in the world? I—who am a man, broken-down, wretched, beggared of all that makes life a pleasure!"

"William, my dear friend!" cried the lawyer, while his eyes twinkled with suppressed triumph. He rose and placed his hand on the other's shoulder.

They were of the same age, these two men, standing in such friendly proximity; but there was a wide difference between them.

Beverley Bogg, with his long, narrow, cunning, cruel face. Judge Vincent, noble, and honest-looking. The lawyer, with his expression of exultant malice, his visitor, with a shadow of deep despair and settled trouble darkening his face, and ageing him before his time.

"You are troubled, William," continued Beverley Bogg. "But you can confide in me—you know it. Think of our long friendship!

We were boys at school together. I was your fag; but I never envied you. We were at college together; you obtained the first honours; I just managed to get my degree; but there was no envy in my heart towards you. We studied law together. I am still a poor plodding barrister; you are a judge; but, William, who can say that envy found a lodging with me then? We both loved the same woman; you married her, but I did not envy you. No! I looked at you on the pinnacle whence you had risen above me, and I *reverenced* you, William."

As he spoke of his freedom from the passion of envy, his face assumed a bitter, sarcastic expression; and when he mentioned *reverence*, the word might have been *hate*, so savagely did it creep forth from his trap-like jaws.

"Heaven is my witness, Beverley, you have nought to envy in my state," said the Judge. "Once I looked forward with feverish delight to the time when I should rise to wealth and honour. I have grasped them, and they are as Dead Sea apples in my grasp."

Was that a sneer on the lawyer's face? If it was, it had passed away with lightning swiftness, and the sorrowing man saw on it only the warm expression of friendship due to him from the companion of his life.

"I had a dream of love," continued the Judge; "you know how bright and beautiful it was. Ah, Beverley! you know how I strove for her—how I won her?"

"I do!" he replied, emphatically.

"How false, how fleeting it proved, you know; how bitter was my awaking from the dear vision, you can guess. My wife—the woman I loved and trusted, the woman on whose faith I would have staked my life, fled from me."

He sank into his seat, and leaning his head on the table, groaned in his agony.

"Why recall these things?" said the lawyer, bending over him. "Why not forget them?"

"You speak of impossibilities," said the Judge, sadly. "The remembrance of these woes, the sting they inflicted, will cling to me my whole life long. But I speak of them now that I may enlist your aid. When she left me, she took with her my boy—my little Paul. For more than ten years I have searched for him in vain. Beverley, help me to find him—restore to me this one gleam of light on my dark way, and I will bless you."

He seized his friend's hand, and looked into his face with desperate eagerness.

"My boy—my only child!" he continued;

"heaven only knows where he may be. Wandering, perhaps, in poverty and sorrow, through the world!"

"Perhaps in ignorance and crime," said the lawyer, in a melancholy voice.

"'Tis that maddens me," almost shrieked the unhappy man. "For the sake of all you hold dear, help me to find him before it is too late. I see it in my waking thoughts, in my dreams at night—my son, my bright, beautiful boy, a felon, a criminal!"

His voice faltered, and once more he relapsed into heavy, sobbing groans.

"Have courage!" said his friend. "I pledge my word I will yet restore to you the son you have lost."

"I would give my fortune freely to the man who gave him back to me," cried the Judge. "Beverley, my friend, I trust you in this, as I have trusted you in the old time."

"And you will find I am true to my resolves," said the lawyer.

Half an hour later, when the pair passed from the office, there was a smile of hope on the Judge's face—one of joy on that of Beverley Bogg.

The lawyer cast a keen glance on his clerk as he went out; but Simkins was working on industriously, and the hole in the wall was carefully plugged up again; but no sooner had he departed, than the man laughed silently, and shook hands with himself gleefully.

"There go the lamb and the wolf!" he said. "Go it, Beverley Bogg, Esq.! I shall help you in the search for little Paul; and who knows but the Judge may give me enough money to render myself, Mrs. Simkins, and all the future olive-branches, independent for life?"

CHAPTER IV

SHUTER'S COURT was situated in one of the dingiest localities in London. It was a small square, surrounded with high houses, and was entered by an arched passage, opening from a narrow street. The pavement of the place was broken and slippery with damp, treacherous to the footing, and perpetually oozing with muddy slime, which sent up its poisonous vapour, and infected the whole place. The houses were dilapidated, tumble-down specimens of architecture, with crumbling walls, broken windows, crazy doors, and tottering chimneys; the inhabitants of this den, squalid, degraded specimens of humanity. Poverty, crime, and disease,—all seemed to have made the place their head-quarters, and to reign with undisputed sway over the population of Shuter's Court.

It was night; and the solitary lamp which stood in the centre of the square was flaring with a dull, red glare, revealing the wretchedness of its surroundings; shining on the begrimed faces of women and children—the brutal ones of men, as they gathered around it in knots, conversing in eager tones, or snarled and fought in their hatred and defiance of each other.

At times, a cry, or a shrill scream, would peal through the court, and pierce through the entrance alley into the street beyond, rising like a higher wave of misery above the tide of sounds in that dreary place, the monotonous beating of shrill voices and laughter, with their undercurrent of hoarse, growling notes.

And this had been Paul's home—*was* all the home to which his memory could turn, in that great crowded city.

He stood even now at the end of the passage, looking down into it, wondering how he could have lived contentedly there, and contrasting its foulness with the purity and freshness of the country from which he had just returned, to take up once more his labour at the crossing.

A fortnight had scarcely elapsed since he had bade Rachel "good-bye," and watched the waggon which was bearing her away from him, and the summer was still reigning in all her splendour and beauty; but eager to redeem his promise to his friend the apple-woman, and rejoin Ray, he had turned away from the pleasures of the green fields and trees, the streams, birds, and flowers, and trudged manfully back to his old haunts; the promised letter from the showman being the one bright hope which cheered and strengthened him in his loneliness and grief.

At length, with a slow step, he walked down the passage, and was swallowed up in the gaping, dismal court.

"Hallo, Paul!" said a stout, florid-looking woman, touching his shoulder, as he stood under the lamp. "So you've come back ag'in, at last! I suppose yer'll be wantin' yer old lodgin' in the garret?"

"Yes, if you please, ma'am," said Paul, shrinking back, with an involuntary shudder, from her grimy touch.

"Then I'm sorry to say yer carn't have it," continued the woman. "And what's more, that I don't think yer will get a hole to sleep in, not in this blessed locality."

"Why not?" said Paul, in astonishment. "I've got money enough to pay a whole week aforehand."

"'Tain't that," said the woman, who was no less than his former landlady. "But we're a doin' a good trade down here, jest now. Them improving comisshuners have been an' had Saddler's Rents, and two or three other places, pulled down since you've bin gone; an' the people have flocked in to us, and we haven't a spare inch of room in all the houses in the courts, from the cellars to the garrets; and sha'n't 'ave, unless the fever comes bad among us ag'in, and thins 'em. There's a cobbler and his famerly in your place. I'd 'vise you to look out somewhere else."

With these words, she hastened away, leaving Paul staring helplessly about him.

"If it was the country," he murmured, "I could sleep in a barn, or under a hedge; but here there's no peace, for the perlice a-tellin' yer to move on all the time. I'll just see the old apple-woman, and get my broom; and then I'll look out for another place."

He turned round, and glanced up to the topmost window of a house facing him.

It was quite dark; not a flicker of candle or firelight shone through the window, to cheer the little wanderer.

"Not come home yet," he said. "I'll wait."

Withdrawing from the crowd, he crouched down on the ground, and leant his back against the wall, with a weary sigh.

His gaze for a time wandered round the court-yard; then, finally, rested on the patch of sky visible above the houses.

In the dark, cloudy canopy, one single star glittered; and Paul fell to thinking how he had lain awake many a night during his excursion, watching the myriads of them twinkling above him, in all their wondrous brilliancy and beauty.

The tears rushed to his eyes; and, seen through them, the bright star gleam spread into arrowy rays that seemed to touch him, and form a golden pathway upwards from the dismal court and its poisonous air and wretchedness.

"Perhaps Ray is looking at it, too," he whispered, while a vague wish crossed him, that both could climb up the ladder of light, and meet in the bright orb. He stretched out his hand, as though he would grasp those shimmering arrows, floating down to his very eyelids, and thus form a link between himself and Rachel; while, from its distant place, the star seemed to smile upon the ragged, solitary child, and his short dream of love and beauty.

An hour passed away; then, across the pavement, came the sound strange shuffling, mingled with an odd stumping noise, which roused Paul from his reverie.

He looked in the direction from whence they came, and rose from his seat, stretching himself.

A new-comer had arrived in the court, who was greeted with many a rough welcome and shout of recognition as he passed on his way.

He was a strange-looking man, with a large head, set upon a massive body, but crippled and shrunken in his lower limbs, which were doubled uselessly under him. He managed to drag himself through the streets by means of a short crutch and a stick; and on his bosom, suspended around his neck by a piece of cord, was a placard, on which was written in very large, very round letters, the words, "Paralyzed from birth. Kind Christian friends, pity me."

It is more than probable that his kind Christian friends would have doubted his need of their pity, had they seen him on his return from his daily labours, and observed the change in him; from the mendicant's pleading, sorrowful face and droning whine, to the jovial expression of the reveller, and the hearty, round tones of merriment and triumph.

At last, he came close to the spot where Paul was standing, and looked into his face inquisitively.

"Why, I'm blest if it ain't young Paul come back from his travels!" he cried. "And what are ye doing 'ere, leaning in that molloncholy fashi'n ag'in the walls; and vere's that blue-eyed lassie, leetle Rachel?"

"Rachel's gone away with some—some friends," said Paul; "and I'm waitin' here to see old Mary, the apple-woman, and git my broom afore I goes to look arter fresh lodgin's."

"The court's full," said the cripple; "and as for old Mary, eighty year and the rheumatiz ha' carried her off at larst, and she'll never more sell apples on Westminster Bridge."

Paul reeled back in astonishment.

"Dead?" he cried.

"Yes, that's it," said the cripple. "Afore it happened, she sent for me, and 'Ned,' says she, 'there's leetle Paul gone out for his country wisit. He owes me five shillings, and there's his broom a-standin' in the corner. Now I shall be dead when he comes back again, so

PAUL UNDERGOES A SEARCHING INVESTIGATION. (See page 12.)

he arn't pay me the cash, an' I don't want it, for I've enough to bury me dacent; but you tell him, if he'll plant a rose-tree at my head, and a gelly-flower at my feet, I'll forgive him the rest on it. I got a fancy for flowers,' says she, 'for I was borned in the country, and lived there till I married; and you take charge on his broom, Ned, and gi'e it to him, wi' my dyin' words. You ha' heard them words, and if you'll come inter my room, I'll gi'e ye back the broom.''

So saying, he hobbled to the step of the door, Paul following him.

The cripple stopped at the first room on the ground-floor, and, taking a key from his pocket, opened the door, and entered, bidding Paul do likewise.

A moment after, the scraping of a match was heard, and the light of a tallow candle revealed the apartment. It was destitute of all furniture, save a mattress, which lay on the floor in one corner of the room, and a tattered blind, which was pinned over the window.

On the floor lay an old besom, worn nearly to the stump, and plentifully bespattered with mud.

This the cripple took up; and turning round to Paul, presented it to him, with a flourish.

"There, now, I've done my biddin'," he said, looking at the lad, with a cunning leer.

"Thank'ee," said Paul; and grasping the handle as if it were an old friend, he was about to depart, when the cripple spoke.

"Don't be in sech a hurry!" he exclaimed. "The court's full; so is all the houses in the streets round here; and yer'll have a trouble to get in anywhere to-night. I feels sociable, like; and, if yer pleases, yer may stay along of me, so as yer pays yer half of the 'spenses. Anyhow, yer can stay to-night.''

"Thank'ee," said Paul, again.

Then, feeling like one in a dream, he sat down on the edge of the mattress, still grasping the broom in his hand, and watching the man as he hobbled himself about on his household labours.

Soon a fire burned in the grate, its glowing flames leaping savagely up, and eclipsing the candle-light—sending a dancing gleam on the yellow walls of the room and the figure of the cripple.

As he moved hither and thither—sometimes in the full radiance of the red light, sometimes in the shadow,—a sensation, half of fear, fell upon the boy.

He looked so ugly, with his broad, grinning face and stunted form, that the child involuntarily likened him to a huge spider creeping about in search of prey, and grasped his broom, as though he would brush him away if he came too near him.

"What is it, leetle Paul?" asked Ned, noting his silence and gloom.

"Nothing, thank'ee," said the boy, humbly; then, with a sudden idea of flight, he started to his feet.

"Halloo!" cried the cripple. "What's the row?" and before Paul had taken three steps, he had planted himself menacingly before the door.

"I—I'm oncy a goin' out for half a hour," stammered Paul.

"What for, eh?" pursued Ned.

"I thinks," said the boy, in desperation, "I'll go to the crossin' for a bit, and take persession on him agin, afore to-morrer. The theayters will be out soon; I may get summut."

"You'll come back ag'in, leetle Paul," said the cripple, poising his head on one side, and scrutinising his face. "I've made up my mind as yer'll stop 'ere to-night, and we're a goin' to have sassingers for supper. If yer don't peromise, I'll lock the door, and yer sharn't stir."

"I'll promise," said Paul, breathlessly, looking in terror at the keyhole.

"You'll come back ag'in to-night?" said Ned, emphatically.

"I'll come back ag'in to-night," repeated Paul, with a spasm at his heart, as he contemplated returning

"Then you may go," concluded Ned, moving on one side. "A boy as a 'oman like Mary would lend five shillin's to, must be in the habit o' keeping his word.''

Without any further reply, the frightened lad dashed past him into the court, and through the passage entrance.

CHAPTER V.

PAUL was about to enter the street beyond, when the sound of voices, in eager conversation, fell upon his ears.

"Perlice," he muttered, as he crouched down in the shadow. "I wonder who they are arter?"

His bare feet had made but little noise, and that little was drowned in the traffic and riot of the place; so that the speakers continued their conversation undisturbed by his proximity.

"Is your whim gratified now?" said a harsh voice. "You asked me to show you one of the haunts which vice and misery make their abode. Do you think, if we searched London over, we should find a more wretched, depraved locality than Shuter's Court?"

"Such places are a blot upon the city," was the answer made in a deep, sad tone; "a stain upon the humanity and charity of every respectable man living within its walls. There is little wonder that crime flourishes and thrives among us, when it is allowed to possess such nurseries and hot-beds as these!"

"There is scarcely a grown man or woman living there," said the hard man, "who is not a felon in the eyes of the law; there is scarcely a child among them who has not commenced the career, which ends in a prison."

Paul shivered in his damp hiding-place, and a sob rose to his throat.

"It is that cuts me to the very heart," said the other; "to think that in one of these dens of infamy my boy may be learning his lesson of evil. Beverley, I cannot rest; every hour I can spare from my duty will I devote to searching these holes and corners of the city; every penny I can spare or save from my income will I devote to the salvation of children such as these. Who knows but that, in so doing, I may draw back my own child from destruction?"

"They will abuse your kindness, laugh at your charity, and disappoint you in the end," said the harsh man. "They are without gratitude—without an inclination to rise above their lot."

Paul shivered still more, and drew closer to the wall, for fear of being perceived.

"I'll begin this very night!" said the kind speaker: "perhaps some one in that loathsome place might know where I can find my child—might be able to tell me something about him."

"If they could, they would not answer you," said his companion. "They would use you as a sponge, from which they could wring what they live, strive, and sin for—money; they would deceive and cajole you, but you would never learn what you thirst to know. Leave it to me; I am experienced in sifting matters, and I pledge my word that if he is among these people, and the slightest clue to his identity remains, I will find him for you. Do you trust me?"

"I do!" said the voice, now a shade sadder.

"You may assist me," answered the other, "but let me direct all inquiries. There is not a detective in all England more true to the trail of a mystery than I am, more expert in taking up, when broken or dim."

He laughed as he spoke, a grating, chuckling laugh, which made Paul drop his broom with sudden terror.

He made a vain effort to grasp it again, but it eluded his hand, and fell with a clatter against the opposite wall, and from thence to the ground.

"Some one listening," said the laugher; and darting down the passage, he stumbled over Paul, whom he seized and brought out in triumph, dragging him and the unlucky broom under the light of a chandler's window, which was near them.

"Now, you young vagabond," he exclaimed, shaking him roughly; "what mischief were you plotting there?"

"I weren't," said Paul, looking up pitifully. "I weren't a doing nothink. I oney dropped my broom, and I'm a-goin' to the crossin', I be."

He tried to wriggle away from his captor's grasp; but holding him tightly, Beverley Bogg —for it was him—bent him back until the light fell full upon his face, and brought his own grim countenance down to a level with it.

"A coincidence!" he muttered, as he examined it narrowly! "A strange meeting!" Then a smile, full of cunning meaning, curled round his lip.

"Do you know me?" he questioned, sharply. "Tell the truth, do you remember me?"

"Yes, I does," said Paul. "You comes across my crossin' every mornin'; you've gived me a copper sometimes, thankee, sir."

He pulled off his ragged little cap, and ducked his head with an awkward reverence to his captor.

"What else do you remember?" pursued Beverley Bogg, still smiling.

"You are the man as come two or three times to see Jacob Prew, afore he was sent to furrin' lands," said Paul.

"He means transported for burglary," continued Mr. Bogg, turning in explanation to his companion. "Jacob Prew was his uncle, or some such relative, and I visited him in one of my searches for information. Well, what else do you remember?"

"Nothink!" said Paul; "oney as Jacob Prew had lots of money arter you'd visited him; and used to send me for a whole bottle of brandy, and drink it all afore the next day was over!"

"He comes of a bad stock, you see," said

Beverley; "hardened to evil from his babyhood. I am interested in this lad—professionally, I mean. I am watching the growth of a felon."

He looked maliciously at his two listeners; so cruelly, that Paul shrank away as far as he could, and shivered more violently than before.

"You speak from hard experience," said his companion. "But it is a bitter truth to set before a child.—Boy," he continued, laying his hand gently on Paul's bare head, "I am Judge Vincent; will you think of my words? The man, or boy, who works honestly, steadily, bravely—no matter how humble his work, no matter how poor and friendless he may be—will never find the way to a prison."

"Thank'ee, sir," said Paul, as he impulsively put up one of his begrimed hands, to touch the kindly one of the Judge. "I knows what yer means. Don't steal nothink, and stick to the crossin' like a brick. Rachel's mother taught me that."

"There's a *leaven* of goodness there, you see," said the Judge, pointing to the court. "Here, my little man, is a shilling for you; and if you come to this address next week, I will see whether I can do anything for you—put you to a school, and give you the chance of becoming an honest man."

"Thank'ee sir," said Paul, taking the shilling, and a card which the Judge offered him.

"Good night, my lad," said the Judge, patting him once more on the head; then taking Beverley Bogg's arm, he walked slowly away; turning once, when nearly out of sight, to look back at Paul, who still stood at the mouth of the alley, apparently watching them.

The lawyer looked back, too.

"Stay here a minute," he said, to the Judge; "there is a question I should like to ask that child."

With a quick step, he retraced his way, and once more stood by Paul's side.

"A word with you, youngster," he said, seizing him by one ear, and tweaking it to and fro as he spoke. "Listen to me."

"I wish yer wouldn't pinch so," said Paul, indignantly. "I should be able to listen a precious sight better if yer didn't."

Beverley laughed; and releasing his ear, took hold of his wrist—the wrist of the hand which still held the shilling and the card.

"I suppose you are thinking of Judge Vincent's words?" he continued. "Making up your mind to be honest and brave? You are a fool for your pains. You were born a vagabond; you will soon be a thief."

"Don't, please," said Paul wondering why the lawyer's face was so cruel and stern; and why his cold blue eyes glared upon him with such hatred. "Don't say that! When I've put a rose-tree at her head, and a gelly-flower at her feet, I'm a-going to be a show-actor, and I'll try not to be wicked, if I can help it—I will, sir."

"What's the use? You *can't* help it!" sneered Beverley Bogg. "When you are a man you will have been to prison many times; you will be quite ready to be made a convict, to work in a gang, with a chain fastened to your leg. It's the truth, I tell you!"

He shook him angrily, and at the same time grasped the edge of the Judge's card; then, with a sudden push, he sent him reeling away against the wall; the card being now in his own grasp, while the shilling dropped upon the muddy pavement.

Paul burst into tears.

"Don't whimper there," said Beverley Bogg. "You are not hurt; and if you think you are, here's money to pay you for it. You'll say I spoke truth when you stand in the prisoner's dock, some day, and Judge Vincent sentences you to gaol."

He drew forth his purse, and taking from it a piece of money, tossed it by the side of the shilling; then, seeing the boy's eyes fixed upon him, made a movement as though he intended to slip the purse again into his pocket, but, instead of doing so, dropped it upon the muddy ground.

Then turning, he ran swiftly down the street, and rejoined his friend.

The short silence at the mouth of the court was broken, for a party of revellers entered the alley, and some foot passengers were rapidly nearing the place; and, realizing these facts, Paul darted quickly forward, picked up the shilling of Judge Vincent, and the purse and gift of Beverley Bogg.

CHAPTER VI.

HOLDING them tightly in his hand, Paul hurried away through the maze of narrow streets to a quieter one, at the end of which stood a dingy, smoke-dried church; having before it a dingy, smoke-dried graveyard. A couple of the iron rails which fenced it in from the street had broken, or been wrenched away; and through the aperture left, Paul squeezed himself, and picking his way among the mounds and stones, ensconced himself behind a tall monument, and sat down on the grass.

Then, carefully putting aside the shilling, he opened the lawyer's purse.

He uttered a cry as he did so.

The moon was shining brightly, and its rays fell full into the pockets of the portmonnaie, gleaming on bright, beautiful pieces of gold and silver.

Paul looked at them with eager eyes; then putting out his forefinger, touched them timidly. They jingled together with a merry, friendly, musical sound, that made the child smile, and touch them again and again.

That jingling might have been so many real voices, for they spoke to the little outcast, sitting alone in the moonlight, under the great monument; voices that reminded him of the shops where he had seen luxuries displayed, for which he had hundreds of times vainly longed.

Voices that reminded him of his past sufferings, of the poverty, hunger, cold, which had so pinched him, and told him those ringing pieces of metal had the power to shield him from them. Voices that spoke of little Ray, and made his heart leap, as he thought of how he could join her now—of how happy he could make her with his wealth. "I'll have boots and new clothes," he said joyfully; "I'll have my hair cut" (this was a great flight of imagination); "an I'll go to her, lookin'—lookin' like any gent—like the Prince of Wales hisself!"

Then he turned the coins out into his cap, and counted them—one, two, three, four, five, six pieces of gold, and ten of silver.

"It's a fortune," he continued joyously; then was silent.

In his hand was a piece he had not yet counted. It was the money tossed him by Beverley Bogg. He looked at it, with an unsmiling face, and dropped it into an empty pocket of the purse.

"This is his'n too," he said, looking at the rest. "I don't feel as though I could spend it; I could chuck it at his head, I could!"

He fell off once more into musing; thinking over the lawyer's words.

"By an' by, you'll steal," he muttered, "then you'll go to prison!"

He chinked the money impulsively.

"I picked this up," he argued; "I didn't prig it; oney I knows as he dropped it—I sawr him do it. You'll go to prison," he repeated, "and Judge Wincent he'll condemn yer!"

He started uneasily; then putting his hand in his pocket, pulled out the shilling, and looked at it earnestly.

It had no voice to speak, but it seemed to look up at him with the face of a frend. "It's werry hard," he said mournfully, casting a glance at the treasure in his other hand; "but he said be honest, and work; that don't mean keep the purse. I'll gi'e it back to 'un, I will, for his sake who spoke so kindly to me to-night."

He closed the purse, and, bending his head until his lips rested on the shilling, he sobbed aloud.

The clock in the ancient turret above him struck eleven. He raised his head. His gaze fell upon the old broom lying at his feet. He took it up, and examined it carefully.

"It's a'most wore out," he remarked, "but it'll larst a little longer. I'll have to go out ag'in to the crossin', that's certain; but I don't care. Some day I'll see him ag'in, an' I'll tell him as I didn't steal the purse. I shouldn't wonder but he'd pat me on the head ag'in. That 'ere other 'un have got the bit of paper he gived me. I'll arsk him for it, when I gi'es him his money."

He smiled now, and, shouldering his broom, picked his way once more between the graves, and squeezed himself into the street.

He stood a moment, thinking.

"I peromised I'd go back," he said, "or I'd go and sleep behind that 'ere stone. I'd never be found out. I'll go; but I won't tell him about the purse—not I."

With slow and reluctant steps, he returned to the court, and the house of Ned, the cripple.

He was busy preparing supper, and looked up with a smile as the boy entered.

"I waited for you," he said, "I knowed you'd come back. Well, what luck?"

"A shillin'," answered Paul; and once more he seated himself on the mattress, and stared alternately at Ned and the fire.

The man was, as he said, sociably inclined, and sat watching the sausages fry, and singing scraps of popular melodies.

"A shillin's very good luck for an hour or two's work. I won't ask for any of it, though. I'll stand treat to-night, in a friendly way."

Presently he handed Paul bread, and a share of the contents of the frying-pan.

As he bent over to take it, the bosom of his jacket gaped wide open, and the purse, which he had thrust there for safe keeping, fell out upon the ground with a heavy bang.

"Halloo!" cried Ned. "What's the meaning of that, young 'un?"

"It isn't mine," answered Paul, flushing

with vexation. "A gent as I knows dropped it."

"Get along wid yer blarney!" interrupted Ned, in a peculiar strain.

"What d' yer mean?" cried Paul. "I tell yer I seen him drop it, and I'm a-goin' to give it him back ag'in. I aren't a thief—I'm an honest boy. D' yer think the old apple-'oman would have trusted me with five shillin's if I wasn't?"

Ned looked at him thoughtfully.

"I was oney a-jokin'," he said. "In course you'll give it back. Though I say, leetle Paul, wouldn't it be jolly to have a lot of money to spend? I wonder how much there is in it? Let's see!"

"I sharn't," said Paul, stoutly. "What's the good? It ain't ourn."

He put it back into his bosom, and took up his broom defiantly.

"Orr right!" said the cripple; "I don't want to see it. Be honest, if yer likes; but it ain't a trade as pays now-a-days."

He lit his pipe, and sang songs, until by-and-by the boy became drowsy, and the sounds of Ned's singing seemed to grow more and more distant, while his figure appeared as it were receding, melting away in the smoke which curled up from the pipe.

His head fell back upon the pillow, his eyelids drooped, and opened wide; then drooped again, and remained closed.

Paul slept.

For awhile, the lulling sound of Ned's voice soothed his light slumber; then it ceased, and Paul partly awoke.

He half-opened his eyes.

The cripple had descended from his chair, and was noiselessly, but with great pains and labour, dragging himself towards the bed.

Paul thought of the spider, and his old terror rushed upon him.

The perspiration broke out upon his forehead, and he scarcely dared breathe, as he watched the man dragging himself nearer and nearer to him.

"The money!" he heard him whisper; "I'll have my share on it—I'll have it all! Give it back? Not when Ned the cripple is at hand to take care on it!"

He had got nearly half a yard nearer.

With a shrill scream of fright, Paul leaped to his feet, seized his broom, and, unlocking the door, escaped into the court; hearing, as he fled from the dangerous locality, the cripple's howl of rage and disappointment, as he lay helpless on the floor.

CHAPTER VII.

THE scene of our story now takes us to a quiet little village, a few miles from London. It was a small straggling place, with one principal street, and boasted, in a mercantile sense, a general store, where candles, tea, sugar, tobacco, treacle, toys, sweetmeats, besides tapes, needles, calico, and a few other articles of haberdashery, were all displayed in the same window, and dispensed behind the same counter.

This shop stood in the centre of the street, and was flanked on the one side by an ale-house, and on the other by the establishment of a venerable doctor and chemist, whose windows were embellished by the three orthodox glass jars, blue, red, and yellow, a small assortment of pill-boxes, labelled "Antibilious" and "Rhubarb," and a few suspicious-looking white jars.

A little below the ale-house, a barber's pole projected into the street; and above the chemist's, a milliner and dressmaker resided, who ornamented her door with a brass plate, and upon it rested her claims to gentility.

It was evening time when Beverley Bogg emerged from the little railway station of the village, and sauntered into the main street, just described.

As he walked leisurely along, he smiled and tapped the ground gently with his cane, looking as though he were well pleased with himself and the world. He smiled as he noted the gable-roofed houses, smiled at the pretentious little shops, and chuckled as he stopped at the door of the general dealer's, into which he entered.

The general dealer was a woman of about thirty years of age, a plump, comely matron, with sparkling brown eyes, waving brown hair, which could scarcely be confined under her cap, but evinced a decided inclination to stray from beneath it, and disport itself into curls of a most bewitching turn and twist. To these beauties were added a pleasant mouth, pearly teeth, and a clear red and white complexion, the whole making the sum total of one of the prettiest little women in merry England. Beverley smiled still more as he watched her for a moment busying herself with tying up minute packages of tea, and unconscious of his presence.

"Ah, Mrs. Scott," he said at length; "so I have stolen a march upon you! I am glad to see you take such interest in your thriving little business."

The widow looked up with a frank, though melancholy smile, and extended her dimpled hand across the counter.

He held it for a moment, looking all the while in her face, with eyes twinkling with malicious amusement.

"It is quite refreshing to me," he continued, "to see your professional zeal. It quite upsets the theory of those among your ancient friends, who voted you a mere butterfly, unable to exist in a less luxurious sphere than you were placed in by the accident of birth. They would marvel to see you here—you who once shone the brightest star in the circles of wealth and beauty—using your dainty fingers in tying up packages of tea, coffee, snuff, or tobacco, as the case may be, for the rough boors around you."

His words were kindly, and his voice hearty; but there was a tone of mockery peeping through them, which jarred on the sensitive nerves of his listener.

"Hush!" she said, imploringly. "Don't speak so of the old time, to-day. Do you not know it is the anniversary of the day when all my trouble began?"

Her voice faltered, and she bent closer over the packages, to hide her tears; but lowly as she bent, Beverley saw all she would have concealed from him, and brightened up; as if the best cordial of happiness for him was the misery of this poor little woman.

"Let us go into the parlour," she said, at last. "I will call Mary to mind the shop. Indeed, I do not think I can endure the noise to-day."

Calling up a neat hand-maiden, she led the way into a small sitting-room at the back of the shop, and placed wine and food before her guest.

"Elderberry," remarked the lawyer, pouring out a glass of the beverage; "and of your own manufacture too, I shouldn't wonder. Marvellous!"

"Ten years of privation, and struggling against evil fortune, are good teachers," said Mrs. Scott. "That is but a simple thing to achieve."

"May I ask what are the weightier ones?" said Beverley, slowly sipping his wine.

"Patience and hope," she said.

Yet, in spite of her words, her voice sounded weary, and her lips drooped in the straight, listless form of misery.

"Patience and hope!" said the lawyer, as though he were repeating the words of a witness, and he was the cross-examiner. "Pa-tience and hope! Very fine; but to what end? What will they bring you?"

"They cannot restore my happiness," she said, "but they may give me peace."

Again Beverley took short sips at the wine, looking at her keenly over the glass.

"It is a year since we met," she said, at last. "Perhaps you have heard something of my child?"

She clasped her hands in entreaty, as she waited for his answer.

Beverley was silent.

"You have!" she cried. "You would never keep me in such suspense, to disappoint me at last!"

"Pardon me," said Beverley, speaking earnestly; "I am thinking how I can best soften the bitter truth I have to tell you—that sentence which for nine long weary years has so tortured you. I have come here to tell you, on this tenth anniversary of your parting from your husband, that I have no news for you of your boy!"

"No news—no news!" she repeated, drearily. "Heaven help me and the poor child!"

Leaning forward, she bent her head upon the table, and sobbed quietly, while Beverley alternately rubbed his hands, sipped wine, and ate cake, and looked as happy as it was possible for him to seem.

At last the woman looked up, and drew her hands across her forehead, thrusting back the waves of bright hair which had fallen across her face.

"Beverley!" she said.

Then stopped for a moment, and looked at him questioningly.

"Well, Catherine?"

"In this quiet, lonely life, so different to the life I was brought up in——"

"So different to the life you were brought up in?" he said, glancing round the humble room, and through the pane of glass in the door, out into the shop. "Well?"

"I have had time to think over many things I never thought of before. I have been looking at myself as I was nearly twelve years ago, when I married William Vincent."

"When you married Mr. Vincent?" said Beverley Bogg, with a savage emphasis on the last words.

"I can see myself just as I was then—a young, giddy, foolish creature."

"You were scarcely eighteen," said the lawyer, musingly.

"Young, giddy, and foolish," continued the unhappy woman; "ill educated to bear the ills of life, unfit to be the wife of a man like him, save in one thing."

"And that was———" questioned her unsympathising guest.

"That I loved him!" said Catherine—"loved him truly, fondly; that I reverenced him, worshipped him, as I did no one else upon this earth!"

Her cheeks flushed, and her eyes grew bright and tender as she spoke impetuously, clasping her hands over her heart, as though the very remembrance of her girlish love had power to make it leap and thrill again.

Beverley turned a shade paler, and bit his lip.

"But still I was unfit for him," she continued; "he was so wise and grave, and I was but a passionate, wilful child, with no sympathy for his duties and studies; nothing but a frivolous pleasure-seeker."

Again she sobbed for a moment, then went on.

"I did not find this out at once. You know how happy we were until little Paul was born. Then he changed. He grew stern and cold, and tired of his home—the home I had failed to make happy for him!"

"Failed to make happy!" repeated Beverley.

"It fretted me to notice this; but instead of trying harder to please him, I let my pride, my self-will, guide me; and I copied his coldness, I shunned his society, and became more frivolous and pleasure-seeking than before. At last, Beverley, you told me the cause of his change. He had met some one more suited to him than his foolish little wife; and—and she had won his heart. I deserved it; but it drove me mad to know how I had lost him. But even then, if I had bravely striven to meet his needs, to atone for my folly, he would have taken me to his heart again."

"You mistake," said Beverley.

"I demanded from you proof of your words."

"And I gave it to you," he said. "You remember the ball at the French Ambassador's,—the scene in the garden, where you saw him with Constance Clayton—saw him embrace her!"

"I remember," said Catherine, wearily. "But even then, had I been wiser, I should have now been his happy, honoured wife, instead of the lonely, wretched woman I am. I listened to my proud, jealous heart, and I left him, forgetting that I had vowed to be faithful and kind while life should last."

"It is too late to think of it now, Catherine," said Beverley Bogg. "There is no recalling the past."

"No recalling it," she said; "but it might be mended. You have been my friend; you are his companion; you know his nature better than any one else. Tell me, may I not go to him?"

"For what purpose?" he questioned, somewhat eagerly.

"I would tell him all my miserable story. I would throw myself at his feet, and never, never rise again until he had forgiven me. Oh, Beverley, he is good and noble! He would not cast me from him when he knows the truth!"

"You say he is good and noble!" said Beverley Bogg. "I know him to be also harsh and proud. Do you know what the world says of you?"

"Of me?"

"That you left your husband because you had discovered you could love another more than him. That this other was the partner of your flight."

"Oh, Beverley, how could they?—how could they?" cried Catherine, in distress. "Was there no one to defend me against so false a slander? Was there no one who answered for a poor friendless woman, and told the world that it lied—cruelly lied?"

"There was one," he said, with a smile which would lead her to suppose he was the individual. "There was one; but the many tongues of scandal would not be stopped, and society still heard the rumour, and believed it."

"And he—my husband?"

"I cannot tell what he thought. I think he deems it true. At any rate, you can see how useless it will be for you to return. His pride would revolt against again receiving a woman to his arms, to share his home, whose name had been bandied about as yours has been for years past."

"Beverley," said Catherine, pitifully, "you know better. You know the purity of my life; how I have toiled and striven, and never by even one act sullied his name. Plead for me; tell him this—all my story since I left him. Promise me you will, for the sake of your old friendship."

She knelt before him, and clasped her hands over his in entreaty.

"It will be of no avail," he said. "Could you bring me his boy——"

"I cannot; you know I cannot," she sobbed. "When I was ill in the hospital—so ill that I knew nothing,—my boy was taken from me.

What right had the parish to give my child to a stranger? You know, as soon as I was well, how I tried to find him; how the person who had adopted him had disappeared, leaving no clue for me to trace my baby."

"Still, if you could bring that boy, perhaps he would forgive you, for the child's sake. There is no other chance."

"Lost! lost! both my husband and my boy!" she said, despairingly.

"If you see him before, you lose your only chance of reconciliation. Catherine, trust me now, as you have always done. Have patience yet for another year. I will strain every nerve to find the child; and, when I succeed, you shall take him to your husband, and ask his pardon."

"And he will not deny it. He will be merciful to me, for little Paul's sake. Beverley, I will obey you; I will wait—still striving for patience and hope."

CHAPTER VIII.

"Is there e'er a letter for Mr. Paul, at this 'ere Ginral Post Orfice?"

As Paul spoke, he looked eagerly into the face of the clerk, and touched his hat reverentially, with an awe begotten in him by the size of the building, its pillared portico, and the majesty of the man, in beadle's costume, who sat keeping watch over the broad flight of steps leading to the entrance.

"Paul, eh?" said the clerk, looking superciliously at the tattered little figure on the other side of the counter. "Letter P," he added, turning to a number of pigeon-holes, each labelled with a single letter of the alphabet, and drawing from one of them a number of letters, which he leisurely examined. "Price, Potter, Paul. This is it, I suppose," he mused, taking out a clumsy-looking, coarse envelope, addressed in a straggling scrawl. "Mr. Paul——"

"Ginral Post Orfice, London," concluded the boy. "That's him, sir."

The clerk tossed it carelessly towards him, and Paul, with a grateful "Thank'ee," seized it, and made a rapid exit from the place, scaring the dignified guardian of the steps with a shrill whoop of defiance, as he darted by him into the street.

With the letter hugged tightly to him, he wandered on, and found a quiet nook at last, where, seating himself on the ground, he first turned the document over and over, and then, with an air of intense enjoyment, broke the seal, and examined the contents of the envelope.

First, a sheet of dingy, whitey-brown letter-paper with strange-looking hieroglyphics, running over its surface in sloping, irregular lines, embellished with sundry smears of ink, and ending with a number of little blots enclosed in a crooked circle, over which was written a solitary word.

Paul mused over it a long while, turning it about in all directions, and winding up with applying it to his nostrils, as though it were a bouquet.

Then he folded it up, muttering, as he did so, the one word, "Baccy."

As he again took up the envelope, he detected the presence of a hard substance within it, and pulling it forth, looked at it earnestly, then uttered a shout of joy.

It was a roughly executed portrait of little Ray, dressed in the new clothes promised to her by the showman. Little Ray, in a red dress, with a blue cloak thrown over a chair beside her, and the identical hat trimmed with yellow ribbons, which he had heard described, dangling from her hand.

Little Ray, with shining boots, and a vision of lace peeping from beneath her scarlet skirt, such a glowing, happy-looking picture, that Paul laughed and cried in a breath, as he gazed upon it, and would have kissed the sweet face glancing into his own, with a smile, had he not feared to dim the gorgeous colours around it. So the time flitted by, until the great clock of St. Paul's sounded the hour, waking him up with its iron tongue.

Then, restoring the portrait and letter to their case, and hiding them carefully in the pocket which held the purse of Beverley Bogg, he shouldered his broom, and trudged off to his labour at the crossing.

It was a dull day; there was a dampness in the air, and a darkness in the sky, which told of rain; and Paul had but a scanty reward in halfpence for his labours; but through the whole of the weary time the child's face wore a happy smile, as he ever and anon touched the letter he had received that morning, and wove bright visions of his future, when he should have joined the good-natured showman.

It was dusk in the evening, when Beverley Bogg, returning home from the office, and reaching the corner of a street which he was accustomed to pass, came face to face with Paul.

A grim look of satisfaction flitted across him, as he caught sight of the boy leaning against the wall, and he quickened his steps, as though he feared he should lose sight of him. But, contrary to his expectations, Paul watched his approach, with an altogther unconcerned air, and even touched his cap, as Beverley reached him, and grasped him by the shoulder.

"Ah, ha!" said the lawyer, with an irrepressible burst of joy; "so I have caught you again! I've been looking for you, at your old crossing, and Shuter's Court, for two weeks in vain. I imagined you had taken yourself off on another trip, for an indefinite period of time."

"I don't live over yonder now," said Paul, pointing in a direction which he meant to signify his former home. "An' I don't sweep that t'other crossin'," neither."

"Which means that you have changed your residence, and your place of business," sneered Beverley Bogg, seizing one of his crisp curls, and pulling it through his fingers in an abstracted sort of manner. "And why, may I ask, did you do so?"

"Acoss the court's a bad place," said Paul, ducking his head, and obtaining a sharp twinge of pain, as he pulled the curl from the lawyer's fingers. "Look 'ere; that night as you and Judge Vincent saw me there, I seed you drop your purse, an' I picked him up. At first, I thort I'd keep him; and then, ag'in, I thort I wouldn't; but would give him back ag'in the very first time as I seed you."

The look of pleasure had vanished from the lawyer's countenance, and he stood frowning darkly upon the eager, happy child.

"So I made up my mind not to say nothink about it in the court; but that werry night Ned the cripple found it out, and he tried to get me to stick to it, and harf the money along of him."

"And, of course, you didn't do it? Oh, no! you didn't touch a penny of the money?" mocked Beverley; speaking as though he very much wished Paul had purloined the contents of the purse.

"In course I didn't," he said, stoutly. "But that very night, when I was asleep——"

"When you were asleep," repeated the lawyer; "well, what then?"

"Why, Ned, he tried to prig it. I woke up, and seed him a-crorlin' along the ground, to get to me, an' I jumped up and run away; an' since then I ain't never been near Shuter's Court, or the old crossin', for I'm afraid to go there. That's how it is you've never seed me, but I've looked out arter you, to give you back the purse, an' there it is; an' every bit of the money safe inside of it!"

He had been fumbling in his jacket pocket as he spoke, and now drew forth the purse, which he handed to the lawyer.

As he did so, the letter slipped from its place, and fluttered to the ground, unperceived by Paul, who was staring at the face above him, and wondering why it looked so angry and disappointed, when its owner had just received his lost property again.

"So you are determined on trying the honesty dodge, I see," said Beverley, setting his foot on the letter. "As I told you once before, you are a fool for your pains."

He dropped his handkerchief, and stooping hastily, picked it up, dexterously gathering in its folds Paul's letter, scowling all the while so fiercely, that the lad forgot to ask him, as he had fully intended, for the card of Judge Vincent, but turning, slowly walked away, puzzling himself over the question of what he had done to awaken the enmity of the rich man.

For a moment, the lawyer stood watching him, then followed at an easy distance, until he had tracked him to his home, in a distant court, when he retraced his steps, rubbing his hands and knitting his brows, in deep thought, chuckling at times, as he thought of the letter he had purloined.

In the meantime, unconscious of these things, Paul had ascended to the little attic closet he claimed as his abode, and lighting a candle, had seated himself, with the intention of enjoying another peep at the letter, and the precious portrait.

As he felt for them vainly in his pocket, his face lengthened and clouded, and with quick alarm he sprang to his feet, shaking himself, and searching everywhere amid his tattered clothing.

It was in vain; there was no letter to be found; and with a sick throb at his heart, and hurried catching of his breath, he realized the truth that he must have dropped them in the street.

Without a moment's delay, even to blow out his candle, or pick up the halfpence which he had in his excitement scattered on the floor, he bounded down the stairs, and slowly retraced his steps to the street corner where he had met Beverley Bogg, and where he had last felt the little packet resting on his bosom.

But here, as before, his search was in vain;

nowhere on the pavement, or in the kennel, though he examined them every step of the way with eager eyes, did he find aught that even looked like a letter; and sadly and moodily, he returned to his squalid home.

The candle had guttered away, in the draft from the open door, and the long wick leant over the neck of the bottle in which it was placed, and dropt greasy tears upon the floor, while a thief had stolen in and gathered up the halfpence.

"There won't be no need to find anybody to read that 'ere letter," said Paul, despairingly; as, heedless of everything about him, he threw himself down, and burying his face in his hands, burst into a passion of tears.

At the same time, Beverley Bogg sat in his dressing-room at home, with the epistle spread out before him, reading it aloud, and laughing every now and then, as he pictured Paul's dismay when he should discover its loss.

"An interesting document," he said, as he concluded the showman's scrawl. "A promising opening for you, little Paul; only I'll take care that you never enter upon it. No, no; we will look after your future, and give you such a profession as will make you an ornament, and a credit to your family, when I restore you to their arms. An interesting letter; and a pretty enclosure, certainly!" he added, looking contemptuously at Rachel's laughing face.

Then, gathering them up, he held them in the flame of a taper, and watched them burn and shrivel away into light, impalpable ashes.

CHAPTER IX.

It was a bright, cheerful morning when a man emerged from a narrow lane-like street, and entered the thoroughfare leading to Beverley Bogg's office.

He was considerably past the prime of life, of medium height, squarely and powerfully built, and was attired in a dress which would mark him as belonging to the lower order of society.

The sun was pouring down with intense heat, and the pavement sent up a white glare, which struck upon the eyes with an almost blinding effect; but, unmindful of these inconveniences, the man walked hurriedly along, seeming to shun the shady side, which the mass of people preferred.

At last, with a sudden dive among the vehicles passing along the road, he crossed, and entered the open door of the lawyer's office.

Simkins, the clerk, was at his post, as usual; his face a trifle redder, and his whole appearance denoting the extremity of humid misery.

He looked up petulantly as the man stepped into the room, bringing with him a current of warm air, and frowned ominously over the little railing which was fixed around the top of his desk. Nothing awed by his assumption of dignity, the intruder returned the stare with double interest, smiling insolently all the while.

"I want Mr. Bogg!" he said, jerking his thumb over his shoulder, in the direction of the inner room; "so you just step in, and tell him that there's a gent waitin' here who can't be refused, not on any account."

"My good man," answered Simkins, shuddering at his audacity, "I can take in no such message. Give me your name, and tell me your business, and I will inquire whether my master will see you."

"I sha'n't do nothing of the kind," he said. "You go an' tell the guv'ner as I'm here, an' I'll bet you a shillin' as he'll see me. Tell him it's a great pusson from abroad, as he once used to know in the way of bisness."

With a look on his face, expressive of his conviction that the visitor would, in spite of his assurance, find no admission to that sacred inner apartment, Simkins took the message in to Beverley Bogg; adding a note of his own at the end thereof, to the effect "that he thought the man was after no good, and that he should advise his master not to see him."

"What business have you to think anything about it?" said Beverley, raising his eyes from the contemplation of a large manuscript. "If you would bestow more thought upon your duties, and less upon that which does not concern you, it would be better for you and more profitable to myself."

Simkins writhed under the reproof, and became a rosier red than before, as, looking behind him, he perceived the room-door was wide open, and concluded, in consequence, that the obnoxious visitor had heard every word, and was probably laughing in his sleeve, and looking upon it as an excellent joke.

"I beg pardon, sir," he stammered, advancing a couple of steps towards the table, then precipitately backing half a dozen, before the uncompromising expression of his master's face—"I beg your pardon, sir—I am sure——"

"Silence!" said Beverley. "Speak another word, and consider yourself to have received a week's notice to quit my service. Out of my way, and let me judge for myself of this man."

He rose to his feet, and thrusting the clerk aside, strode to the door, and looked out.

The person under inspection was quietly leaning on the mantel-piece, with his back to the private room, and was quietly smoking.

"Now, then," roared the lawyer, angrily; "what are you doing with that pipe?—and what do you want here?"

Simkins, from his position behind Beverley Bogg, saw all, and rubbed his hands with delight at this rough reception of the shabby, presuming stranger.

"Well," said the man, coolly pressing down the contents of the bowl with his huge, dirty thumb, "in the first place, I'm a-smokin' this pipe, and very much I enjoys it, on this brilin' 'ot day. In the second place," he continued, between a series of puffs, "I wants to see you partickler, Mister Beverley Bogg."

As he spoke, he turned round, and displayed his face to the lawyer.

Beverley started, and looked as intensely surprised as it was possible for him to do.

"Jones!" he said, at last. "Ah! yes, walk in—walk in, Mr. *Jones!*"

"I'm agreeable," said the man Jones, swinging himself round on his heels, and walking into the private room, smoking furiously all the while.

Simkins fell back aghast at the turn in affairs, and remained still, leaning in a helpless manner against the wall.

"Now, then," said Beverley Bogg, sternly, "what are you waiting for, idling your time? Leave the room—and don't forget the caution I gave you a short time back. Go, and remember I am not to be disturbed."

With the look of bewilderment still upon his face, Simkins obeyed, and returned to his desk, where, as he seated himself, he heard the key click in the lock of the inner door.

The sound roused him. He elevated his head, and snuffed at the air.

"There's something in it," he remarked, with the old cunning twinkle growing in his eyes. "I've been here fifteen years come Christmas, and never, in all that time, have I known a cigar or pipe to be smoked in these rooms. Yet this man—this plebeian Jones—can indulge, without reproof, in shag, and that of the rankest kind."

He curled his pursey little mouth into an expression of disgust; and listened intently, with his pen poised in his hand, ready to be thrust into the ink at the first alarm.

But as all remained safe, he smiled contentedly, and with careful fingers extracted the plug from the wall, and applied his eye to the opening.

Through the crack in the opposite wall he could see into his master's room.

He could obtain but a small view, but that little must have been highly satisfactory, for he lifted his head quickly, winked his right eye, and rubbed his hands in a manner which denoted jollity and satisfaction.

Then he looked again.

Beverley Bogg and the stranger, Jones, were sitting side by side, their heads bent together, and they were talking earnestly.

He moved his eye, and applied his ear to the tube.

That was apparently unsatisfactory, for he removed it, his round face lengthening into positive dismay.

"Whispering!" he said, briefly; then again applied his ear with redoubled vigilance.

After awhile his perseverance met a slight reward. The voices became gradually louder, and at last he caught a stray sentence.

It was Beverley Bogg who spoke.

"You cannot have kept your share of the compact," he said.

"Ain't I?" answered Jones, contradictorily. "I tells you I've had a heap of trouble with the boy! Haven't I kicked, and cuffed, and half-starved him? Haven't I given him the treatment that makes thieves of most all the young 'un's in my class of life—the very treatment that made me what I am? Oh, don't you go to accusin' of me of not keeping the bargain! I tell you, I've made the life of that child a trouble to hisself; and if he ain't a-done nothink desperate yet, it ain't acoss I've bin a-usin' of him too well."

The little round clerk lifted his face. He looked scared, and whispered, in horror, "Oh, lor'!"

Then he listened again.

"The result is not satisfactory," said the lawyer. "I tried him the other day. I dropped my purse at his feet——"

"And he stuck to it," said Jones. "Oh, trust him for that!"

"He returned it," interposed the lawyer.

"What!" Jones's tone was depressed. "I niver heeard tell of the like on it before!"

"He has got some notion of *honesty* in him," sneered Beverley,—"of working for his living, and such-like ideas."

"It ain't my fault," said the man. "Ask anybody that knows me, and they'll tell you that Jacob Prew, as took his trial for burglary (which deed was a thing as I'm purfeshunally proud on),—ask 'em, I say, of Jacob Prew—returned to his native land on a ticket-of-leave—and they'll tell you as I've edicated some of the cleverest hands in our line of business."

"You fool!" interrupted Beverley Bog. "Can't you sink your identity in a place like this? Here, I know nothing of Jacob Prew. I recognise only Peter Jones, an agent, who gathers legal information for me."

"You're a sharp 'un!" said Jacob Prew, *alias* Peter Jones, in an admiring tone. "But how about the boy, Paul?"

"Silence!" said Beverley. "I'll have no names here. Call him the child—anything but a name. You know my wishes. Make him what you are—a pest to the world, an outcast, a felon, a wretch from whom every honest man will shrink with aversion and disgust, and I shall be satisfied. See here! Set that boy in the prisoner's box before another year is over, and I'll pay you a hundred pounds on his committal to prison."

"Agreed!" said the convict. "I'll do it, if I have to force his hands into pilfering."

"Good gracious!" said the clerk, recoiling from the wall with a white face, and in his excitement nearly toppling backwards over the stool.

He caught the desk just in time to save himself, but his feet came with a heavy kick against one of its legs, and nearly frightened him backwards again.

He hastily covered the hole in the wall, and, picking up his pen, wrote diligently.

Not a moment too soon, for the inner door opened quickly, and the lawyer's head was protruded.

"What page of that document are you now writing?" he queried, sharply.

"Number five, sir," said Simkins.

"Very good," said Beverley, and again closing the door.

The little clerk laughed. For once, he had outwitted the lawyer.

He had finished page six, and had commenced the seventh.

It was nearly ten minutes before Simkins could summon courage enough to return to his eavesdropping, and when he did so, the conference was almost ended.

"Where is he to be found?"

The convict was asking the question, as he filled another pipe, preparatory to taking his departure.

"Here," said Beverley Bogg, as he handed him a small card, on which he had been writing.

"Then I'll be off at once; there's nothing like strikin' while the iron's hot," said Jacob Prew, rising. "I shall soon come to you for that hundred pounds."

The clerk put in the plug, and applied himself to his work, and presently heard the inner room-door open, and the heavy step of the visitor, as he emerged therefrom. Still he did not look, and could barely repress a shudder as the man, crossing the floor, came up close to him, and thrust his face betwixt him and the light.

"I say," he sneered, "wouldn't you like to be confidential clerk to Mister Bogg?"

With a laugh, he walked away, stopping on the threshold to light his pipe.

"He shall find out I *am* his confidential clerk a little bit sooner than he will find agreeable!" muttered the clerk, as he clenched his fist, and shook it fiercely under cover of the desk.

"How many pages?" called Beverley from his room.

"Going seven," he answered, scowling until his rosy face was wrinkled and puckered like a winter apple.

Then something like tears glistened in his eyes, and one fell upon the deed he was preparing—the strangest baptism paper had ever received in a lawyer's office; and he bent over his work, saying, in a tone of pity, "Poor Paul—poor little Paul!"

CHAPTER X.

WHEN he had reached the end of the street, Jacob Prew stopped and read the card; then, thrusting it into his jacket, sauntered into an eating-house, and lounged away an hour, feasting on the various dainties vended there, ever and anon gaily rattling some money which he had received from his employer.

Thus, leaving the place, he wandered on, and rested again at an inn a mile or two away—a quiet house, where no one knew him, or troubled themselves about him or his affairs.

Then, in a succession of strolling and resting, eating and drinking, he contrived to pass away the time until the evening came on, and deepened into the darkness of night.

Thus, with a firmer step, and the reflex of a settled purpose in his face, he bent his steps towards another quarter of the City.

Through the gaily lighted portion, with a slinking motion; into the poor regions beyond, with an assured air; and so on, until he came to the court whither the lawyer had tracked Paul on the previous night. He walked boldly down it, and, standing in a dark corner, kept a sharp look-out.

Presently, the boy came pattering past him, his broom over his shoulder, and a shadow of gloom and weariness resting over him, darkening his face, making his figure droop, and imparting to his whole appearance a look of dejection and misery.

Jacob grinned wickedly, and followed up the stairs, only a little way behind him, up to the tiny cupboard-like room, which he reached just as the boy had lighted his candle.

He stood at the door for a moment, then stepped in, and closing it behind him, stooped, and laid his heavy hand upon the child's shoulder.

Paul looked up, and recognising the face, turned pale with terror, unable to speak or move.

Jacob laughed a little.

"You didn't expect to see *me* so soon?" he said. "I don't wonder you are surprised. Quite glad, aren't you, that old Prew's come back ag'in to look after you?"

Still Paul was silent, but his eyes wandered round him, as if he were searching for a loop-hole of escape.

"Bless the boy, he's struck dumb with astonishment!" continued Jacob. "You little knows how I've been thinkin' of you, since I went away; for many's the time as I've said to myself, 'I wonder what's become of Paul—of litttle Paul, as I've kep' ever since he was a baby!'"

The child trembled as he heard the mocking voice, and tried faintly to release himself.

Jacob held him fast.

"But, you see, I've come back ag'in, though I suppose as how you'd gived me up, and thought as you'd seen the last of me. But 'tain't so; I'm come back agin from Australey, to look after you; and I tell you what, Paul, we'll never part ag'in!"

Tears of intense agony welled to the boy's eyes, and rolled down his cheeks.

"This room arn't big enough for both on us, so we'll go back to Shuter's Court, and I'll promise you we shall be comfortable. Oh, yes, we shall live like two doves, you and me, little Paul!"

It was plain, however, that the lad had a very hopeless idea of any comfort to be derived from living with the convict, for, with a piteous cry, he slid from the rough, grasping hand, and fell upon his knees, his face convulsed with terror.

Again Jacob laughed.

"Come along," he said; "I've no time to lose."

He raised him, and once more resuming his grasp of Paul's shoulder, forced him from the room down the stairs, and out into the street.

There he hailed a cab, and, lifting his prisoner into it, was driven rapidly away to Shuter's Court.

Arriving there, the boy was lifted from the cab, and led into the dreaded place.

His heart sank heavily, as the flare of the well-known lamp fell upon him, and the old, familiar, ragged people flitted about him.

"Seems like old times, eh?" said Jacob. "Oh, but we will have some fine times here!"

Heavier, heavier fell the child's heart; then it gave a sickening throb.

They were close by the house where Ned the cripple lived, and he could see the light burning in the window.

He could have cried aloud, but he knew it was useless, and he yielded with passive despair when his captor drew him into the passage, and stopping at the room-door, rapped in a peculiar manner with his knuckles.

It was opened quickly, and Ned uttered a loud shout of joy as he recognised his visitor.

"I've been expectin' you for a week past!" he cried. "Everything is ready for you. Come in—come in! This *is* a pleasure!"

"Served four years, and took care to be on my good behaviour, so I've a ticket of leave; and here I am ag'in, hearty as ever."

He entered the room as he spoke, dragging Paul with him.

"And here's little Paul," continued Ned, turning round, and thrusting him maliciously with his crutch—"little Paul, as treated me, so bad when I was willin' to act a friend's part by him. But I don't bear malice—not I."

He looked very much as though bearing malice was nothing uncommon to him; and in spite of his protestation of forgiveness, Paul knew he had made an enemy.

"And you give the purse back again—you did!" said the cripple. "You are one of the honest ones, *you* are. Do you hear that, Jacob?"

Both of the men burst out laughing, as though this were a great joke; and one pulled his hair, while the other struck him playful, yet painful, blows with his guiding-stick.

Then they fell to carousing, and Paul, as he had done once before, seated himself on the edge of the mattress, and looked on until, far into the night, he fell asleep, as he was still watching the revelry, and dreamt that the cripple was stealing to the bed-side to murder him with the crutch, and that Beverley Bogg and Jacob Prew were cheering him on. Once only in the vision he saw Judge Vincent's hand held out to save him, but it faded away, and he awoke to see the light still burning in the room, and the two men talking eagerly, as they caroused.

CHAPTER XI.

SIMKINS hailed with delight the hour which released him from his labours.

Never had clock so musical a tone, in his ears, as the one which struck four in the bare office in which he passed the greater portion of his life.

He leaped down joyfully from his perch, thrust his papers into the desk, closing it with a sharp bang, which brought Beverley Bogg from his den.

"Afraid to give a minute over time," he grumbled. "You are not so particular to being a few after it in the morning, I suppose?"

"I am proud to say I am *punctual*, sir," retorted the clerk, diligently polishing his hat with his coat-sleeve, "as the clock strikes nine."

"Bah!" said his employer; and without any further adieu, he walked away.

"Good riddance!" said Simkins, walking into the private room. He looked about the table and on the floor, but the lawyer had been careful, and not a scrap of writing lay about—not a piece of blotting paper, even, from which prying eyes could glean aught of his private business.

"Done!" said Simkins; then, as a relief to his overcharged feelings, he glared savagely at the stuffed easy chair, and shook his fist at that innocent article of furniture with unparalleled ferocity.

After this, he sank into it, in a high state of perspiration, and fanned himself with a sheet of blank foolscap paper, which lay ready to his hand. His brief rest over, he arose, locked the outer door of the office, and, delivering it to the old woman, who was waiting in the passage, took his departure.

He lived a little way out of the City, and had to run for the railway station, arriving there just five minutes after his usual train had departed.

He bore it well, though, and seating himself on a bench, which uncomfortably reminded him of his office stool, he fell into deep thought.

It was full an hour after his time when he arrived at his destination, and his face became broad with happiness as he turned into the road leading to his home.

And, truly, it was a home which was calculated to inspire him with cheerfulness.

A neat little cottage, standing in a shady lane, with a stretch of green meadow around it.

There was a small garden in the front, fenced in with green palings, and filled with bright flowers; and a larger garden at the back, where Simkins cultivated potatoes in one patch, lettuces and onions in another, and cabbage in a third; around these patches was a bordering of parsley; and interspersed among them, gooseberry and currant bushes; and all round the boundary wall, scarlet runners, trained upon pieces of twine.

His front garden boasted of an arbour, festooned with peas, where Simkins enjoyed his pipe in the evening, and watched the lovers come sauntering along the lane.

The back garden boasted a pigsty, and in the sty was a fat pig, of wonderful intelligence and appetite, who was predestined to slaughter on the forthcoming Christmas season.

Altogether, it was such a rustic, happy-looking place, that it was no wonder Simkins's face became more and more genial as he neared it, until it looked like one broad smile.

But when he turned a bend in the lane, and caught a full view of the garden gate, he looked more beaming and beneficent than before. A round, rosy woman stood there, dressed in a pink dress of a most coquettish make. This was Mrs. Simkins.

In her arms she held a round, rosy baby; and climbing up the paling, and hanging on to her skirts, were four other children, all very clean, very shining, and excited.

These were the olive-branch Simkinses, and they all, baby not excepted, set up a joyful yell when they espied their parent plodding along the dusty road; and the elder ones, bursting away from maternal control, rushed to meet, and hang on his hands and coat-tails during the remainder of the journey.

"Bless me, John!" chirruped the little woman, as soon as he came within earshot, —"bless me, John! I thought you were never coming home. I was afraid there had been an accident on the rail, and I've been quite fidgetty. I'm so glad to see you home safe!"

FALLEN AMONG THIEVES. (See page 5.)

"Not more than I am to see you," said Simkins, chucking the baby under the chin, who, in return, grasped his whiskers, and crowed in concert with the general shout of joy.

Then Mrs. Simkins put up her face to be kissed, forgetting that she stood at the gate, and ignoring the passers by; and John took the baby, and in a tumultuous state of joy, the jubilant procession passed into the cottage.

Simkins had a boarder, an elderly gentleman, who had achieved an independency in the wine trade, and had settled down to the enjoyment of a quiet life; though how he could term it a quiet one, surrounded as he generally was by those rampant young Simkinses, was a puzzling question.

He was a genial old fellow, and a liberal man to boot, and the clerk greatly rejoiced in this household acquisition, and the pleasant consequent addition to the yearly income of eighty pounds, earned in the lawyer's office.

Many marvelled how he managed to obtain so dainty an establishment with his slender means, but Mrs. Simkins had been possessed of a fortune of one hundred and fifty pounds when he had married her, and he had been a careful man, and had, during a long course of yearly pinchings and economy, saved fifty more; and with part of this money they had furnished the little cottage where they now resided, and the residue had helped them in many a strait during the earlier years of their wedded life, before Mr. Phipps had come to board with them, and when the little olive branches springing into existence rendered it a hard matter to keep things square and comfortable.

Of late years, the pair had formed the ambitious project of buying the cottage, so endeared had it become to them during the happy years of their wedded life.

Simkins had even entered upon negotiations with the landlord, and he being a kind-hearted man, had consented to letting them give the price by instalments, of which more than fifty pounds had already been paid.

And yet, in spite of these subjects for congratulation, when the flush of the excitement consequent on his return had faded, the clerk became silent and thoughtful, and could not be roused either by the excellence of his evening meal, or the attentions and blandishments of his family, and the genial boarder, who had produced a bottle of old port, and insisted on everybody drinking John's health.

So the depression spread over the social circle, and they all became silent and thoughtful likewise.

At last he perceived this, and calling up the ghost of a smile, pulled four pennies from his pocket, which he distributed among the children, who at once, with a whoop, departed to spend them in indigestible dainties.

Then drawing his chair round to the window, Simkins beckoned his wife to him.

Baby in arms, she went, and seating herself in a rocking-chair by his side, looked at him with loving eyes,

The boarder lit a long pipe, and, by special invitation, joined the group.

"Mary," said the clerk to his wife, "I wish to put a case before you. Mr. Phipps, I wish also to lay it before you."

Both nodded, and he proceeded.

"Suppose I had gained the information that a great wrong was being perpetrated on an innocent person—a wrong which I might prevent—how is it my duty to act?"

"Like a man, and put a stop to it at once," said Phipps, decidedly.

"Stop a minute — don't you speak yet, Mary," he continued, addressing his wife. "Suppose that the man who is about to commit this crime were a rich man? Suppose, for instance, he proved to be my master, Beverley Bogg? How then?"

"That would not make any difference," she said, in a low voice.

"Have you thought of the consequences of my thwarting him?" said Simkins. "I should lose my situation, which would greatly reduce our little income—would expose us to hardship and want. Then I could not go on paying for the house; we may be called on to make many sacrifices, and endure much—not only ourselves, but the children, too! We may meet with a reward from those whom I aid by revealing the plot; but it is as well to look the worst in the face. And, now we have done so, what do you think?"

"Still I say, reveal the wrong-doing, and trust to providence for the rest," said the little wife by his side.

"My sentiments," remarked Phipps.

"Vice never prospered yet," she continued; "and I should fear we should never be happy again if you did not do the right thing, and help the poor and distressed against the injustice or tyranny of the rich, come what may of your endeavours."

"I've made up my mind!" said Simkins, starting up, and seizing his hat from its peg.

"I'm going to London this evening, to tell everything to the proper party. Nobody shall ever say that John Simkins failed, when put to the pinch, to behave like an honourable man and a Christian."

After kissing his wife, he left the house, and proceeded to the railway station, from whence he was soon speeding to London.

Arrived there, he wended his way to the mansion of Judge Vincent.

He was rather astonished, on entering the square in which it was situated, to perceive that the ground was littered with straw; but, quickly passing along, he soon reached the door of the house, and rang the bell.

The servant who answered it knew him, for he had often been there before, on errands for Beverley Bogg.

"Is the Judge at home?" inquired Simkins.

"Yes," said the footman; "but you can't see him. He has taken it into his head of late to go out roaming the streets at all hours of the day and night; and the result is, that as he was rambling in the City to-day, he had a sunstroke, and is ill in bed. The doctor says he will have brain-fever, and it is doubtful whether he will ever recover."

Simkins turned sadly away.

"Fate seems to be against you, little Paul," he said. "But I'll keep my eyes and ears open, and save you yet."

CHAPTER XII.

IT was the evening after the commencement of Judge Vincent's illness, and his housekeeper sat in her room, alone, sadly musing on her master's condition, and the comfortless report she had just received from the doctor concerning him.

"He is a strong man, but it will take all his strength to pull him through this illness."

She had repeated it over and over to herself, and had talked about it lugubriously with the butler, until her spirits had sank to the lowest ebb, and her mind was filled with hopeless forebodings.

She had just arrived at the conclusion that she needed some solace in her misery, and had determined on taking it in the form of tea, with a slight sprinkling of brandy therein, when a visitor was announced.

Mrs. Bentley looked up in surprise, and with an air of not being best pleased with the interruption, set her teapot aside, and shaking out the folds of her black silk dress, prepared to impress the intruder with a true estimate of her dignity.

Soon, a woman, dressed in a costume of sober brown hue, with her face closely concealed by a veil, entered the room.

There was an air of dignity and self-respect in her manner, as she stood just within the door, which was not without its effect on the worthy housekeeper, for, in a mollified tone, she invited her to take a seat.

The stranger sank into a chair, clasping and unclasping her hands nervously, but uttering no words, though Mrs. Bentley waited vainly for her to speak.

At last the silence became insupportable to the curious old soul, and bending forward in a vain endeavour to pierce the thickness of the woman's veil, she inquired her business.

Still, there was no answer; but, suddenly, the veil was thrown aside by the wearer, revealing a face which was still, in a great measure, concealed by the border of a close cap, and a green shade, which was worn over the eyes, and covered a great portion of the features.

What remained in view was, however, young-looking and pretty; and a strange feeling stirred Mrs. Bentley's heart as she gazed earnestly before her, watching her visitor's lips move in a vain effort to speak.

"Don't trouble to begin just yet," she said, with a gentle consideration unusual to her; "I dare say you are tired; rest a moment first."

"Don't you know me, Mrs. Bentley?" cried the woman, tearing off the green shade, and looking with imploring eyes at the housekeeper.

The old servant uttered a scream, and recoiled in amazement from her guest.

"Lor'! it's—it's Mrs. Vincent!" she gasped. "And we have all thought you dead years ago! Why have you come here?"

"Why?" sobbed Catherine. "Because I read in the newspaper that my husband was ill. Where should my place be but at his side?"

"Then you should never have left him!" said Mrs. Bentley, striving hard to put on a show of virtuous indignation, and failing signally in the attempt. "If you had not, this might never have happened."

"Don't speak so," cried Catherine, excitedly. "You pity him for what he has suffered, but you can never know all the misery I have endured since that wretched day when I listened to the dictates of my folly, and wrecked my happiness."

"I can guess, madam," said the housekeeper.

"Sooner or later, every sin brings its own punishment. This has been a sore trial for me. I have known my master from his boyhood; I often nursed you when you were a baby; and when you became his wife, I knelt and thanked heaven for the joy I deemed it had bestowed upon both you and Mr. William. I did not think this would have been the end of it. The Judge, a lonely, heart-broken man; you a lonely miserable woman, whom the world looks upon with scornful eyes, and speaks of with a bitter tongue!"

The tears ran over the old woman's wrinkled cheeks, and she wrung her hands in distress.

"I did not think it would come to this—that you would ever be forced to steal in disguise into your own husband's house, and that I should feel like a guilty thing in allowing you to remain here—in holding conversation with you!"

"Before heaven," said Catherine, solemnly, "I am innocent of the dreadful wrong you would lay at my door! In spite of my flight from him—in spite of the suspicions with which evil tongues have blackened my name, I have been true and loyal to my husband in thought and deed! There are those who have known every step of my life since I went away, and they will tell you I have lived purely, labouring with my hands for my daily bread. In one thing only have I wronged him, and that was when I doubted his love and faith."

"Heaven grant you may be able to prove it!" said the old woman, heartily, though with something of doubt still lingering in her tones.

"And now, madam, tell me of little Paul?"

"Hush!" said Catherine; "do not speak to me of him; you will drive me mad!"

"Is he dead, then?" cried Mrs. Bentley.

"Worse! When I was ill in the hospital, he was stolen from me—my poor baby!—and I have never seen him since, though I have searched until my very heart is sick and weary."

The housekeeper uttered a cry of dismay.

"Oh, madam!" she said, at length, "what misery your foolishness has wrought my poor master! I know how his love clings to his child."

"You kill me, Bentley!" said Catherine. "Have you no pity for me? Think of it; my young life wrecked, my happiness lost for ever; and I, with such a length of time to live and suffer before me!"

"I pity ye both," sobbed the housekeeper.

"If any sacrifice, any labour of mine, could restore to me my boy again, I would give it, no matter what it cost me. I would send him to his father, and be content to live and suffer on alone; but I cannot find him."

"Why did you come here, poor child?" said Bentley, gently smoothing her hair. "It ca do no good."

"I came to throw myself upon your mercy," returned Catherine; "to say to you, 'Let me see my husband.'"

"It is impossible," answered the housekeeper; "and it would avail you nothing. Even were I to admit you to the chamber, he would not know you. He is delirious; brain fever has set in."

"Bentley, I implore you to have mercy on me! You have been wedded, and you know how dreadful a thing it would be were death to snatch him away, and I never to see his face again! You have loved,—you cannot have forgotten it! Think of it, and pity me! Let me go to him, for I love him! I have loved him so fondly, so despairingly, for years!"

"I don't know, I'm sure," said Mrs. Bentley. "I'm not hard-hearted, but I've served him for years, and I've never disobeyed him. I do not think, madam, he would see you if he were well, and I am afraid I should do wrong to let you go to him now he is ill and helpless."

"I will not stay long," pleaded Catherine. "I will go the instant you bid me to. I came to implore you to let me nurse him, but I will not urge you. Let me see him now, and I will go away directly—I will never trouble you again!"

"Right or wrong, I've no heart to refuse you," said Bentley. "So follow me, remembering I rely on your promise to come away when I summon you."

Thus speaking, the old woman once more adjusted the veil over Catherine's face, and led the way to the sick-room.

As they approached it, they could hear the Judge's uneasy muttering, and for an instant Catherine leant against the wall, her courage failing at the sound of his voice.

"Come, madam," said the housekeeper; and, seizing her arm for support, Catherine passed into the room.

At a few words from Bentley, the nurse left them; and, with a low cry, the wife sprang to the bedside, and sinking on her knees, threw back her veil, and gazed with passionate, sorrowful love into the sick man's face.

There was no recognition of her in his face;

he rolled his head feebly from side to side, and called pitifully for some one to bring him his boy, his "little Paul."

She seized his hands, and covered them with kisses; then leant her forehead upon his bosom, and spoke to him in gentle, loving tones.

"William—William—my husband—"

Still no recognition—no reply.

"William, have you no word for me? It is I, your wife—Catherine—who have always loved and been true to you!"

He looked at her then, and smiled sadly. Then he laid one hand upon her head, and smoothed the shining waves of her hair.

"It is a fair face—a fair face!" he said, touching her cheek softly with his fingers. "But take her away; they are all alike—false! I loved one, and she deceived me! Take her away, and bring my boy—my child—Paul! I want no one else!"

He was growing excited, and he thrust her away so roughly that she staggered, and would have fallen, but for the hand of the housekeeper.

"You see, Mrs. Vincent," she said, calling her by that name for the first time during the interview,—"you see, it is of no use. You only make him worse. I believe you now. I believe you to be a true, honourable lady, and I pity you; but, for his sake, you must go. I promise you I will let you know every day how he is; and, if the worst happens, I will send for you. Cheer up, madam, and hope, as I do, that all may yet be well."

"I cannot," said Catherine. "It was my mad folly which robbed him of his child. I can never again approach him, unless I restore Paul to his arms."

Bending once more over the bed, she kissed the Judge's face; then, turning drew down her veil, and left the room, followed by the plaintive entreaty he was still making, that some one would bring him his boy.

CHAPTER XIII.

On the bank of the river, between Bermondsey and Rotherhithe, stood an old house, ruined and dilapidated, and long since passed out of the range of habitable places.

It was the property of a miserly old man, who had of late years converted it into a storehouse for the various kinds of merchandise in which he traded.

Every room had its furniture of huge bales piled around the walls and over the windows, plunging them into a continuous state of semi-darkness.

They were often removed—old ones carried away, and new ones inserted into their places; but it was beyond the memory of the oldest inhabitant of the district that any of them had ever seen those windows undarkened, or caught a glimpse of the interior of the mysterious dwelling.

Old James Berry, the owner thereof, in spite of his miserly habits, was a man of good repute among his neighbours. His sole exemption to his parsimonious tendency was made in favour of a chapel, which he zealously and regularly attended, and to which he annually subscribed the sum of ten pounds, besides a donation for the charity-school in connection with it.

In consequence of this munificence, he enjoyed the favourable opinion of his pastor, who never failed, when occasion offered, to speak a word in his praise.

James Berry was, besides, an industrious man—never away from his business. Not a package or bale was piled away in the warehouse but he superintended the work—watching his men with sharp eyes, and taking upon himself the duties of day watchman and guardian of the establishment.

From morning until night he might be seen at his post; walking in the yard attached to the premises, or moving about the darkened chambers like a seedy, morose ghost, come to do penance in his earthly habitation. It was night, and all along the river-banks the gloomy old wharves were deserted and still; while the old warehouse loomed up against the dark sky, looking more dilapidated and gloomy than ever.

In his little sentry-box in the yard, lying away from the river, sat the night watchman, a burly, faithful dependant of the old man; and in his kennel in the yard, facing the water, lay a huge mastiff, the property of the watchman.

As midnight stole on, the man in the box became gradually more wakeful—listening intently to every sound which now and then rose upon the air.

At last a tapping was heard at the heavy doors leading into the street beyond.

With a quick step, he rose from his seat, and, opening a small wicket, looked out.

Crouching against the wall, in the deep shadow, stood his master and another man.

In an instant the door was opened widely enough to admit them; and they passed in through the yard and into the dismal-looking house.

"The first here, as usual," said the watchman; and turning the key, he stood ready at the wicket, awaiting a fresh arrival.

Presently they came—two more men, slinking along in the dark, who were instantly admitted; and without a word of greeting to the porter, silently as shadows flitted across the yard, and likewise entered the warehouse.

Then came a solitary individual of like pattern with those preceding him; and he, too, obtained an entrance, and followed in the wake of the others.

After this, the watchman closed the wicket, and proceeded to fasten the doors, shooting huge bolts into their sockets, and dropping massive bars into their places, in a manner which rendered the entrance almost impregnable; for it, as well as the surrounding wall, was headed by a cheveaux-de-frise of sharp iron spikes, which grimly threatened to impale any individual who should dare attempt to cross them.

This task accomplished, the man retired to his box, and, lighting a pipe, sat down to enjoy a quiet perusal of a daily paper, which he had evidently hoarded for the occasion.

In the meantime the mastiff on the other side had also been keeping an alert look-out; which was presently rewarded by a glimpse of a boat, which suddenly shot into view, revealed by its crossing a patch of moonlight, then once more passing into the shadows thrown on the river by the wharves.

The mastiff eyed it attentively as it neared him, then seemed to recognise it—for he suffered it to draw near the landing-place without uttering a single note of warning. He even gave a little whine of satisfaction as a burly, thick-set man, who had been rowing, leaped out, and drew the boat to shore.

The whine became more intensely joyous as the new-comer bent down, and lifted to *terra firma* no less a person than Ned, the cripple, whom he set safely down, and placed the crutches beside him.

After patting the dog's rough head, Ned hobbled as fast as he could to the back door of the house, and was received by the men, who hoisted him in their arms and carried him in.

There was one still remaining in the boat—one who was crouched down in the bottom, and who looked with terror on the dark night, the dark river, the black old house, the burly man, and the huge dog. This was Paul.

"Now, then," said his companion, Jacob Prew; "look alive! Out with you, or I'll tell Nero to pull you ashore!"

The dog grinned, and displayed his teeth; and Paul, alarmed still more at the menace, leaped to his feet to Jacob's side, trembling as Nero came sniffing round him, as though he were striving to ascertain whether the child would prove a palatable morsel for his supper.

One moment only Jacob delayed to fasten the boat to a stake driven for that purpose into the ground, and to place the oars ready for use at the shortest notice.

This done, he seized Paul by the hand, and dragged him also into the warehouse.

The boy was glad to escape from Nero's vicinity—to feel him no longer sniffing at his legs, with his cold nose intruding through the rents in his garments; but he shivered with a new terror as he entered the black passage, and was led into a ghostly chamber, where, through a trap-door, and down a steep flight of stairs, they passed into the cellar.

In one corner, where a heavy bale had been thrust aside, was another open trap, from which came a glare of light.

At the foot of this stood a ladder, and down it Jacob Prew led the terrified boy.

They were standing in a low vault, excavated beneath the cellar, in the midst of half a dozen men, who stretched out their hands in cordial greeting to the returned convict. As they crowded around him, Paul had leisure to look around him.

The vault was seemingly of immense strength, the roof shaped like an arch, and the walls being formed of thick blocks of rough-hewn stone.

In one corner of the place was a furnace, under which burned the fire which cast the lurid glow into the cellar above.

This furnace, for the smelting of metal, was constructed after the most ingenious of modern principles, and the flue being fashioned to consume its own smoke, but very little escaped into the open air, and that little was so artfully carried away, that it failed to attract attention in the night darkness, neither was its place of exit visible in the broad daylight.

Protruding from the walls were five slabs of stone, forming as many tables, over which were spread many tools, and some plaster-casts of coins.

It was noticeable that one of these tables was lower than the rest, being but little more than half a yard from the ground, and that it had, beside, no seat before it, like the others.

In another corner of the place was a low door, thickly studded with nails, and the whole vault was lighted into painful brilliancy by powerful gas-jets set over each work-table.

From a survey of these things, Paul's eyes rested on the door, and he was wondering what could be on the other side of it, when James Berry, observing him, left the group around Jacob Prew, and went to his side.

"So," he said, looking keenly at him, "you are the boy spoken of by my most estimable friend yonder?"

"I don't know, sir," said Paul, heartily wishing himself out of the place.

"And I suppose you haven't the slightest idea of what you were brought here for, eh?"

"No, sir!" answered Paul, removing his glance from the door, and fixing it on the miser.

"Well," said James Berry, "for once in my life, I'll be good-natured, and tell you."

"Yes, tell him," interposed Ned, who had placed himself quite close to them.

"I've heard such a good account of you from your kind uncle," said James Berry, smiling benevolently upon Paul.

"Oh, such a very good account!" chorussed the cripple, leering worse than ever; "and of such a *very* good little boy!"

"All about your honesty," said James; "how you gave the lawyer back his purse, and earned your living at the crossing, without ever so much as stealing a penny."

"Or a ha'penny," said Ned.

"Now hearing this, when your kind uncle told me about you, I made up my mind I'd help to make a man of you."

"Only hear *that*, Paul!" said the cripple.

"So this is what I'm going to do," resumed the old man. "I'm going to have you taught a trade, and it'll be your own fault if, in time, it doesn't make you a rich man."

"And you'll begin this very night, and be apprenticed to me?" said Ned. "Do you hear *that*, little Paul?"

Then the child spoke for the first time.

"Not to him—not to him, please sir!" he gasped, looking entreatingly into old Berry's face.

"Why not?" he answered; "your kind uncle wishes it."

"And we are so very fond of one another!" said Ned, with another terrible leer. "Oh, I couldn't get along without you, nohow! *Could* I, now?" he added, turning to the warehouse master.

Then both of the men laughed, and nodded, and winked at each other, and seemed to look upon the whole affair as the best joke which ever existed, and Paul's little trembling figure as a comical picture thrown in to illustrate it.

He looked at them for a moment, then burst into tears.

He was bewildered by the novelty of the place, frightened at the two men, and their manner of speaking; for when old Berry spoke of the kind uncle, and Ned of the affection and friendship, the child instinctively interpreted the one as sarcasm, the other as covert threats and hatred.

He glanced once more at the door in the wall, as though he meditated instant flight, and thought longingly of the river, and the free open air it was so impossible for him to reach.

"You are wonderin' what is behind that door," said old Berry, eyeing the boy. "Well, as that will be part of your work, I'll show you myself."

As he spoke, he took Paul by the hand, and led him to the door in question.

"To begin first with the lock," he said, taking hold of a small knob and turning it; "you see, it opens quite easily; not the slightest trouble. The difficulty is on the other side, for there it can't be opened at all; you would have to beat it down to get in, and that would not be very easy. Now, boy, let me see you open it."

Paul turned the handle, and slowly drew the door open.

A narrow passage met his view, and following his teacher, he entered it, the glare of gas-light from the vault making the way quite visible.

It was a steep passage, sloping upward until it reached the outer air, where it was covered by a trap, formed of one of the paving-stones of the yard, into which it opened.

This was held firmly in its place by means of a thick cable, one end of which was firmly knotted in a staple, wedged and soldered into the stone itself, and secured there by means of iron plates riveted closely around them.

At the end of the cable was a stout hook, which was passed through the ring of an enormous weight of iron, sunk into a hole in the ground.

The cord was, when attached to the weight, so tightly drawn, that there was only a slight slackness of about an inch and a half, to allow the hook to be readily fastened and unfastened.

The slab itself was only large enough to ad-

AN UNHEEDED APPEAL. (See page 94.)

mit of the passage of one person at a time; and though the weight attached to it would render it a task of great difficulty to remove it from the outside, it could be easily raised from within by merely slipping the hook from the ring of the iron weight.

These things were explained to Paul by the old man, who made him perform each of the tasks of fastening, unfastening, and lifting the stone trap, which was approached by a flight of steps fixed firmly against the wall underneath it. This accomplished to his satisfaction the man led him through the aperture.

The two stood in the open air, while the stone, which Paul had thrust upward, had fallen against a pile of old bales, composed of the bundles of rotting straw which had accumulated in the yard during many years of unpacking and unloading of goods, and which were artfully disposed to catch the slab, and prevent any noise from its backward fall. They were in a little lane, irregular, often obstructed by straw bales on one side, and wood litter on the other; and at the end of it Paul could see the river running away with the shining moon-gleams, and the deep, mysterious shadows resting on its bosom.

"Now we'll return," said his tutor. "This will be part of your duties. Are you listening?"

"Yes," said Paul, following him back, but with his eyes turned on the scene behind him, his ears filled with the musical voices of wind and tide that seemed to be calling him away.

Old Berry looked at him angrily.

"What are you staring there for?" he asked, "Do you see anything?"

"No, sir," stammered Paul, facing about, and fixing his eyes sadly on the gloomy-looking house.

"You are thinking how you would like to run away from me to the end of the yard where the boat lies—how you would like to jump into that boat and float away!"

Paul hung his head guiltily, but made no reply.

"You had better try it—try if Nero will let you pass unmolested."

As he spoke, he whistled softly, and was answered by the low, hoarse growling of the mastiff.

Paul shrank closer to his master, and remembered the white, sharp teeth of the dog—the teeth that looked as though they were ready, and only waiting an opportunity to tear and torture him.

He quickened his steps, and had soon passed through the trap and down the steps, where he fixed the hook in the iron weight.

When they re-entered the cellar, the men were busy at work at the stone tables, with the exception of one, who stood by the furnace feeding the fire, and watching the seething metal.

"Now you've seen all there is to be seen," said Berry, "I'll finish the directions I began to explain to you in the yard. You will have to watch this door, and the trap at the end of the passage. When we give the alarm, if you hear any suspicious sounds, such as the ringing of yon bell" (he pointed to a small bell which hung in a corner, near the roof),—" should you hear that bell ring, or the dog bark, open the door, and loosen the hook on the trap from the iron ring. After you have done that, you can look out for yourself—go where you like; but don't try the escape dodge before either of those things happen. Remember there are seven of us against you, and that Nero watches the path to the river! And now go to work, and learn your trade."

He pushed the boy over to where Ned was busily employed with a graver's tool, delicately touching up a number of plaster casts which lay scattered over his table.

By his side stood Jacob Prew, pouring molten metal into several little moulds, and every man in the room seemed to be employed fashioning or touching the coins.

"Do you know what these are?" said Ned, holding up what seemed to be a shining new half-sovereign.

"Money!" said Paul.

"Yes, it's money; and so true an imitation of the real coin, that I'd defy any one to prove it was struck here, instead of in the Mint! I made it what it is."

A light broke in upon Paul's mind.

He had heard of men who robbed society at large by manufacturing false money, and he now knew he was in the company of a band of these coiners.

He had not much leisure to think of it, for Ned made constant demands upon his time and attention; and, at last, with malicious zeal for his advancement in this new business, put into his hand a cast and a tool, and directed him how to work on it.

"There's nothing like making a beginning," he said. "Of course, you'll spoil that, and many more; but, against the time you are as old as I am, you will be one of the cleverest coiners in all England. You will, little Paul; so work—work, I tell you!"

"Yes, work," said Jacob Prew, "or it will be worse for you," as he cast an approving glance at Ned.

Paul looked at the two men with pitiful, imploring eyes. But he read no mercy in their stern faces; and, with a heavy heart, he took the tool and the cast, and knelt at the table by Ned's side, working while he looked on, and gave the boy his first lesson. Every touch of the instrument on the plaster was a throb of sorrow, as he thought of Judge Vincent and his kind words, and how they had been contradicted by Beverley Bogg.

He was beginning to think the lawyer spoke truth when he had told him it was useless to strive for the right, and that a prison would be his portion, as he looked at the counterfeit money lying before him, and felt the tool for perfecting it in his fingers.

The tears rushed to his eyes, blinding him, and forcing him to look up.

Ned picked up the work, and looked at it keenly. "Spiled, as I said," he remarked; "but very good for the fust. You're a-gettin' along, Paul."

The tears rolled down the boy's cheek, as he bent his head to hide them, pondering on the question whether that meant he was getting along the road to the prisoner's dock.

"He's a-weepin' with joy," said Jacob. "Dry your eyes, and take this as an encouragement to you."

He picked up a base shilling, which was lying near, and placed it before him.

Paul made no effort to touch it.

"Pick it up, or I'll fetch Nero in to yer!" shouted the man. "Put it into yer pocket; and minds you *spends* it afore to-morrer night, or I'll know the reason why!"

The child obeyed, and dropped the coin into his ragged pocket.

The two men laughed in derision, and just then Paul heard from the yard a low bark, ending in a moan, as of pain, from the mastiff who guarded.

Without a moment's hesitation, he dashed aside his work, threw open the door, and before the coiners had recovered from their sudden alarm, stood at the end of the outer passage, and slipped the hook from its hold.

CHAPTER XIV.

For an hour, the man in the sentry-box had read and smoked on undisturbed, and the yard seemed as quiet and deserted as though there had been no intruders on its solitude.

Then from beneath a stack of wood, resting in one corner, a man crawled forth, and was presently followed by a companion.

They were police-officers, fully equipped and armed, who had been smuggled into the yard with a load of goods in the evening, and who had remained hidden there for several long, weary hours, watching and waiting.

Instead of their usual heavy boots, their feet were cased in felt slippers, which made no noise as they crept in the direction of the sentry-box.

At length they stood close to it, and one of them cautiously peeped in.

The watchman sat with his shoulder turned to the door, which was partly ajar, and was so absorbed in his paper and pipe, that he was unconscious of anything else.

The officer made a sign to his companion, and, with bated breath, moved round to the entrance of the box.

In an instant, the door was pulled open, and before the sentinel well knew what had happened, he found himself confronted by the very power he was charged to guard his comrades from.

He looked quickly to where a wire hung dangling from the wall.

It was connected with the bell in the vault, and he had but to touch it, to give his accomplices the alarm.

He stretched out his hand, but before he could reach it, he felt the cold muzzle of a pistol pressing against his forehead.

He dropped it again quickly, and remained passive while the officers gagged him, and slipped on the handcuffs.

Then, in a low voice, one of them bade him rise, and lead them round to the yard facing the river.

"You have a dog there," whispered the man, "and you must silence him, and keep him from attacking us, or——"

The watchman knew what the unfinished sentence implied, for he felt the pistol pressed this time against the back of his head.

With a motion of his pinioned hands, he intimated his desire that the gag should be removed.

"If you attempt to escape, you die!" said the officer, removing the gag.

"I must *speak* to the dog," whispered the watchman, huskily. "Don't fear; I shan't forfeit my life to save *them* from the hulks."

He led the way as he spoke, shuddering as every step that he took seemed to press the rim of the pistol to his head.

"One moment," said the other officer.

He passed to the door of the yard, which he quietly unbolted and unbarred.

Looking into the street, he made a sign, and instantly, from the dark side of the way, there stepped into the light a police force of over twenty men, who noiselessly entered the premises, and divided themselves into three groups.

One party advanced to the door of the house, another ranged themselves in the yard, and the third followed the officers who had first entered down the narrow lane, which, on one side of the house, formed the communication between the front and back of the place.

These again, weapons in hand, placed themselves in order to receive an attack, while the adventurous pair forced their prisoner to advance towards the dog, who, appeased by the presence of his master, lay quietly watching the proceedings, the only noise he made being the measured beating of his tail on the pavement. When the three men approached, he looked uneasily up, and, at a closer view of the policeman, uttered a sharp, low bark.

Instantly one of them bent, and struck him on the head with the heavy life-preserver. With a whine, it sank down, and turning on its side, remained motionless.

These were the sounds which had alarmed Paul. In the meantime, a body of the police had penetrated the house, and were stealthily moving towards the cellars.

Before they could enter the vault, the coiners had taken the alarm and fled.

But one man remained behind, helpless and deserted by his companions in crime.

It was Ned the cripple!

He could make but small resistance, and was easily handcuffed and secured; and leaving two of the men to guard him, the men dashed out through the underground passage into the yard, where a sharp struggle was taking place between the gang and the police stationed there. The aid of this reinforcement turned the balance of victory completely against the coiners; and, with the exception of one, who had escaped at the commencement of the fray, the whole were taken prisoners; and among them were old Berry and Jacob Prew.

"There must have been a traitor in the camp!" muttered the old man.

"There, you are mistaken," answered a policeman. "Detective Ford had his suspicions, and watched the place. He has watched you men in and out for many a time during the past two months, and he has come down upon you at last. I'm sorry for you, Mr. Berry; you had such a very good character in the neighbourhood; but that is all blown to the wind. Ah, Prew! I haven't forgotten you during the past four years! So you're back again! You'll lose your ticket of leave, I'm afraid!"

"I'm in for a lifer!" growled Jacob; "but I'd have put up with it without grumbling, if you had only caught the boy."

"What boy?" said the policeman. "We have seen none!"

"Then he is got off! I'm sorry for that," muttered Jacob. Then he relapsed into silence, and no effort of his captors could induce him to speak again.

But Paul had not yet made his escape.

He had rushed up the steps at the sound of alarm, and thrusting up the trap, had passed through it before either of the gang had reached him.

As he was about to dash towards the river, he had seen at the end of the lane, in the lumber, a policeman pass, and instantly perceiving how the case stood, had hid among the bales of straw, where he lay trembling and listening to the sounds of strife, not daring to move his position to obtain a peep of what was going on, lest he should be perceived by the policemen who were examining the premises. He lay in his little nook, scarcely breathing, lest he should be discovered and dragged forth.

Presently, he heard the prisoners removed, and knew that a guard had been set over the house; for after the departing footsteps had died away, he heard the measured tramp of the sentinel as he paced to and fro before the river.

For an hour, Paul lay in his hiding-place, and for an hour did the watcher tread his beat, without pause.

Then he seemed to become weary, for once. As he neared the child, he yawned, and stretched himself, and stamped impatiently on the ground. At last his patience gave way before the monotony of his vigil in the lonely yard.

"I'll just go round, and speak to Bill a moment," he said in a half whisper.

And so he took his departure up the path connecting with the front yard, where another policeman was stationed, and soon the pair were engaged in animated conversation on the events of the evening.

Paul listened awhile. All in the yard was still; the dog had never uttered a single sound since it had given the alarm; and he had heard the policeman retreat from his post.

Now was his time.

He slipped from among the bales, and ran to the river side. In his flight he passed the dead body of the mastiff, and, with a shudder, quickened his pace.

When he had reached the landing-place, he discovered that the boat had been removed.

"I don't care," he said; "I can swim."

Taking off his jacket, he tied it over his head like a night-cap; then, without hesitation slipped into the water, and swam on with the tide.

CHAPTER XV.

THE current bore Paul easily on until he was past all danger from pursuit, when he landed, and struck off into the town.

He hurried along in the darkness without daring to stay to rest, his wet clothes clinging to him, and chilling him to the bone.

Towards morning, he stood in one of the busiest streets in Bermondsey.

It was nearly five o'clock, when, reaching a railway arch, he sat down exhausted, and faint with hunger. In about half an hour's time, a man came and set up a coffee-stand and a fire brazier under the same shelter, and clinked the coffee-cups in a manner which provoked to the extreme the appetite of the jaded boy.

He crouched a little nearer to the glowing fire, stretching himself out to catch its heat, and looking hungrily at the thick slices of bread and butter which the man was piling up in tempting heaps upon the snowy cloth.

At last, the early workmen began to throng around the social board, and Paul's mouth watered as he watched them devour the edibles, and sip the steaming-hot and fragrant coffee.

He turned the counterfeit shilling, which Ned had given him, over in his pocket, and debated within himself as to the expediency of spending part of it in a good refreshing meal.

He held it a long time in his hand, then, at last, with a sigh, dropped it, and it rolled away once more into a corner of his ragged pocket.

"I can't!" he said. "I suppose I must do without it!"—and, rising, he moved slowly away, as though he feared to trust himself near the tempting spot.

Just then, two young workmen came along, laughing and talking, evidently in the best of tempers and in high spirits.

As they neared Paul, the younger looked at him, then touched his companion's arm.

"I say," he said, "look at that poor little chap: I warrant he has slept out all night, and hasn't a farthing to keep him from starving. Here! take that—buy a cup of coffee," he added, tossing the child a penny.

Paul stooped to pick it up, when another rattled on the pavement beside it.

It was the second workman who threw it; and Paul, grasping them tightly, turned back, and followed them to the coffee-stall.

"A cup of corfee," he said, thrusting his ragged arm in between a little crowd of customers, "and a penn'orth of bread and butter, please."

His two friends had already commenced their meal, but, with ready good nature, they made room for him, and pulled him close to the board.

"Here, Jim," said one, "give him a full cup and a couple of thick slices for his money. I believe he is half starved, and his clothes are as damp as though he had been dipped into a water-butt."

"Here!" said the coffee-vendor, handing him a liberal allowance in exchange for his money; "go and sit by the fire."

So the lad shrank closely to the cheerful glow, and warmed his shivering limbs, and eat his breakfast, all the while casting grateful glances upon the tender-hearted workmen.

As he finished the last morsel of bread, his head resting against the wall behind him, he fell asleep, and was only aroused by the breakfast merchant shaking him gently by the shoulder.

"Now, my little man," he said, "I'd advise you to wake up, and get on somewhere. I'm going."

Paul rubbed his eyes. The fire was out, and the stall, with its tempting paraphernalia, was packed up, and reposed in a truck, ready to be wheeled away.

He rose to his feet.

"Here's a few bits of bread that was left," said the man, handing him something screwed up in a piece of newspaper. "And now get along, or the perlice will be after you."

In an instant Paul was wide awake, trembling as he thought of his night adventure and escape, and expecting every moment to hear the sounds of pursuit.

He had caught Jacob Prew's question, as to whether the officers had captured a boy; and he imagined every arm of the law in London was stretched out to take him—that he would be found out, and dragged off to share the coiner's prison.

"Thank'ee—I'll go," he said; and, seizing the proffered gift, he hastened away.

On, through the great city, until the maze of houses was passed, and he began to see around him green lanes and suburban residences, and knew he was once more entering the country.

Never during the day had he flagged in his plodding pace, so powerfully had he been urged on by his fears; and the evening time found him sitting, worn out and spent, by the roadside, looking with dim eyes at the windows of a pretty villa facing him, and listening dreamily to the sound of children's voices as they played in the garden.

His little package of food lay by his side but little diminished, for he had lost all thought of hunger in his desire for safety.

The windows seemed to be winking at him in the red light thrown upon them by the departing day, and their brightness made him dizzy; but still he stared on at them, unable to look another way.

The children's voices, too, seemed to float further and further away from him, as though they were being carried from him, on a rushing tide.

Then, by degrees, he fancied it was not the voices, but himself, who was drifting, drifting he knew not whither.

The white road, the trees, the villa, seemed slipping away.

He stretched out his hand to save himself, but a film gathered over his eyes, and it fell powerless by his side.

Then all was a blank, and Paul lay on the path, beside his little parcel, white and still.

CHAPTER XVI.

AT the drawing-room window of the villa, Constance Clayton stood by her husband's side, watching their children, as they tumbled and romped on the lawn.

She was a tall, queenly woman, with a beautiful face, and a rare fascination lurking in her smile and glance; and her husband gazed upon her fondly as he smoothed the braids of her purple black hair.

"To-morrow," he said, "will be the twelfth anniversary of our wedding-day."

"Twelve years!" she repeated; "what a long time it seems to speak about, and yet it has passed like a dream!"

"You have been happy, then?" said her husband, smiling, with the certainty that her answer would be favourable.

"Yes, happy," she said, looking at the gay children as they chased each other among the flowers.

"When I think over the blessings which have fallen to our lot," he continued, "I cannot help contrasting it with the lonely, melancholy life of your cousin Vincent—robbed of his wife, his child, and all that makes a man's heart cheerful and light. Happy as we are, I would give ten years of my life to see him what he was before this terrible blight fell over his path."

"Poor Cousin William!" said Constance. "It is over ten years since his wife deserted him. He has never been the same genial man he was before that took place."

"I owe him everything!" said Mr. Clayton, impetuously. "My good name, my prosperity, even the love of my wife and children. It is the one dark spot on my bliss when I think of his misery. If I were to live to be a thousand years old, I should never forget that past horror of my life, in which he proved himself so noble, so true, and merciful."

"Heaven bless him!" murmured Constance, —"heaven bless him for his kindness to us in the day of need!"

"It was, indeed, a time of need," said her husband; "when I, who should have scorned aught that was weak, unmanly, or dishonest— who should have striven to secure the happiness of the woman I had married, yielded to every temptation that crossed my path, and finally committed a crime which would have ruined my fame and prospects for ever had I not been dealt with more mercifully than I deserved by the man I had injured—had not you been the truest among women. When I think of the past, I shudder to remember that, to-day, my children might have blushed to own me, as a forger, a felon, had it not been for you and your devoted love."

"You praise me more than I deserve," said Constance. "Our deepest thanks are due to my cousin Vincent. I did no more than I had vowed to do, when I clung to, and supported you in the hour of danger; but never, never can I forget his kindness to us. On that dreadful afternoon when you returned home from your business, and told me you had— had——"

"Forged your cousin's name to a bill, drawn the money, and squandered it in the haunts of vice and dissipation," he said, interrupting her; "when, mad with the fear of detection, exposure, and disgrace, I came to you, the wife I had neglected and betrayed, and confessed my miserable folly, you comforted and cheered me, you took me to your heart, instead of casting me off in scorn and disgust, and you worked my salvation!"

His voice was low and tender, and he held her in his arms, his eyes beaming with gratitude and affection.

"Again I repeat it, you praise me too highly," she said. "Ah, Richard, that love is worth nothing which will not stand fast in the day of trouble. My whole heart bows in grateful remembrance to him who succoured us both from impending ruin. I can live the whole scene with its terror and joy over again, when I think of it. It was not long before I had resolved what to do in the terrible emergency, and went down that very day from our old Manchester home to London, to throw myself on William's mercy. When I arrived at his house, I found it brilliantly lighted, and filled with gay company. I remembered that it was a *fête* in honour of his young wife, whom I had never seen, and of whom he spoke so lovingly and proudly in his letters."

"Yes, I remember," said her husband. "She was never worthy of his love—a creature so false, so frail, and fickle!"

"Judge not," said Constance, half-playfully, half-reprovingly. "We do not know her temptations, how strong they were, or how weak her moral nature! Well, I saw my cousin, and I told him all. I begged him to pardon you, for my sake—for the sake of the happy hours we had spent together in our youth, when he called me sister! And he did pardon me—he spoke cheering words, and assured me that none but himself should know the story of your errors. Oh, Richard, how blest I felt, when, in the happy reaction of feeling, my strong composure gave way, and I wept on his shoulder, as I had done in the past times, when he had soothed my childish griefs. Oh, how I thanked him when he brought us here, and made your future his care, placing you in the position you now occupy, with so much of honour and prosperity!"

"With heaven's blessing," he said, "it shall never be otherwise. For your sake and that of our children, I will cling to the right. I am glad we spoke of this; it does a man good to look back, at times, upon the slips and stumbles he has made on the shoals and quicksands he has safely crossed!"

"Never, on this day," said Constance, "do I turn to the past, and contrast it with our present happiness, but I pray for the peace of our dear benefactor, and grieve that the only recollections it can bring him are the desertion of his wife and the loss of his boy. If only it could happen that the child could be restored to him, how thankful, how rejoiced I should be!"

"I fear it will never be," said Mr. Clayton; "it is most likely that the boy is dead. But hark!" he cried, as a noise of shouts and frightened young voices arose without. "What is that?"

As they hurried into the garden, they perceived children gathered round the gate, looking through the bars with wondering wide-open eyes, and shouting for their parents.

Quickly Mr. Clayton sprang forward and passed into the road, where, lying by the side of the way, was Paul.

"It's a poor, destitute boy," he said, as, stooping tenderly, he raised him in his arms, and bore him towards the house, while the children stood together filled with awe, and whispering that the white face, which rested on their father's shoulder, was that of a "dead boy!"

CHAPTER XVII.

ON the evening after the capture of the coiners, Beverley Bogg sat in the bedroom of Judge Vincent, who was now convalescent, and slowly fighting his way back to health and strength.

The evening was drawing on, and the room was nearly dark, save for a feeble gleam of waning light which stole in between the window-curtains, and rested on the sick man's face as he reclined in an arm-chair, looking up at the twilight sky. From his corner, in the dark, Beverley Bogg watched him, with a look of settled anxiety resting upon his grim face.

In truth, the lawyer had, at that time, sore matter for thought.

He had that very morning heard of the capture of the coiners, and had received a message from Jacob Prew which had drawn him to visit the convict in his prison-cell, where he learned that Paul had, for the time, at least, escaped from his clutches—from the snare which, if it had succeeded, would have seen the wily lawyer's scheme of vengeance partly fulfilled. In addition to this, he had found a letter from Catherine Vincent awaiting him, in which she begged his pardon and indulgence for the step she had taken—that she had determined upon giving up her business, and devoting herself to a search for her boy.

THE LITTLE WAYFARER MEETS WITH SUCCOUR. (See page K.)

Almost mad with rage, he had started off to the village where she had resided, to find her place deserted, and a stranger standing behind the counter where she had formerly presided.

At the station, too, he had heard news which still more angered him—namely, that she had taken a ticket to London; and he now sat thinking how he should best keep the husband and wife from meeting—how he should draw the mother and son once again into his power.

And all the while, with his face screened by the gathering night, he went on planning his future movements, and talking to his sick affectionate friend in the softest accents of friendship and interest, not one note in his voice betraying the passion of fear, hatred, and disappointment which was raging within him.

"I see the postman crossing the road," said the Judge, with a smile. "More letters for me, I suppose. Business must be attended to. The world will have its dues, no matter whether its debtor be tied to his sick-chamber, or struggling painfully to bind up the links of a broken life, or the pulses of a broken heart."

He sighed heavily, while clanging on the bell, far below, came the postman's summons.

A few moments later, a servant entered the room, bearing the letters on a salver.

"Take them, Beverley," said Judge Vincent, "and read them aloud; my eyes are still weak, and I cannot exhaust my small stock of patience in deciphering the cramped hands of some of my usual correspondents."

"With pleasure, my dear William; with pleasure," he answered, rising hastily, and possessing himself of the leters. "Light the lamp at this table, John," he continued to the servant; "I will sit here, so that the glare will not disturb your master."

The servant obeyed.

The lamp was placed on a small table at the other end of the room, so that he was behind his friend, with his back turned slightly towards him.

There was silence for a moment, during which the lawyer spread the epistles before him, his eye running rapidly over the different handwritings in which they were addressed.

They were all of them seemingly from male correspondents, and he smiled with relief as he failed to detect among them the delicate hand of Catherine Vincent. Then the smile vanished, and he frowned more deeply than ever, as he glanced on one missive, which he had until then overlooked.

It was the usual coarse blue envelope, but Beverley looked at it as though it had been the Gorgon's head, and pushed it aside, covering it with his sleeve. One keen glance at the Judge assured him that he was not watched, and in another moment the letter was slipped from the table into his own pocket, after which he quietly opened the remainder, and read them to his friend, clutching the one he had stolen with a cruel and relentless grip.

"Nothing but business," he said, as he concluded the last of them. "But do you know, William, it has struck me that some day, while reading your usual budget, you might come across a letter from the wife who deserted you so many years ago!"

Judge Vincent looked at him with a startled glance of inquiry.

"What do you mean, Beverley?" he said, sharply. "Surely, surely there is nothing——"

"Here?" said the lawyer, finishing the sentence for him, and gently tapping the papers strewn over the table. "Oh, no; there is nothing of the kind here!"

"After so many years," continued the sick man, musingly, "I do not think she would come back to trouble me again. Besides, it is most probable she is dead!"

"You have no proof of the fact," said Beverley. "People often turn up unexpectedly, when they have been given over for deceased or lost for ever. Why should not Catherine Vincent?"

"Ay, ay; why should she not?" said the Judge, who had, from Beverley's suggestion, evidently gathered fresh ground for thought.

"Women who have gone astray in their youth are constantly striving to retrace their steps in their more mature days," he continued. "We are always hearing of such cases. By this time *she* must be weary of her present situation. I prophecy you will have her either writing or coming back to you soon, if she be still alive."

"You think so?" cried the Judge, eagerly.

"Yes, I think so; there will be a pitiful story made up, in which she will prate of penitence, of past and present suffering, and plead for your pardon."

"Sin, sorrow, and suffering!" said the Judge, "Poor Catherine!—poor child!"

The lawyer frowned, as he noted the tender pity in his friend's voice.

"You think only of *her*," he said. "In your generous heart you have no remembrance of the wrong she did you."

"I loved her," persisted the sick man. "I can never forget *that*. You who knew her in those days, can understand the feelings with which I now regard her—with sorrow for her fall, with pity for her suffering, but not with harshness or malice."

"You think of her in her youth and beauty," said Beverley Bogg, replying angrily to his sentiment of forgiveness. "Do you imagine she is now anything resembling the girl you married twelve years ago? Think of your experience in the police-court; of the wrinkled, prematurely old, and faded women you see there; ay, not only aged, but squalid and degraded—beings you shrink from even while you compassionate them—and then reflect such may be Catherine Vincent, if she lives!"

"How terrible must be the trials which would drag down one of her refinement of nature and education to such a level," said the Judge. "Still, Beverley, in spite of all, I could pity and forgive her."

"You remember only *Catherine*," continued the lawer, hoarsely. "You do not think of the child she stole from you in his babyhood. If she is degraded, so is your boy. Think of him breathing the pestilential air of such a place as Shuter's Court, for instance! Sucking in vice and contamination with every respiration! Picture him as one of the young felons whom you have sentenced to prisons and reformatories!"

"Hush, hush, Beverley!" said the Judge, raising his hands imploringly. "You sicken me: you drown all gentleness in my heart towards one I would fain pardon."

The lawyer's eyes sparkled, and he leant forward in his chair, with his back to the dim light, so that the working of his features was undiscernible, gazing straight before him, and gesticulating, as though he saw all he was describing, and was pointing it out to his listener.

"Picture him growing into manhood, warped and twisted morally, by the hard world he has lived in—a reprobate, a scoffer, a scoundrel, whom it would be your duty, the duty of all honest men, to drive from among them!"

Judge Vincent wrung his thin fingers in agony, as the stern voice of the lawyer drew the terrible sketch.

"And all this, mark me—all this, I say, through no fault of his own! The work of the woman who ought to have cherished and fostered him in goodness; but who, instead of so doing, has, by her own sin, made him familiar with vice, and forced him into its practice. Think of it, William Vincent, and if you can forgive her the pain she has caused *you*, the loneliness of *your* life; ask your heart if you can, when you remember your boy, ruined through her act, made a terror to you, when he should have been your greatest comfort and hope!"

He rose from his chair as he spoke, glaring before him, with one finger outstretched, as though the spirit of prophecy were upon him— as though he were denouncing an actual sentence upon the persons he hated, and his words stung the Judge into fresh anger against the woman who had wronged him.

"You are right," he said; "I do not think of her as she is. You, who knew her as I did, in her gay youth and beauty, in her seeming innocence and purity, cannot wonder at it. But I forget, when I remember her, that she is the woman who has drawn down upon me the bitterest dishonour and sorrow which can fall upon man. Yet, even that I could have pardoned, had not her wrong-doing recoiled upon our innocent boy. But this I swear, Beverley—could I see her now, kneeling at my feet, with all her loveliness and brightness clinging around her yet, I would spurn her as I would a poisonous reptile, unless she could bring my boy in her hands to plead for her, with his young life and heart unsullied by guilt."

"Now you are yourself again," said Beverley Bogg, with a look of triumphant malice. "I feared that in case she should again appear, you would relent towards her, and, by so doing, again expose yourself to evil, through the wiles of a designing woman."

"Ay, ay!" said the Judge, looking at him with a smile, which was more melancholy than any burst of passion could have been. "You are ever the same—the cool astute lawyer and councillor—and yet so true and hearty a friend!"

He seized Beverley's hand as he spoke, and pressed it fervently.

"Let us sit down, and talk more calmly," he continued. "This excitement has wearied me."

Beverley shook his head.

"The fact is," he said, "I have been contemplating my departure for the last half-hour, but could not bear to leave you. I have an important case in hand, and have promised a legal friend to step in and talk it quietly over, this evening. So, you see, I must go. As you say, be we ever so indisposed, business must meet with its just due of attention."

He was burning with impatience to open the letter he had stolen, and ascertain its contents.

"Yes, I see," said the sick man. "The world rolls on without me, and I am not much missed there, I know. So much the better; the doctor has ordered me abroad, as the only means of re-establishing my health. It will be a sore effort for me to quit London, but it is my only resource. To you, old friend, I leave the task which it is the aim of my life to accomplish—the search for my lost child!"

"You may leave it safely in my hands," said Beverley, delighted at the information he had just gathered. "I shall leave no stone unturned in my search. I must, one day, be successful. Let us hope for the best."

"You give me fresh courage," said the Judge. "Ah, Beverley, who knows, we may yet be in time to save him; and, if so, I can never be thankful enough to the Providence which has preserved him from the dangers besetting him."

"Never, never!" responded his friend; and again he smiled, as he reflected how strong a power it would need to extricate Paul from the toils he would weave about him in the future, when he once more held him in his hands.

"And if, in the course of your labours, you should meet with—with—*her*, in your just dealing, remember mercy!" continued the Judge. "Shield her from poverty, lest she be cast into further crime. I would not have her dealt remorselessly with, though I never wish to look on her false face, or hear her false voice, again!"

"Ever noble and generous!" said Beverley Bogg, taking up his hat and umbrella, in readiness to depart. "I will deal with her as I would with an erring sister. And now, for the present, good-bye. To-morrow—to-morrow, my good friend, I will step in, and read those business intruders the letters you so dread. To-morrow, I will answer them for you, if you will."

He took his leave, with a warm, smiling friendliness, pausing a moment at the door to look back mockingly on the Judge, who had fallen back in his chair, and was looking through a mist of tears up at the sky, where one star was peeping forth from a black cloud. Like Paul, on his return to the squalid court, the man was looking up at the tiny sparkler, wishing and longing; and, though still sorrowful, was weaving visions of peace for the future time.

Once in the street, Beverley Bogg drew forth the letter; and, withdrawing to a distance, stood beneath a gas-lamp, and once more examined the address.

"I could swear to it," he said to himself. "It *is* his writing. What can he have to say to Judge Vincent?"

He hurried on, and presently entered an hotel which was near; and obtaining a private room, locked himself in, sat down, and, with fingers trembling with eagerness, opened the missive, and began to read it.

Before he had got through half a dozen lines, his face assumed an expression of angry astonishment.

"The ingrate!" he muttered, looking down on the open paper—"the wretched, skulking spy! Aha! So he thought to overreach *me*—to play the eavesdropper, and enrich himself by betraying me to my 'injured patron and friend!'" he continued, reading from the epistle. "He shall find out his mistake—he shall obtain his reward earlier than he looked for it! Oh," he said, savagely bringing his clenched fist down upon the offending paper, "had I him here—had I the wretch Simkins in my power, I would destroy *him* as remorselessly as I would this letter!"

He tore it into atoms as he spoke, and, gathering the pieces into his kerchief, unlocked the door and passed out, muttering curses against his clerk as he wended his way home through the deepening night.

CHAPTER XVIII.

BENEATH the room where Judge Vincent sat was a small parlour, which had in bygone times been a favourite sitting-room with the Judge and his young wife.

Now it was almost always deserted, save when the servants paid it their usual visit, or the old housekeeper peeped in with a saddened face as she remembered the happy pair she had seen there so often, and in whom she had felt such pride.

But on this evening, the good dame had taken her post in the dainty chamber; and with her, reclining in a low rocking-chair, still clad in her dress of sober brown, was Catherine Vincent.

There was no light in the room beyond that of the moon; and the heavy crimson curtains drooping over the window shut out even that, save where it stole in a broad white patch across the floor, revealing the rose-buds, lilies, and forget-me-nots which twined themselves, in a rich, fantastic pattern, over the dark green carpet.

"It is just as you left it, madam," the housekeeper said, referring to the room. "Not a thing in it has been displaced—not an ornament broken or removed. I would discharge the housemaid, however efficient, who injured anything here."

"You have not lost your old pride in this chamber, I see," said Catherine.

"I have not lost my old love for it," said the woman. "It seems but yesterday that Mister William came to me, and, with such a happy smile on his handsome lips, told me he was going to bring home his wife—the very wife I would have chosen for him out of all the world if I had been privileged to name her."

Catherine listened eagerly to the housekeeper's reminiscences, the tears gathering in her eyes as the old woman called back the past time.

"And so, he said," she continued, " we must make the house ready to receive her—everything pretty and bright, like her own sweet self. Ah, madam! that was a busy time! What with the upholsterers and others, I had my hands full for a long time; and a great delight I took in my labour, seeing it was all for those I had loved and served so long."

Faster and faster fell Catherine's tears, dropping over her white-clasped hands and the wedding-ring, which had been placed on her finger by the gallant bridegroom—the ardent lover of the housekeeper's story.

"But of all the rooms, this was the one we had most pleasure in. Your morning-room, he called it; and here we took such pains to have everything beautiful, yet home-like, about you; everything that you could admire, and not tire of seeing day after day. The piano, your work-table, your writing-desk, the very carpet, were studied, and thought of for weeks before they were purchased for your use. The vases and statuettes were brought from Italy, and the pictures on the walls cost a mint of money. Every wish, every taste of yours, was studied here; it was as though he told the tale of his love in every piece of furniture, that it might speak to and cheer you, by repeating it over and over again, when you had thrown off every other tie, and came to brighten his home."

Lower, still lower, drooped Catherine's head, and a heavy sob throbbed through the darkness.

"And it was my pride to see you both here—the handsomest pair in all England, and the happiest, too; to hear your gay voices blending—to listen to the music which came hence, and floated over the whole house! Ah! yes, madam, it is little wonder that I love the room!"

The old woman was weeping now, and her voice trembled as she still spoke on.

"It is little wonder that my pride in it has not waned, even though the freshness has gone from its fittings, as the freshness and happiness has vanished from both of your lives. It is little wonder that I will not have things disturbed; for though you had deserted it, and he shuns it as he would a haunted chamber, yet it was one spot where I could sometimes sit and think of the happy past, until I could almost believe the miserable present a dream, from which I am about to wake."

Catherine knelt at her feet, and leant her head on the housekeeper's knee.

"I'm a foolish old creature to talk so," she continued, gently smoothing Catherine's hair, and half-unconsciously drawing from it the pins which confined it in those neat braids so that it fell over her shoulders, and after awhile twined itself into soft curls. "I'm a foolish old woman, dear lady; but I cannot help thinking all will come right in the end, and that I shall see you and Mister William sitting here as in the old days; that the infant's toy lying on the rug, where it fell from your boy's baby fingers, will yet be looked at and laughed at by him, when the three now parted are united again."

Then both the women wept, with their hands firmly entwined; and the darkness deepened, and the moonlight crept in a longer line into the chamber, and touched Catherine's hair with a gleam of silver light.

For the first time since the housekeeper had began to recall the memories of the past, she spoke.

"Bless you," she said, "for your kindly words, for your faith in me, for your bright prophecy of the future."

"If I had not faith in you, dear Mrs. Vincent, you would not enter this room," said the trusty servant. "You should not find a shelter here for one hour. But I believe in you, as I do in my master himself. I have not one single hard thought remaining in my mind. I would stake my life on your truth and honour."

"Bless you again," said Catherine. "You give me fresh strength and hope. Never, but in one respect, have I wronged my husband—in doubting his love for me, in believing he had proved untrue, and, in my mad jealousy, flying from him. The one act, which has entailed so fearful a punishment upon me, such undeserved misery on others!"

"Jealousy is a green-eyed monster, that is certain," said the old lady, in a moralising tone; "but I cannot help wondering how it should ever have come between you and my master!"

"I cannot tell you the story yet," pursued Catherine. "But I had proofs that my husband loved another, and, in my misery, I left him."

"I don't care if you had gospel proofs of it," cried her listener; "I'd not believe them. Why, the Judge loved the very ground you trod! It's the way of you young people; when you have no real troubles, you must make imaginary ones, to plague yourselves, and a pretty piece of unhappiness your fancied one has wrought!"

Catherine looked up beseechingly, and laid her finger on the speaker's lips.

"No! I'll not scold again," she said, answering the mute appeal. "Besides, that won't mend matters. We must try to make things smooth again, dear lady, which will be much better."

"Much better, if it can be done," said Catherine.

"We will try," continued her friend. "No one but myself knows who you are. All the servants imagine it is my niece come to pay me a visit; and we have no visitors, but my master's old companion, Mr. Beverley Bogg, who was here this evening, and has only just left."

"I did not know that," stammered Catherine "Are you sure he is gone?"

"Quite!" answered the housekeeper. "Would you like to see him? You say he is friendly to you?"

"I would rather not," said Catherine. "He wished me to have patience, and wait until he had found my boy, before I came to plead with William for pardon; but I could not. It seemed so long and weary a time. Do you not think if any one can trace her child, a mother can, guided by her motherly love, and the endurance it plants in her heart and nature? But he cannot understand this; how should he—a man of the world, though kind and generous? No! I would rather he did not know I am here; he might be angry, and command me to return; and how could I refuse to obey one who has proved himself my disinterested friend?"

"You are right," assented the housekeeper, "and we will keep the secret to ourselves.

Still, I shall always admire and like Mister Bogg for his kindness to you, though I must say I did not think him capable of it. You will stay here, Mrs. Vincent, and I'll speak to my master, prepare him to see you—to hear your story, and to judge your cause himself· Who knows but illness may have softened him—may have lessened his anger towards you, and disposed him to pardon and take you back again!"

"Do you think so?" said Catherine. "Oh! if it could be so, I could never be grateful enough for the joy it would shed upon my heart. I love him so—my noble husband! and together we would search for lost little Paul."

"With a much greater chance of finding him," continued the worthy dame. "So let the matter be for a day or two. I have no doubt, if we work wisely, all will be well."

There was silence after this; and at last the housekeeper nodded in her chair, and fell asleep; while Catherine sat thinking in the darkness, and drawing shadowy pictures of the happiness she had there enjoyed.

At last she arose from her seat, and moved softly about, touching the furniture with gentle hands, resting her cheeks against the chairs he had sat in, the window-curtains he had so often arranged, and, in a whisper, murmuring loving words which gushed upward from her full heart.

In one corner of the room was a tiny *bassinette*, with cloudy lace curtains shrouding it, looped back with rose-coloured ribbons; and kneeling there, she bent her face upon its pillow and kissed it, sobbing and praying for the babe it had once sheltered.

Then she stole on to the piano, and with one hand timidly touched the keys.

It was as sweet and tuneful as when she had first tried it; the loving care of the faithful servant had kept it in order and good condition. Nothing in the sacred chamber was suffered to go to ruin. Gradually, as her fingers moved over the keys, she forgot her caution, the need for secrecy, and sitting down before the instrument, her hands wandered away over the familiar notes, awaking a low, dreamy melody, which could scarcely be heard without the apartment. And, by degrees, she forgot also the present time, and began to live again in the past, and conjured up by the magic of her music the spirits which had brightened it, to cheer and bear her company again.

There was her husband in his accustomed chair—a gallant, loving husband—who was listening, as was his wont, to the melody;

there was a baby in the cradle, lulled to sleep; and she was no longer a toil-worn, suffering woman, but a happy young wife and mother, with joy and peace brooding in her heart, like mated doves.

And all the while, the tired housekeeper nodded on, slumbering deeply, and in no measure disturbed by the unwonted music in the long silent chamber. And as the pictures grew more real and vivid in Catherine's mind, so the music swelled louder and more joyously, rippling off into long-forgotten cadences, tunes which her husband had once loved and praised. Strange sounds in the dreary house, where no harmony was ever heard; strange sounds to float upward to the sick man in his chamber, alone with his racking thoughts; strange, familiar sounds which made him start and gasp for breath, which made him think for a moment that he was dreaming, and then suddenly gave him strength enough to rise and steal down stairs to the door of the chamber he had not entered for more than ten dismal years.

He stood in the passage, with a white face, listening—listening intently, trying to fashion an answer to the questioning fears crowding over him.

For years it had been to him a haunted room. Had the ghosts who had scared him from crossing its threshold assumed tangible forms, and was the dreamy melody swelling around him—now rising into joyous peals, now sinking into tender cadences—a voice calling him on to witness the shadows of his departed happiness in the deserted chamber?

His hand instinctively wandered to the handle of the door. He turned it, and crossed the threshold.

The music thrilled around him triumphantly, then died away in a plaintive wail, and, once again rising, merged into an air he had heard his wife play in the days which could never come back to him.

Oh, false music! to rise so lovingly on the air — speaking, in every throbbing note, of peace to the heart, which could know neither pleasure nor rest!

Oh, false music!—false as the fair hands which should have clung, through good or evil report, to the haunted man, but fell away at the first breath of suspicion and doubt!

Oh, false music!—yet with such a charm in every chord—a fascination which would not be resisted, but drew the listener step by step to the dark corner where the piano stood!

Every pressure of the carpet beneath his feet, every touch of his hand upon the furniture lying in his way, had a voice to speak to him of her for whose comfort they had been placed there.

Every voice carried him back a step into the past, until, when he had reached the other side of the room, he remembered no more that he was a sorrowful, heart-stricken man, but was again the gay bridegroom—the loving, trusting husband, with the halo of his lost happiness gathering brightly around him.

Oh, sweet, compassionate music, full of kindly pleadings! what sorrow that thy voice should ever sink into silence, taking thy pleasant visions back into the land of oblivion!

Still it murmured on; and, standing by the piano, Judge Vincent saw shadowy white hands moving over the keys — a shadowy woman's form bending over them, which took no heed of him, and seemed unconscious of his presence.

As his eyes grew accustomed to the deeper gloom, he saw the wavy curls, which floated over her shoulders, and drooped across her face.

Was he still dreaming, still under the glamour which had lured him into the room?

It was the figure of the woman he had loved and lost, which sat before him; and, with a rush of reviving affection, he laid his hand upon her shoulder.

"Catherine!" he whispered.

The music ended in a sudden discord, as her fingers fell helplessly upon the notes.

The old housekeeper awoke from her sleep with a start, to discover her master in the room, and his wife kneeling humbly at his feet—her hands clasped as though she were begging forgiveness.

"Light!" he said in a stern voice.

The woman lit a lamp; and throwing her apron over her face, withdrew to the window-seat, and rocked to and fro in her fear and excitement.

He was looking down at Catherine's face.

Still beautiful and fresh, and but little changed during the dreary years of their separation.

Still beautiful and still innocent in its expression, as the tender eyes looked up at him, pleading for his mercy.

"Catherine!" he said again. "Oh, heaven! he spoke truly to-night, when he prophesied your return!"

Still she was silent, and he went on.

"Ay, come back to me, with all her loveliness undimmed—come back with all her sin upon her head."

"No, no, William!" she cried. "Not that—not that! I have been true to you!"

"Hear her!" he answered. "*She* speaks of truth—the woman whose heart is false to its very core! I doubt not she will deny she has ever wronged me!"

"Nay; I own it!" she said. "I did you wrong when I doubted your love, and gave way to the jealousy which spurred me on to leave you; but, beyond that, I do deny that I have been aught but a faithful wife to you."

"Said I not she would?" he cried bitterly. "She would make herself an angel in my eyes! So, madam, you plead guiltless to my charge? But you lie when you speak of your faith to me. Do I look like a man whose life has been cheered by a loving wife? Where is the comfort and peace of my home? Where is my child—the child you stole from me when you forsook your duty, and left the husband you had vowed to cling to, for better or worse, until death should divide us? Oh, woman! speak not of your faith!"

"William, pity me!" she sobbed.

"You cannot clear yourself," he said. "But one thing you shall answer, if I tear the truth from you. Tell me of my boy—where shall I find him?"

"I do not know," she replied; "I swear it! He was stolen from me years ago, and I have never seen him since. Oh, husband, forgive me!"

"Forgive you?" he said, angrily. "Never! Not if on your dying bed you implored me to do so! False wife!—false mother!—untrue to the holiest ties of your nature!—go! Take with you the scorn of the man you have betrayed! Take with you the knowledge that the child you have so injured will live to hate the sound of the word mother—to curse it, as I do."

He flung off her arms, which she had thrown round him in agony, striving to stay the torrent of his anger, and passed from the room, closing the door after him with a heavy bang; while Catherine bent forward in despair, her face once more resting on the baby's pillow, her hand touching a broken toy.

CHAPTER XIX.

THE fate of the coiners had been decided; and Jacob Prew, with Ned the cripple, had received the sentence of transportation; Jacob for the remaining term of his natural life, and Ned for fourteen years.

And on the same morning when they started for Portland, Judge Vincent had departed for the Continent, leaving only with his banker and Bogg the address where he might be found, so fearful was he lest his wife should again intrude on him.

And all this while, Paul had been sheltered by Constance Clayton, who, full of pity for the young outcast, had nursed him through the long and severe illness which had followed his escape; and while Bogg had sent his agents to scour the country round, execrating his ill luck in not finding the boy, he lay snugly housed in the pretty villa. This, one astute detective had passed in his search, never dreaming that it could shelter the little vagabond he was set to hunt down, but went on whistling and peering with his sharp professional eyes behind hedges, in country copses, in empty huts and wayside barns, and was, at last, rewarded by coming upon a homeless wanderer, in a village some twenty miles ahead of the right place, whom he had dragged triumphantly to the metropolis, and into the presence of his employer. But at this point, on receiving a torrent of reproaches instead of the reward and thanks he had expected, the astute officer had retired to try another trail, and the boy he had captured was left to add one more item to the stray waifs homeless and starving in the streets of London.

Bogg had, in truth, much to try him at this time, for added to the escape of Paul from his hands, was this new dread of Catherine Vincent which had come upon him.

He had heard from the Judge of her return to her home—of her meeting with him; and though he rejoiced that he had so adroitly paved the way for her repulse by her husband, he was troubled because he was ignorant of her proceedings, and knew not in what way she would next set to work to regain her former position, and effect a reconciliation

It was in vain that he had questioned the housekeeper. The old woman had obstinately refused to answer him; and baffled and mortified, he had set his wits to work to circumvent Catherine when need should arise.

He had kept a sharp eye on his clerk, Simkins, as also on the Judge's letters, under pretence of reading and answering them, and thus sparing him any exertion in his weakness.

Upon the plea of wishing to be near him, and enjoying his friendship during the last days of his sojourn in England, he had taken up his quarters in his friend's house, and daily repaired there after his labours in the City were ended.

But as the time passed on, and no new event took place to disquiet him, his spirits lightened, and after seeing Judge Vincent safely on board the vessel, after watching it commence its journey, he had turned his face homeward, rejoicing that the one peril was past; and full of revenge and malice, setting himself in order to accuse his clerk of betraying him, and dismiss him from his service.

He had carried out his resolve, and Simkins had received notice to vacate the high office-stool; which he had done, without the least show of regret, having rather electrified his master by his outspoken comments on the transactions he had overheard through the medium of his funnel in the wall; which comments being of anything but a flattering nature as regarded Bogg himself, had excited the wily lawyer to the verge of distraction, and had made an inveterate enemy for the little, round, rosy clerk to cope with.

After watching Simkins turn the corner of the street, Bogg had locked the office-door, and putting up the ambiguous notice of "Back again in an hour," had departed likewise, having, after much consideration, resolved to visit Constance Clayton, and close up every avenue against Catherine, should she make an attempt in that direction.

It was on this day, or rather the preceding night, that Paul had first awoke to consciousness from the fever and delirium which had followed his escape from the coiners; a delirium in which he had raved vaguely of his former life and trials, and made his hearers shudder as they thought of his hardships, and the scenes of sorrow, and perhaps crime, in which, young as he was, he had borne his part.

The sun was struggling through the closed blind which shaded his room, when Paul awoke, and gazed around, wondering where he was, and how he came there.

For a time, he watched the motes floating in a standing ray of golden light, whirling about in it, and assuming every colour of the rainbow. Then, by slow degrees, his eyes wandered round the room with its shining furniture, to the white counterpane which covered his bed, and bristled all over in little knobs, as though the fabric, growing angry at being looked at, had twisted itself up to expostulate with the invalid for his impertinence. Paul gazed at the knots a little while, then put out his finger and touched them; then, by a natural transition, looked at his hand, so thin and white; then at the sleeve which covered his arm; then at the ceiling, and then at the walls, which were covered with paper, where roses and violets bloomed on a white ground, and made the whole room gay.

There was a picture at the foot of the bed; and being, by this time, rather weary of twisting his head about, he lay still on his back, and stedfastly surveyed it.

The painting was set in a gold frame, of elaborate workmanship, and represented a cherub's head.

It was a chubby specimen of the cherub tribe, with very blue eyes, which seemed to have been squeezed into about half their natural dimensions by the plump and rosy cheeks; and to have attained thereby a leering expression, somewhat at variance with its angelic character.

The cheeks were indented with two very deep and palpable dimples, having a perceptible connection with a little pursed-up mouth, which was smiling in a jocular manner, refreshing to behold.

Beneath the mouth was an extremely pink double chin, and the forehead was surmounted by a luxuriant crop of well-curled hair, above which peeped the tips of a pair of golden-feathered wings, supposed to be attached to the cherub's shoulders.

So Paul stared at the cherub, and the cherub stared at Paul, as though it were making fun of him for lying there so weak and thin, and altogether miserable, while it (the cherub) was so fat, and altogether jolly and comfortable; and Paul's eyes were just beginning to wink and blink, which gave him the idea that the cherub was nodding tipsily, when a hand was laid on his shoulder, and roused him to wakefulness again.

Paul turned his head, and then, with a cry of terror, hid it under the bedclothes, trembling convulsively.

It was Bogg who stood beside him.

"So you are the poor little boy the lady downstairs told me of; the boy whom all good Christians should pity?" said the lawyer, after listening at the door to assure himself that there was no one coming. "Upon my word, you are in nice, easy quarters; and seem to be enjoying yourself, too."

Paul lay silent.

"So this is how you managed to escape the police!" continued Beverley, pulling his shelter remorselessly away, and fixing his eyes on the boy's white face. "I wonder what these kind people would do were I to tell them you were one of the gang of coiners and thieves who have just been transported? I wonder whether they would lot you lie there, and feed and wait on you as though you were a gentleman's son, or whether they would send you to prison? Shall we try?"

"Oh, no! please, sir, don't!" gasped Paul, as his persecutor made a feint of moving away. "I couldn't help it. Jacob and Ned, they made me go; they'd 'a' killed me else. And I never spent the shillin' they gived me—the bad 'un, you know; it's in my trousis pocket—arsk the lady if it ain't; and don't send for the perlice, don't now, sir!"

His voice had grown shrill in his terror; and Beverley angrily laid his hand upon the child's lips.

"Be quiet, or I will," he threatened. "Do you think I want everybody in the house to know I'd speak to a vagabond like you? Oh, yes; *of course* you couldn't help it! *Of course* you are innocent! You are going the right way to be transported at last; you are, Paul— you are, whatever you may say to the contrary!"

The boy sobbed aloud at the direful words, and the cherub looked at him, and seen through the medium of his tears, seemed to be laughing more broadly than ever.

There was an ugly leer on the lawyer's face, and Paul listened more despondingly than ever.

"If you do not want the police to find you out, never mention to the people of this house that you know me; never mention that you came from Shuter's Court, in London. I would advise you not even to tell them that your name is Paul. Do you hear?"

"Yes; I hear, sir," said the child, lifting his eyes meekly to the lawyer's face. "I twigs, too. I'll not say as I come from London; and I'll not tell what my name is, either; nor that I knows you; *though* you could tell 'em as I ain't a thief—for I gived you back the purse and all the money in it, I did!" he continued.

His weak voice grew weaker as he spoke, and his pale cheeks paler with fatigue; but Beverley Bogg only looked more amused and pleased, and playfully laid his fingers on the thin arm lying outside the bed.

"You've been very ill," he said.

"Yes, sir, thank'ee," answered Paul.

"Ah!"

The exclamation came forth from Bogg's lips, with a prolonged chuckle of pleasure.

"You like this sort of thing?" he continued, touching the white shirt-sleeve. "You would like to be a gentleman; eh, Paul?"

"Yes; I rather think I would," he answered.

"*Honesty* will never do it," said the lawyer. "It's a game which does not pay."

He turned and walked to the window, and looked out through the vine-tree which grew around it—at the garden, and the children who were playing there; and just then Mrs Clayton entered the room.

"So you found out my patient?" she said, as she advanced to Paul's side, and smoothed the pillows, and laid her hand upon his forehead in a motherly fashion very pleasant to the child.

"Your directions were so clear, I could not fail," he said, looking at the sick boy and his gentle nurse, with a benignant smile. "Oh, yes! I found him out! I found him out! And who is he, and what is he, I should like to know? What is his name?"

"I do not know," she replied. "I have not questioned him. Child, what is your name?"

Paul shifted about uneasily, but made no reply.

"Tell us," persisted Constance. "Do not be afraid to speak. This good gentleman has heard your story—how we found you ill upon the ground; and he has such an interest in you, that he has come up-stairs to see you, and learn all about you. Is it not so?"

"Oh, yes!" said Bogg. "I take an interest —I may say a very great interest, in him. What is your name, my man—*John?*"

"Ye-es, sir—thank'ee, sir," said Paul, who had been hopelessly fishing for one. "That's him; that'll do."

"Oh! Then, *John*," he said, "you had better go to sleep, and we'll defer questioning you for a time. You've got no father, no mother, no friends?—you are a stray waif in the world?"

"Yes," said Paul, between the pause.

"Then we know all you can tell. So, *John*, go to sleep; and when you wake, do not forget that there is a kind gentleman, who takes great interest in you, always on the look-out."

He beckoned Mrs. Clayton from the room, and Paul drew a sigh of relief as the skirts of his coat vanished through the doorway.

Then he looked at the cherub.

It was laughing more heartily, and it seemed as though the object of its mirth was Bogg's philanthropy.

CHAPTER XX.

The time passed by; the summer deepened into autumn; and Paul no longer lay on a sick-bed, but moved about the house and gardens, with fresh colour glowing on his cheeks, and a new light sparkling in his eyes—the light of happiness.

And yet, sometimes, it was dimmed; when Bogg paid his visits to the house, ostensibly to bring news of Judge Vincent, but, in reality, to keep an eye upon the boy, and re-establish his power over him.

He made a show of patronising Paul, and brought him occasional gifts, proffering them with such a kindly air, that Mr. and Mrs. Clayton began to deem him truly benevolent, and to wonder why the world gave him the character of being so hard a man. But, to the boy, there was something in the lawyer's cold, gray eyes which filled him with fear; he felt, instinctively, that in spite of his ostentatious kindness, the lawyer was his enemy; and he laid aside the presents with an indifference which astonished his protectors, and drew upon him the imputation of ingratitude.

It was in vain he endeavoured to hide himself at the period of Bogg's visits; for, no matter in what corner he was concealed—in the out-houses or gardens—the man ferreted him out, congratulated him on his change in fortune, and spoke of his interest in him in a manner which filled Paul with dread, and made him feel more and more keenly that he was an enemy. As the time passed on, the conviction and the dread grew deeper and deeper, until it culminated in an agony of fear and desperation on a day when he learnt that Bogg had proposed to employ him in his office, and superintend his future career, and that his offer had been accepted by Mr. Clayton.

That night, the child's little bed was empty; for, while the rest of the household was sleeping, he had climbed from his window, and escaped into the open country, wandering he knew not whither; and once again the lawyer cursed the unlucky chance which had enabled Paul to slip through his fingers.

Two days later brought the lad near to a small country town. Here he learnt with joy that there was a fair in the place, and that there would be the usual gathering of shows to amuse the fair-goers, and draw the money from their pockets.

A ray of hope sprung up in his heart.

Probably Morrison, the showman, would be there, and he should meet again with Rachel, and with friends. He hurried on, with fresh spirit; and, at mid-day, entered the market-place, tired and dusty, and set to work eagerly to discover the well-known tent.

There were wild beasts, marionettes, panoramas, and, to his great joy, a theatre with a painted front, and a stretch of dingy canvas behind, which looked familiar to him.

There was a clown, too, on the platform, and a bespangled lady, diligently dancing a Highland fling; while, besides this, was a man, standing apart, in a melodramatic attitude, whom Paul could have sworn was the "Black Pirate of the Blue Sea," for there were displayed on him the gay stockings, and half maritime dress he remembered as having formed the costume of that renowned brave.

With the view of surprising Rachel, he ran behind a pump which stood near, and with the help of a little water and his pocket-handkerchief, performed a hasty toilet, and then boldly hastened on to the foot of the steps leading to the show.

He looked up at the people on the platform, and, for the first time, a feeling of disappointment came over him.

Their faces were strange, and the pictures over the entrance did not seem the same to him.

A man came bustling forward from among the crowd, and placed his foot on the first step of the ladder.

As they caught sight of him, the dancer danced more zealously, and the band played a yet louder strain.

"Are you going up?" he said, to Paul.

"If you please, sir, whose theayter is it?" questioned the boy.

"Why, mine," answered the man; "and my name's Jenkins. You had better come up, and see the tragedy of 'The Babes in the Wood.' Half-price for children!"

"Where's—where's Mr. Morrison's tent?" said Paul. "Ain't he here?"

"Morrison? No!" answered the showman; "he is not in this quarter of the country at all; and I know nothing of him."

He walked away, as he spoke, and Paul stole to a quiet corner, behind a door, and wept in his desolation.

He realized how completely circumstances had broken the link between himself and Rachel.

———

CHAPTER XXI.

"Nursed by hunger and want,
Taught *out of Nature's* page,
Singing I plod, by wayward fancy led."
VAGABOND.

NINE years had passed away.

It was autumn time; the hop-picking season was just over, and the country lanes and roads were populous with bands of labourers, who were deserting the fields and gardens, after gathering in the rich harvest of blossoms. By the side of one of these roads, half sitting, half reclining, lay a youth of about twenty-one years of age; a tall, handsome, sturdy fellow, with bold, flashing eyes, and a luxuriant crop of curly black hair.

He was dressed in a rough suit of fustian, travel-stained and dusty, and was regaling himself by smoking a pipe—short, black, well used, and as vagabond-looking as himself.

At times he watched the smoke curling upward in slender rings; at others, bent his gaze upon the clear blue morning sky, or the groups of travellers passing by, laden with their household goods—the pots and pans, beds, and other necessaries needful during their period of camping out in the hop plantations.

For all, the youth had a pleasant word; a jest for the men, a cheering one for the jaded women and children; sometimes bestowing upon the younger of the latter a few ripe berries which he had gathered, and which lay in his hat beside him.

And from all—from men, women, and children—he in his turn received friendly greetings and adieus, as the wanderers passed on their way, leaving him alone by the roadside.

"There they go!" he said, as the latest family faded away in the distance—" there they go, my companions of many a merry day, leaving me once more to be merry alone! And *that*, I know, I can be; with tobacco to fill my pipe, and money to line my pocket, I am happy as a king."

Then, in a mellow voice, he trolled out a few lines of an old ballad, ending with

"I care for nobody, and nobody cares for me!"

He paused a few moments at the last words, then repeated the line again, more softly and slowly, as though he were reflecting upon it.

"It was not so once," he remarked; then relapsed into silence, and, with a soft sigh, lit his pipe, which had gone out, and smoked furiously.

By-and-by there was a noise far down the road—the noise of wheels rumbling merrily over the hard track, and blending in, like a deep bass, with the sounds of happy voices and laughter.

The youth raised his head, and looked in the direction whence they came.

There was a cloud of dust rolling along, and in the midst of the cloud was a pleasure-van, drawn by a pair of stout horses.

As they drew nearer, he could see a group of heads peering from under the tent-like covering of the vehicle; and when they were nearly close to him, he saw, too, that all were blooming and bright, and full of enjoyment, fun, and mischief.

Some were men's faces, and some belonged to the gentler sex; and, moreover, all the male heads were crowned with jaunty-looking caps, and the female ones with coquettish bonnets and gipsy hats, more or less embellished with flowers, lace, and ribbon, and looking very lively and bright under the tilt of the waggon.

"A pleasure party," said the youth; then stretching himself more at his ease, he withdrew his attention from them, and fixed it upon his pipe and a white cloud sailing far, far above his head.

A little to the right stood a rustic inn; and, opposite to him a clear stream of water rushed, with a musical gurgle, from a pipe projected through the bank of a field, and splashed into the way-side ditch, where it ran coyly away, and hid itself among the long grass and brambles.

There was a shout from a chorus of feminine voices as a dozen feminine eyes spied out the crystal water; and in a moment the waggon was stopped, and half a dozen swains nimbly alighted, and offered their hands to assist the ladies down.

The ladies uttered timid little screams, and poised themselves on the shafts, or stood trembling just on the brink of the back descent, making believe to be very much alarmed as they viewed their elevated positions; and finally resigning themselves, with many tremours, to the officious cavaliers, who lifted them down, and carried them off to the tempting rural fountain.

The lounger on the opposite bank had looked on, considerably amused; then he had caught a glimpse of a pretty ankle, peeping one instant from under an array of embroidered skirts, as its owner, in her turn, made the perilous descent.

And seeing that the ankle was so pretty, he had raised his eyes to her face, and there they remained fixed.

It was the face of a girl of sixteen, framed with golden brown curls, and lit by large, deep blue, laughter-loving eyes—a face half childish, half womanly, and wholly beautiful,—which took him by surprise with its loveliness, and, holding his own orbs captive, forced him to gaze upon it.

She was standing by the side of a portly, middle-aged man, with both little pink, dimpled hands clasped over his arm, and her curls blowing across his shoulder as she looked up, talking in a sweet, arch manner, perfectly irresistible.

The youth involuntarily drew the pipe from his mouth, and stared as though he were envying the portly man his privilege of being clasped with those delicate, caressing hands, and looked at by those eyes.

They had moved nearer to him during their conversation, until he could catch their words, and he listened eagerly.

"How sorry I shall be to leave this," she said, "and go to London, to be pent up in its labyrinths of streets and brick houses!"

"I wonder whether you will remember it," said the man. "It's years since you were there, you know."

"Don't speak of that time, father," said the girl. "I cannot bear even to think of it. Remember London? Of course I can! It is a dreary, desolate, hard city; all smoke and fog, through which a ray of pure sunshine never beams."

The man put one fat finger under her chin, looking quizzically at her, and once again the youth fell into the sin of envy and jealousy.

"Very prettily expressed," said the middle-aged gentleman; "full of true pathos. You will make a capital sentimental actress. But, there! I almost forget your experience of London was not over pleasant; and, after all, I own that for beauty it doesn't compare with the country. Still, as far as the sunshine goes, I'm not afraid to risk it. We shall always have plenty of that so long as we keep you, little Ray."

The listening youth started, and a flush crossed his swarthy face, while he still more earnestly gazed on the figure of the young girl; then, with the same close scrutiny, examined that of her companion.

There was no mistaking it : though clad in a better garb than he had worn on his first introduction to him, and vastly increased in importance of demeanour, it was Morrison, the showman, who stood in the road, and the girl was Rachel.

"At last," murmured the youth, who was no other than Paul,—"at last we meet again, dear little Rachel!"

His dark eyes dwelt on her with a passionate, imploring glance, as though he was waiting for her to recognise him; but without casting one look in his direction, she tripped gaily on towards the inn, still clasping the showman's arm, with her muslin dress fluttering round her like an azure cloud.

Paul's lip trembled with disappointment, and for a moment he leant his head upon his hands in gloomy thought, then raised it again, smiling.

"Why, what a fool I am," he said, "making myself miserable because she did not remember me, when I have been looking at her sweet face for the last five minutes, and failed to remember her! Besides, how could I expect her to know little Paul in the great hulking fellow lying here?"

He sat thoughtfully watching the merrymakers at the spring, with the smile deepening on his lips, as though he were fashioning some pleasant scheme in his mind.

Presently the party moved away, and likewise entered the inn, at the door of which the van now stood, while the horses plunged their heads in a trough of water standing there; and the driver drank deeply from a foaming pot of " brown October."

Paul was alone, and rising to his feet, shook himself much as a Newfoundland dog would on emerging from the water.

Then, stooping, he pulled up a long handful of grass, and, with it, dusted his boots and clothes; after which, he crossed the road, and laved his face and hands in the mimic fountain.

He looked a noble specimen of rough humanity as he stood there, with his shoulders well thrown back, and his broad chest heaving with excitement; and the water-drops hanging in his tangled curls, and glistening like diamonds in the sun; and yet, over his whole countenance might be traced the innocent, trusting expression which had been once the great charm of the child, Paul.

After awhile, he put on his battered felt hat, and strode towards the inn.

The waggoner, who was now varying his enjoyment by eating energetically of a huge hunk of bread and bacon, looked up as he approached.

"Good morning," said Paul, with a pleasant smile. "A fine day, isn't it?"

"To be sure, it is," said the man, good-humouredly. "On the tramp, eh?"

Paul nodded his head.

"Have a drink?" said the driver, pointing to the jug of ale.

Paul complied with the request, and took a hearty draught.

"Thanks!" he said, putting the jug down.

"Good, isn't it?" remarked the jolly waggoner, with a laugh. "And plenty more where that come from; so don't spare it. They don't do things by half, when they sets about it," he added, pointing with his clasp-knife to the inn. "I never was out with such an-out-and-out good-natured party in all my life. 'Eat and drink, and don't be afeared,' says they; and I'm doing it, with a good will."

"Pleasure party?" questioned Paul.

"Picnic, leastways," answered the waggoner. "They are the theayter people, from the town down yonders, and they are a-going up to the woods, to make a day of it."

"Do ye think they'd give me a job?" said Paul. "I'm known in these parts. I've been hop-picking here every season for the last nine years; and the landlady of the inn will give me a good word, if it is wanted. I've done many a day's work for her, and have given satisfaction."

"Now, driver, we're ready," shouted Morrison, through the parlour window. "If we don't make haste, we shall not reach the woods to-day."

"Wait a bit," said the man, to Paul, as he arose, and closed his knife, after gulping down the last mouthful of his meal. "There'll be somebody wanted to carry the baskets down into the woods, and help with the horses, and so on. I'll see."

He sauntered into the house, and, after a few moments, Morrison peeped at Paul, and then came the landlady, and looked also.

"Ah! so it's you, Captain!" she cried. "I've been expecting you to come along, knowing that the hop season is over, and seeing the labourers go by."

Paul touched his hat, and made an awkward bow. He was somewhat confused, for behind the landlady and Morrison he saw a whole battery of eyes fixed upon him.

"Recommend him? Of course, I can," continued the woman. "I've known him now for nine years, and never has he done a dishonest or uncivil thing all the time. Never drunk, never rude-spoken; and as industrious a lad as any in all England, though he does lead a wandering life, I must say."

"That'll do, then," said Morrison. "You may bring him along, driver. We shall find him plenty of work, never fear."

Paul smiled joyfully, and walking to the horses' side, smoothed their rugged coats, and leant his cheek against their noses, talking to them as though they were old friends.

"He's a good lad—a good lad!" said the landlady. "I remember well when he came here first, a poor, tired, ragged child, as it made your heart bleed to see. I gave him food, and a bed; but, bless you! in the morning, he was up like the lark, and had polished the grates, and cleaned the knives and forks, as independent as you please, sir."

"He looks that," said Morrison, watching.

"I'd a kept him, but he would go on; so I gave him a shilling, and off he started to the hop-picking, and got work in a garden about five miles off, through a note as my good man gave him. And a tidy sum he earned and saved; and every year since, he comes and takes his place there; though he might, long ago, have got into decent service here, or in the town where you've been staying, for he works about there all the winter and spring; and many would be glad to get him, only, as I said before, he is of a roving disposition, and never so happy as when wandering about the lanes and fields, singing and working, and getting as brown and lusty as a gipsy in the sun. He'll make a good husband for a lass, some day, for he's not so poor, and has a tidy sum, nigh upon twenty pounds, which I have in my hands, to keep for him."

"Quite a respectable vagrant," said Morrison, who had listened with great interest to the story. "And a splendid fellow to boot. And pray, what is his name?"

"That I do not know," said the woman. "We always call him Captain; for, you see, he was first captain of the children among the hop-pickers, and now he's head of the young men and women, being a kind of overseer in the garden where he works. We never thought of asking for another name."

"'What's in a name?'" quoth Morrison, rising from his seat, and pressing an extra silver piece into the landlady's hand. "But prithee, friends, let us be going. Come, Rachel."

Paul stood by the waggon, ready to lend a helping hand, if required; and many a kindly glance was vouchsafed him by the fair ones of the party, as they looked on his handsome face, and thought of his romantic history.

At last came Rachel's turn.

She came smiling to the horses' side, touching them with her pretty hands, and chirruping to them in a voice like a bird.

But never a glance did she cast upon Paul, only swept him with her fluttering robes and ribbons, making his heart throb and his cheeks burn, and yet strangely disappointing his expectations of recognition.

He stretched out his hand to assist her to mount, but, with a charming gesture of disdain, she turned, and beckoning one of an eager group of admirers, was straightway lifted to an elevated perch on the front seat, by the driver, from which she looked down upon humble Paul, with a scornful pout on her ripe lips, and the air of a young queen. He turned sadly away, and stooped, apparently to examine the horse's girths, but in reality to hide his chagrin and vexation.

"She has forgotten me," he muttered; then, with a sudden access of pride, leaped to a seat on the shafts, and threw up his head with a manful air.

The waggoner cracked his whip, and the vehicle went on its way, Rachel laughing merrily, and regarding with scornful glances the moody face of Paul.

CHAPTER XXII.

"I CARE for nobody, and nobody cares for me." It was in vain Paul strove to sing the old song, as he sat in the shade of a giant oak-tree, awaiting the return of the pic-nic party from the woods. "I care for nobody." His wounded pride sent the words out with a burst, and made them ring through the silence around him.

"Nobody cares for me." Pride was vanquished by the line, and his voice quivered sadly as he sung, dropping with each word, until it ceased, and Paul was as grave and melancholy as the woods themselves in the gathering dusk of night.

He could never sing the ditty again, "I care for nobody."

Deep down in his heart, underlying his anger and pride, was the knowledge that he had fallen from his former state of careless freedom—that he could never again be the same youth in mind and spirit as he had been on the morning of that day when he had sat by the wayside, watching his comrades pass by from the hop-picking, and hearing the pleasure-van rumble in the distance.

He drew out his pipe—the companion of so many of his lonely or weary hours—and, filling it, tried to solace himself with a whiff of his favourite weed.

All smoke—that is, not only the tobacco, but the idea of comfort. Through and through his mind rang the ghost of his ditty, singing, in a low, mocking tone, "Nobody cares for me."

He dashed the pipe from his lips, and looked sullenly up through the branches of the trees at the dull, gray sky, and listened to the sounds rising dreamily around him.

Suddenly, the evening wind seemed to gather intelligence, and to read his thoughts, and went rustling through the crisp leaves, whispering to them the name which had haunted him through the livelong day.

"Rachel, Rachel—little Ray!" it sang; and all the voices of the hoary wood took it up, and chanted, in chorus, "Rachel, Rachel! Little Ray! Pretty Ray! Proud Ray!" until his heart leaped and his pulses throbbed tumultuously as he listened.

And the clouds drifting overhead, and the shadows moving stealthily around him, took fresh forms in the magic of his solitude, until he saw her face bending over him from the sky, or her form lurking under the trees, ready to spring forward and greet him.

And so he lay, dreaming his love-dream, under the whispering oak-tree, while the merry pleasure-party chased each other through the dingles, dells, and woodland paths, and the jolly waggoner sat on the shafts of his van, diligently selecting the choice portions of the remnants of the feast, and as diligently devouring them, while he marvelled at his companion's stupidity in letting such a rare opportunity slipby without improving it.

The evening deepened, and the moon crept up slowly into the heavens, while the stars came out one by one, and clustered around her.

Still, Paul kept his old place, with the neglected pipe grasped in his hand, and filled with gray ashes.

Poor old pipe! It seemed to be mourning its owner's inconstancy, and the end of the pleasant times when the pair had been sufficient for each other.

Ah, Paul! it looked as though it had learnt your song; and that, if it could have spoken, it would have sighed through its blackened bowl, and shrilled through the broken stem, which had been so often pressed lovingly in your lips, "Nobody cares for me!"

Certainly, Paul did not; for, at last, he heard coming from the distance the gay tones

PAUL BECOMES SENSIBLE OF HIS DEGRADED POSITION. (*See page* 51.)

of Rachel, as she came towards him, laughing, and chatting, and full of holiday gaiety and mirth.

Nearer and nearer, until he could see her robes glimmer through the trees.

Nearer, nearer, until he could almost touch her with his hand; still she never saw him, for he was crouched in a black shadow, and she was looking up at her escort, as she passed by, and moving to a tree a few yards from the great oak, sat down, with her back turned towards the lonely watcher.

The wind blew in her face, gently lifting her curls, and catching her words, wafted them on to Paul.

"Triumph!" she said, in a joyful voice. "I see no reason why I should not succeed in the metropolis as well as in the provinces, Father Morrison."

"That's the true spirit in which to make a venture," replied the ex-showman. "Faint heart, you know, never won anything worth having yet."

His words must have reassured the unseen listener, for he smiled and bent forward more eagerly to catch her answer.

"I shall not fail through want of courage," she said, proudly. "I shall think no more of playing to a London audience, to the critics and connoisseurs of the dramatic art, than I do of appearing before the people in the villages and country towns."

Ah! what a pretty accent of scorn she threw into her voice, as though, secure in her youth and beauty, she could defy the world.

Morrison laughed aloud, and pulled one of her long curls.

"I shouldn't wonder," he said, "if you ultimately became a great star, and ended your career by marrying a lord."

"Suppose I should?" said Rachel, gleefully; "a lord with no end of money! How glorious it would be!"

"Silks, satins, carriages, servants!" continued Morrison, carrying out her humour, and still laughing.

"And you and ther to help enjoy them," she added. "I couldn't do without *you*."

"Perhaps you wouldn't care for me and my old lady then," he bantered. "We shouldn't be grand enough, I expect."

"How ungrateful you must think me!" said Rachel. "As though I could *ever* forget all the kindness you have shown me for so many years!"

"Then you have not forgotten little Paul?" said Morrison.

"No!" she answered. "I have not forgotten him."

"By right—I mean, romantic right," he continued, "now I come to think of it, you ought not to marry a lord."

"Why not?" she asked.

"Suppose, in London, we should meet with your childhood's hero?"

"And what if we do?" she said. "I cannot see why the meeting should affect me. What is he to me now?—what can he be in the future?"

"He has been a friend and protector," answered Morrison, reproachfully. "You should bear it in mind."

"And so I do," she said. "I would repay him, were we to meet again, by good services, with money—but with nothing further."

The listener by the oak-tree drew a gasping sigh.

She went on speaking impetuously: "Think, Father Morrison, what he must be by this time! Would he be a fitting associate for *me* —the Paul who has grown up in ignorance, and squalor, and degradation?"

"I do not think so," said Morrison; but without noticing it, she continued her vehement speech.

"I cannot bear to think of him, and the past. I pray we may never meet again. Only think how I should suffer were my story revived! Were the people I now meet to discover that I was formerly nothing but a beggar child, who stood by a London crossing, asking alms, how they would scorn and despise me I could not bear it, father; it would crush all my energy and ambition. Oh! never speak of it, of him again, if you love me—if you would make me happy!"

Her voice ended in sobs, and she withdrew from the place with her companion, leaving Paul once more alone.

"I love her—I would die to make her happy!" he whispered. "She shall never know that we have met again!" And bowing his head until his forehead rested on the cool, soft grass, he fell into a bitter reverie, looking with loathing eyes upon himself, and the degradation of his life, while the wind soughed on, muttering to the leaves the burden of its former song, "Pretty Ray! proud Ray!" and darkness settled slowly over the hoary woods.

CHAPTER XXIII.

Rachel's first benefit.

It was placarded on every dead wall in the town, and smaller heralds of the momentous event greeted the folks as they passed through the streets, staring in resplendent hues from the shop windows, or else thrust themselves ostentatiously into notice in the interiors of ale-houses, and other public resorts.

Such a bill as it was!

Daring in design, and prodigal in its promise of entertainment.

It was little marvel that the townsfolk read it with an ever-increasing interest, which culminated in a rush from the upper class of inhabitants for the box-office, where they purchased tickets and secured places with a prodigality which both astonished and delighted Morrison; and on the night itself, a rush from middle and lower rank for all the public entrances to the temple of art, where they jostled, and crowded, and inconvenienced each other's elbows, sides, and toes in a barbarous and reckless fashion, until the above-mentioned portals were unclosed. Then they tumbled in pell-mell, and sat for the space of half an hour closely packed, and gradually warming into a state of high fever heat and perspiration, staring at an indistinct drop-scene, and listening to the persevering efforts of the orchestra—on this occasion, six strong—to keep time and tune, without once achieving that desirable state of things.

Among the pit audience was Paul, who had crushed himself into a front row, and had worked himself into a state of painful excitement in his waiting and longing to see Rachel once more before he let her pass on her way, and out of his life for ever.

The orchestra waxed feeble for a moment, the musicians were becoming tired of their labour, and just then a bell tinkled behind the curtain.

The music burst out in one tremendous chorus, every instrument for itself, without care for the others, faster and louder—louder and faster; and then, crash! All was still.

The musicians laid down their arms, and looked round on the audience with red faces and shining brows; while, in their turns, the audience cheered, and, awakened by the tinkle of the bell, applauded and shuffled their feet, and, in the midst of the clamour, the curtain rolled up, and disclosed the first scene of the play — "The Lady of Lyons," with Rachel for *Pauline*. A story of love and pride, something akin to Paul's story; and he looked and listened entranced—this modern *Claude Melnotte*, who had dared to love one so much above his sphere, in her grace, refinement, loveliness, and genius, when contrasted with his own ignorance and lowly estate.

There was not a sorrow which fell upon the heart of the hero of the play which did not touch that of the lover sitting in the pit of the little theatre. There was not a sentence of love spoken by Pauline which did not make his pulses leap, and his cheeks burn, as he wished himself the happy man to whom they were spoken.

There was not a word of her passionate scorn of the mock prince, the gardener's son, which did not make him shrink, and make him more and more ashamed of his vagabond life, and the idle way in which he had floated on with the stream of time, content so long as he had food and shelter, and caring nothing that he had no honourable name or place in the world.

True, he had wronged no man; he had been honest and truthful in his dealings with his neighbours, but since the night when he sat under the tree, and listened to Rachel's talk, he had begun to realize that man owes a duty to himself as well as his fellow, and that he had wronged *himself* by his inaction. That he had cheated his noble nature out of its due, and lied to it, when he had persuaded himself that he could always be content to live in a manner no far different to that of the lower animal creation, ignoring all ambition to rise, and forgetting he was endowed with a reasonable brain and intellect.

And so, when the play had ended, Paul's resolve was taken, for Rachel's sake, to strive and struggle against his ignorance; to win himself a name and fame, so that even she might be proud to know him, and recognise in the man who had fought bravely against his disadvantages and difficulties, the Paul of her childhood. And in the meanwhile, that he might continue near her, and by her presence nerve himself to his duties, he that very night saw Mr. Morrison, and prevailed upon him to engage him as a scene-shifter and general servant in the London theatre, which that thriving and enterprising manager had been enabled to lease for the ensuing winter season.

A lowly position, but Paul aspired to head the boards, and looked upon it as a promising commencement; and having settled his plans, he forthwith fell to building castles in the air.

—castles in which he saw himself rising into good repute—castles in which he was installed with Rachel, both happy in their mutual respect and love.

CHAPTER XXIV.

THE years that had rolled on, touching with new beauty those who were just springing up to maturity, had not fallen lightly upon Lawyer Bogg.

Once more it was morning; not the warm summer, but the dreary gray of autumn time; and once more he sat in his accustomed chair in the office.

The place was little changed.

Somewhat dingier and gloomy, but as hard and cold-looking as it had been nine years before. The old clock ticked on in the outer office with the same metallic click in its pendulum as it had in the past.

The old desk stood in its accustomed place, a little darker, and more polished by age, but in other respects unaltered; and behind the desk sat a clerk, nibbling the end of his pen, and looking with a vacant stare through the window, as though he were watching for the departed summer sunbeams.

He was an old man, with a frosty head, more than half bald; and as unlike the round, rosy Simkins as a man well could be; but he matched the place, for it, like himself, looked old, and bare, and frosty; and the master, sitting in his easy chair in the inner room, fast growing aged, and his hard nature becoming harder and harder, as the flying years ground him beneath their feet, and pressed him closer into the dust and mire of the world.

It was no longer Beverley Bogg, the upright, stalwart man, glorying in his strength; but Beverley Bogg, with thin, grizzled locks—bent, worn out, and feeble,—tottering on his way.

Yet the face was the same.

There was the same cruel expression on it—glittering in his eyes—lurking in every wrinkle—culminating in his heavy, trap-like jaws.

And yet, looking on it, one could see that a change had passed over it—not altering its former characteristics, but, as it were, blending and weaving itself into it indelibly.

It was a look of care and sorrow.

He was reading the newspaper; and in the hand which held it, the knotty joints and purple veins stood out boldly.

He was perusing the columns which record the criminal deeds of the day—reading them with a fixedness of interest, but with an expression of weary disappointment.

"Nine years!" he muttered. "For nine years, every morning, have I looked here for some token of him, and there is none yet."

He sighed, and tossed down the paper, and sat, with gloomy eyes, looking at the table.

After a while, he broke once more into uneasy whispering, clutching and unclutching his hands impatiently.

"Nine years of reverses and failures, of baffled scheming and trouble; and yet I will not give up—not while I have one spark of life and energy in my veins! Come what may, destruction, despair, I will keep the vow I made more than twenty years ago. How far back they seem; the days of my prosperity and youth!"

Once again he was silent, but his eyes had wandered to the wall, where the crack still remained opposite to which Simkins had drilled his acoustic tube.

"I wonder what is become of him?" he mused. "I have stopped up the hole he made in the wall, but could not stop up his memory, and force him to forget what he heard and saw through it. Suppose some day he should meet Judge Vincent, and disclose the secret? He tried it once ; why not again? If it were done now, it would ruin me. But it cannot be. Why should I frighten myself with idle shadows?"

"That's more than I can answer," said a voice from the threshold. "Still, I am wise enough to warn you that it is a most dangerous habit to think aloud; and you seem to have fallen into it lately."

The speaker, a young man of about thirty years of age, lounged into the room, banging the door, and threw himself upon one of the ancient, slippery, uncomfortable chairs, but started up immediately, and pushed it away with his foot.

"Why, in the name of goodness, do you have such chairs?" he asked, coarsely. "If I had my way, I'd throw the whole lot out into the street!"

"Ha, ha! Dick, my boy, so there you are at last!" said the lawyer, his face flushing with pleasure. And rising from his seat, without noticing the youth's ungraciousness, he walked over to where he stood sulkily leaning against the wall; and clasped his hand, looking at him fondly, and with every line in his face softening. There was sufficient likeness between them to mark them at a first glance as father and son. The same tall figures and square shoulders, the same expression in their faces.

What Beverley Bogg had been in his youth, the son was; what the son might be in his old age, even so was Beverley Bogg.

"Yes, it's I, as you can see, dad," said Richard, withdrawing his hand, "And I'm back at last."

As he spoke, he advanced to the easy chair, his father's especial seat, and seating himself in it, sprawled his long legs across the floor, and leant his head back in a manner at once careless and defiant.

"Have you been home?" questioned Bogg, standing by his side.

"Yes."

"Your mother has been very anxious about you," continued the father; "I may say we have been very anxious."

"Have you really?" said Bogg the younger, altering his position so as to render it easier.

The movement brought his head nearer to Beverley, and, with a tender touch, the lawyer began to smooth his hair, looking down at him all the while with an expression which would have astonished his acquaintances and clients, had they been able to see it!

"Why do you stay away so long, Dick, my lad?" said his father. "Think what we must suffer, not knowing where you are, for weeks together."

"Oh, bother!" said the youth, impatiently; twisting away his head from the caressing fingers. "If that's how you are going to welcome me, I'm off again."

He made as though he would have risen; but his father detained him, with a tremulous hand.

"Don't be angry," he pleaded.

"It's always the way. One would imagine I am still a baby, not to be trusted out of your sight. And I should like to know what encouragement there is in our family for a young fellow to remain at home? When I go there, the old woman whimpers and cries, and whines until it drives me frantic; and when I come here, you put on the injured parent. A pleasant berth I should have if I stopped at home!"

How cruelly he spoke, flinging off the detaining grasp, and snapping his jaws, with the exact trap-like trick of his father!

"If you would only try it," said Beverley, "I will take care everything is pleasant for you. There shall be no more repining to drive you away. You may invite your friends."

"Oh, pshaw!" interrupted Dick. "Treat them with weak tea and currant wine, and amuse them with a quiet rubber at whist! It wouldn't answer. We young men of the present day like to see life."

"Oh, Dick, my boy!" said the lawyer, with a burst of feeling, "you are treading the road to ruin!"

"Now you are beginning!" replied the hopeful youth. "If it is not enough to wear out the patience of Job! But there, amuse yourself," he continued; "I'll take a nap the while!"

He closed his eyes, and pretended to sleep, smiling insolently the while.

"Think of us!" pleaded his father; "think how lonely we must be when you are away!"

There was no reply; Dick dropped his head a little farther back, and snored gently.

The tears were rolling down his father's cheek.

"We have loved you your whole life long!" he continued; "we love you so now!"

His voice rose higher, as he pleaded, and the youth opened his eyes angrily.

"Do you want everybody to hear you?" he said, coarsely. "A pretty idea they will have of you, if they happen to catch you raving like an idiot! Another word like that, and I'm off."

Beverley wiped away his tears, and seated himself moodily in one of the inconvenient chairs.

"That's more like!" said his son. "And now, if you please, we will proceed to business."

"I knew it—I knew it!" muttered the lawyer. "It is always the same!"

Dick took no notice of the speech.

"I want a hundred pounds!" he continued, briefly.

"What?" said Bogg, in a low tone. "A hundred pounds? You had three hundred a fortnight ago!"

"And have parted with it," answered Dick; "so there's no other remedy but for you to behave handsomely, and hand me over the hundred."

Still insolent, but added to it was a fierce, relentless tone, which made the old man shudder, and yet angered him.

"Not a hundred farthings!" he replied, in accents of concentrated rage. "You shall pillage me no longer. Oh, I know you for a base, undutiful son! A *roué*, a gambler, a spendthrift! I tell you, boy, you shall have no more money of me to waste in riot! Go! I refuse to give you what you demand!"

"You do, eh?" said Richard, rising. "Very well; you cannot blame me for getting it on my own responsibility in the best way I can."

"You would *steal* it!" hissed Beverley Bogg, "as you did when you broke open my strong-box! Thief! ingrate!"

"I want the money, and I *will* have it!" said Dick; then noticing his father's suppressed fury, approached him, and spoke in a conciliating manner. "Come, father, don't let us weary ourselves with useless contention, for, believe me, it *is* useless. My need for the money is imperative."

"Richard," said Beverley Bogg, speaking more calmly, "listen to me; and, believe me, I speak the truth when I say that I am on the brink of ruin!"

"Father," cried the young spendthrift, in dismay, "how can that be? I was always told you were a rich and thriving man."

"I was once," he answered. "It is not so now. For years I have been speculating, and losing; until there is but a narrow step between us and beggary."

"A pretty look-out, indeed!" said Richard.

"My private fortune is gone; all we have to rely on is the money I make by my professional duties. I have but one hope left me to retrieve myself."

"What is it?" questioned Richard, somewhat eagerly.

"The fortune of Judge Vincent," answered Bogg. "I speak plainly — for why should I have any disguise with you? He trusts me implicitly; he will do whatever I counsel him to, for we have been friends for years."

"Exactly so," said Richard, laughing. "I tell you what, father; if I were not your son, the last relationship in which I would stand in as regards you would be as your friend."

"I am manager of a company, in which I have persuaded him to invest. Next week I draw the first cheque from his banker. That money—all I extract from him afterwards—I shall keep. All he will get will be false receipts for shares which I never purchased."

He had spoken in a low, whispering voice, so that not a sound relating to his infamous plan should pass beyond his son's ears, and now looked at him with a gleam of triumph lighting up his haggard face.

"Very pretty!" said Richard, in the same wary tone. "I must once more repeat that you use your friends well."

"I hate him!" returned the lawyer. "I have hated him for years! It will be the next best revenge to the one I planned years ago, and which partly failed, to see him a beggar, and to know his downfall was my act!"

Richard whistled softly.

"Ah, well," he said; "work out your own little game! I care nothing about the means employed, so that you compass a fortune. I cannot think what could have induced a clear-headed man like you to speculate, and lose, as you have been doing."

"My love for you," answered Beverley. "I wished to leave you the owner of a colossal fortune; you are all I have to care for in the world. And now hear me; I will let you have this hundred pounds to-morrow, on the understanding that you do not harass me again for money. When I can safely spare it, I will offer it to you; but remember, if by your thoughtless extravagance you embarrass me now, you will ruin your own future."

"Trust me," said Richard. "I will be careful how I act. With a fortune in perspective, I can afford to practise a little self-denial. And to-morrow, you say, I shall have the money?"

"Yes, yes; to-morrow!" answered Beverley. "I will manage to raise it by then."

"Then I'll no longer interrupt your professional labours," continued Richard. "I'll make myself scarce."

"You will come home to night?" asked his father, imploringly.

"Yes; I should like to know a little more of this affair."

He drew out his cigar-case, and selecting a cigar, lit it, put on his hat, and in a few moments he was gone.

Gone, without a word of thanks or kindness to the man who, in spite of his evil nature, yet had one soft spot in his heart, and gave it up to his child.

"Gone!"

The lawyer uttered the word with a groan; then tottering to the door, he locked it, and returning to his seat, bent his head on the table, and wept.

CHAPTER XXV.

In a street near to the Strand lived Levi Nathans, a Jew. The house was old, and quaint in appearance, with a dark entrance leading to ancient-looking rooms; sombre, old-fashioned staircases, which groaned beneath every tread; and branching passages, opening on chambers and nooks in unexpected places, and among which any one uninitiated in the mysteries of the dwelling might wander as in a maze, without arriving at their point of destination.

The house had dwindled down through several stages of decay, until it had been sold for a moderate price to Levi Nathans, who used it as a lodging-house for clerks and the higher classes of trades-people, and made a thriving living out of his bargain.

Levi had bought the tenement years before, when he had been, comparatively speaking, a young man, and he had brought a young wife to share it with him.

But before the first year of their occupancy had passed she had lost all her bloom, and had grown so pale, and thin, and shadowy, that she looked not unlike a ghost as she moved about the gloomy rooms and corridors.

And before the second year had flown, Mrs Nathan had died, and been buried; and Levi was left in his antiquated dwelling, alone.

He had loved his wife, and the place seemed dreary enough when she was gone; but still he remained in it, growing old with it, until the lapse of thirty winters saw him looking as dim, and antiquated, and aged as his residence.

He was a little man, with a thin, wiry frame, and a small, round head, bald-pated, and adorned with a scanty remnant of silver hair, which looked like a piece of meagre fringe fastened around it. His face was weazened and wrinkled, with a large hooked nose, a pair of sharp, bead-like black eyes, while a long white beard covered his mouth and chin, and fell down over his breast. His hands were small, and transparently thin, with a faint, yellowish, wax-like hue pervading them; and from feebleness, and a habit he had acquired of leaning on a stout staff as he walked, his shoulders had contracted a permanent curve.

He, moreover, always dressed in the fashion of his youth, wearing the old conventional velvet knee-breeches, black worsted stockings, high-heeled, silver-buckled shoes, long velvet waistcoat, full-skirted velvet coat, and ruffled shirt of ancient days.

With the exception of his linen, the colour of his attire was solely black, fastened with silver buttons, and buckles that gleamed with dead whiteness from the sombre velvet.

He looked, as he wandered about his crazy house—sometimes peeping from the door, sometimes staring from the windows—like a spirit of the departed old time, come back to examine, and marvel at, the improvements, changes, and follies of modern days.

Levi had never thought of taking another wife. He had hired a housekeeper—a widow of his nation and tribe, who had a daughter of about his own age.

The girl's name was Marah.

In her mother's time she had frequented the house most perseveringly, and had paid delicate and flattering attentions to its master, who, however, seemed totally unconscious to them, and remained blind and deaf to the blandishments of the Jewish maiden.

In course of time the *housekeeper* waxed aged, feeble, and, at last, there was another death in the ancient mansion, and once again Levi was left to shift for himself. It was then that he had cast his eyes upon Marah, with some show of interest.

She was still a spinster, and had arrived at the discreet age of fifty, and he thought it no imprudent act to offer her the post her mother left vacant in his home.

She accepted it joyfully.

It may be that some remnant of her aspirations to fill the position she had once coveted still remained alive in her heart; but if it were so, she must have discovered, by degrees how vain were her hopes, for nigh upon twenty years had slipped by, and she was still only the hired housekeeper to Levi Nathan.

She was a quaint old woman, much uglier, in her age, than her master; and, she too, was small of stature and slim in figure, with a hooked nose and white hair.

She also dressed in the olden style, with a high mob-cap poised upon her shaking head, and her chintz gown tucked through her pocket-hole, under which gleamed the gaudy red of her quilted petticoat.

She wore a queer little apron, full of pockets, and round her waist was a belt, attached to which, by a steel chain, was a bunch of keys, which jingled as she walked, and chimed in weirdly with the pit-pat of her high-heeled slippers on the floor,

One involuntarily thought of the "Lady at Banbury Cross," "who had music wherever she went," when they saw Marah, and listened to the clatter of her keys and her footsteps.

It was Marah's province to look after the lodgers, to receive their rents, give the necessary receipts, and hand over the money to her master; a duty which she performed with the most rigid fidelity.

It was also her task to prepare and cook the frugal family meals, and to superintend the operations of a small girl of fourteen, who ran on errands, cleaned boots, answered the door, and performed sundry other laborious and dingy duties pertaining to the establishment.

It was in this house that Paul settled himself on his return to London with Morrison, now arisen to the dignity of a West End manager.

He had rented a small room, which stood alone at the end of a rambling landing-place; a dark little room, with a diamond-paned lattice-window, and walls panelled with oak, which had grown black through age.

A room full of odd corners, with queer cupboards cropping up in them; a room where, seated at night, one could hear the rats and mice busy at work under the floor and wainscoting, and the roar of the city, subdued and shut out, until it sounded only like the distant murmur of the sea.

And yet, though his lodging was so snug, Paul spent very little of his time there.

It was wonderful what a friendship sprang up between him and his landlord, and how the old man, who had been isolated from the world for so many long and weary years, clung to the simple-hearted, handsome youth who had come to live under his roof-tree.

It was wonderful to see lines of laughter trace themselves among the wrinkles in his face, as during the hours of Paul's leisure they sat together in Levi's own particular den—a room decorated with articles of *vertu*, as quaint as their owner and, more than all beautiful and precious in Paul's eyes, with books, arranged in a glass-case, sealed volumes, whose mysteries he longed to penetrate.

It was not long before he confided his desire to his new friend, who forthwith took him in hand, and began to press him up the hill of learning; and many were the bursts of laughter which issued from that room, as Paul plodded over his pot-hooks and hangers, his alphabet and figures; and old Levi looked on, and explained, and taught, and enjoyed his novel employment with more zest than he had enjoyed anything since his wife's death.

A quick and persevering pupil was Paul. His brain, which had lain fallow for so many years, was like rich earth; and the seeds of knowledge, dropped by Levi's skilful hand, took root, and blossomed, and teemed into life with a rapidity surprising both to the teacher and the scholar; and, before much time had elapsed, Paul had mastered the simple rudiments of science, and was taking bolder flights into the realms of literature than was afforded him in his primer and table-books.

And ever as the master grew more cheerful, and the pupil more hopeful, old Marah became more and more morose, and gloomy.

It was Sunday evening, and Marah sat in the kitchen, listening to the mirthful sounds pealing from Levi's room, and becoming angrier every moment as they increased in intensity.

In a scullery, opening from the kitchen, stood Sue, the small serving-maid, washing cups and saucers at the sink, and looking with half-frightened glances upon the crone, who, in her tucked-up dress, red petticoat, and malignant face, looked not unlike a bad fairy, working an adverse spell.

"Ay, ay; laugh on!" quoth Marah, as she seized the poker, and vigorously stirred the fire. " Laugh on! the old fool and the young one! If I had my way, you should both laugh on the other side of your mouths!"

She emphasized her speech by tapping on the floor with the poker, and then, bending forward, clutched the head of it with both hands, and resting her chin on them, stared into the fire.

The girl in the scullery almost dropped a cup; then, in a fright, pushed the partition door gently open with her foot, shutting out the kitchen gaslight, which cheered her place of retreat, and stood in the semi-darkness, peeping and trembling violently.

"I hate 'em both!" continued Marah. "Him for slighting me for so many years, when I might reasonably have expected him to marry me, and now neglecting me in my old days, and taking up with a stranger! And the young man—oh! I owe him no good will for coming here, and putting himself where I ought to stand, first in Levi's good will! Oh, yes! I hate 'em—hate 'em both!"

She tapped on the hearthstone with the poker, as she spoke. Just then another faint peal of laughter came echoing down the stairs and into the room.

Marah started up, and setting the poker down, drew off her boots, and placed them in the corner; then rising, hobbled from the room, leaving the little servant whimpering with fear in the scullery.

Up the stairs, along the hall, to the door of Levi's chamber went Marah; and having arrived there, she knelt down, and looked through the large keyhole, from which the key had long since vanished, never to be found again.

In his arm-chair sat Levi, with a long-stemmed, huge-bowled pipe in his mouth, from which he was blowing a thick cloud; while Paul emulated his example, and held his black pipe between his lips, with an air of enjoyment.

The evening lesson, which had caused so much amusement, was over, and the books lay open on the table.

"You are getting on, lad," said Levi, holding the mouth-piece of his pipe between his thumb and finger, and looking curiously down the tube; "you are getting on, as you'll get on in the world, until you win her you love, and everything else which can make you happy. You love, Paul—you love this pretty maiden with the proud heart?"

Paul nodded his head, and sighed.

The old man's voice was clear, and every word was distinctly audible to the listener outside.

"Yes, yes," resumed Levi; "of course you do! I know what that love is—the hope that comes only once in a lifetime; the joy that can never come again when once it is lost."

Paul looked at his old, wrinkled face, and wondered how such a passion could ever have dwelt in him, and Levi seemed to read his thoughts.

"You forget I have been young," he said. "I was so years ago; and I, too, loved, and married, and brought my wife home to this very house, and here she died."

There was a simple pathos in his tone which went to Paul's heart, and, with an involuntary expression of sympathy, he bent forward, and caught the old man's hand in his own.

"She died," said Levi; "or this dull house might, in time, have been made cheerful by the sounds of children's voices and footsteps—my dull life have been brightened by them. But it was not to be so. She passed away, and I have been alone ever since."

His pipe had gone out, but he made no effort to kindle it, as he sat looking down its stem, and recounting his history.

"I never filled up her place. There was no face in the whole world could win me a moment from the memory of Leah."

"I wonder you never married your housekeeper!" said Paul.

"What, Marah?" cried Levi, in surprise. "No, no, boy! Marah is a faithful servant, but she was ever too like her own name—'bitter'—to take my sweet wife's place."

The spy at the keyhole flushed angrily, and bit her lips.

"I have been a lonely man for many years, and, like my house, I have fallen behind the times and fashions. You are the first person who has roused any interest in me, Paul, for more than a quarter of a century."

Paul smiled gratefully, and pressed the hand he still held.

"All the love I felt for Leah, all the sorrow her death cost me, as the long years rolled by, turned their channels, and centred upon myself. I lived for myself, I worked for myself. I hoarded money for myself. I should have become a miser, had I not fallen in with you. See here!"

He opened a strong-box which stood in a corner of his room, and drew forth a leathern bag of respectable proportions.

"All gold," he continued, shaking it slightly; "scraped together for no other purpose than that I might toy with it. Nobody knew of it. I kept it as a pleasure for myself, in this box, where I hoard my precious things—my wife's wedding-gown and jewels. Look!"

He lifted out a leathern case, and placed it in Paul's hand.

He opened it, and drew forth a string of glittering emeralds and creamy pearls, then a brooch, then a bracelet, and looked at them with wondering eyes.

"They are very fair," said Levi, smiling; "and some day they may shine on your bride, for I love you well, boy—I love you well."

He took the case from Paul, replaced the gems in it, and, putting his treasures carefully away, locked the chest, and again sat down to smoke; while Marah, rose from her knees, returned to the kitchen, and, sitting in her former place, put her feet on the fender, leant her head on her hand, and stared into the fire.

CHAPTER XXVI

"THIS may really be said to close our winter season, and a right jovial ending it is."

So spoke Morrison as he stood on the wharf by Westminster Bridge, looking with admiring eyes upon a small Richmond steamboat, which lay there waiting for passengers, with the smoke puffing in a black column from her funnel, and the water gently surging beneath her.

"Such a winter as we have made of it, too!" he continued. "Not a theatre in all London has done a more flourishing business. At this rate, I expect I shall soon make a fortune."

He looked with a pleasant smile upon Rachel and his wife, who were standing on either side of him, and still went on speaking.

"It is a little better than the old days in the caravan; and you find more congenial employment than sitting all day in the tent entrance, taking money from the rustics on the head of the big drum, eh, dame?"

That worthy woman, however, instead of replying, tossed her head indignantly, and gazed up the river, muttering, "I wish you wouldn't always be talking about things you would show your good sense best by forgetting."

"Like the rest of them," said Morrison, with unruffled good humour. "You cannot bear to remember you have ever been in the valley of humiliation. Now it is different with me; I *like* to look back on the rough places I have trod; it makes the smooth seem so much more enjoyable. But there! I don't blame you; it's the way of the world, and you women follow it most diligently."

He patted Rachel's shoulder, and laughed in his wife's ruffled face, then sauntered up and down, with his hands in his pockets, looking at everything round him, with a most genial expression of countenance.

"Here they come!" he cried, as a party of happy, laughing folks of both sexes came towards the wharf. "I do not believe there's a manager in London can boast of such a company as mine. There's De Nevier and his wife, and a girl with the baby! Did you ever see such a heavy villain before? And there's Merton and his betrothed behind them! You wouldn't think he was a low comedian, to look at his face. And there's Brian, our sentimental man, looking as merry as a clown in the pantomime. How are you, boys?" he continued.

This greeting was accorded to the whole troop as they came near him, and delivered with a vigour which called up fresh smiles on every face.

This meeting no sooner over, than another party arrived.

The workmen of the theatre, with their wives, and children, and sweethearts; a motley, merry crowd, gay in all the hues of the rainbow, and as noisy and blithe as crickets.

"But where's the Captain?" cried Morrison, as his sharp eye ran quickly over them. "I never knew him late before. Ah! there he is!"

He pointed, as he spoke, to Paul, who was patiently trudging along, with a boy of five years of age hanging to his coat-tail, and a baby in his arms; while, behind, a meek-looking woman came slowly on, leading a man, whose pale face and feeble frame showed traces of sickness.

"Just like him!" said Morrison, to those standing near. "There's poor Smith, just recovering from his fall from the flats, and the Captain has stayed behind to help him along. There's not many young fellows would do what he is doing. I honour him for it."

Rachel looked at Paul, and a scornful smile curled her lips.

"I see nothing in it," she said. "He is only a scene-shifter—a man without a name."

Morrison looked at her rebukingly.

"That is his *misfortune*," he said; "not his *fault*. It is well for *us* that every one does not judge of people by your standard. Child, you forget your first glimpse of London, years ago!"

Rachel's face flushed with anger and mortification, and turning away, she stood on the edge of the wharf, looking down into the water, as memories of the past she so hated came crowding over her.

"I engaged him as Captain," continued Morrison, "and I have never asked him for another name. He serves me honestly, and that is sufficient."

"That's the young hop-picker you met with in Kent, is it not?" lisped a young lady. "How handsome he is, and what a romantic history!"

"Yes; he's a strange sort of fellow," said Merton, the low comedian. "Quite a phenomenon. Why, the other day I went to the theatre unexpectedly in the afternoon, and there he was, unconscious of my presence, in the full glory of a solitary and private rehearsal of *Claude Melnotte*. From memory, too, and spoken in splendid style. It's my opinion," he added, apart to Morrison, "that if some one would take him in hand, he would make a good figure on the boards in a year or two's time."

A look of interest gathered on the manager's face.

"I did not know he was a scholar," he answered. "Perhaps I shall attend to your suggestion. Well, Smith," he said, advancing towards the invalid, who had by that time reached the landing-place; "I am glad to see you among us again. You've got as pretty a load as ever you will carry in all your life," he added to Paul. "And now if my laggard friend, our lawyer's son, had arrived, we would go on board. It is a pity to lose a moment of this glorious day."

The loiterer, however, did not keep him waiting much longer; but in a few moments joined the party. It was Richard Bogg, and he brought a youth of his own age, Charles, the eldst son of Constance Clayton, one of the children who had been playing in the garden of the villa, when Paul had sunk by the roadside, after his flight from the coiners.

Neither, however, recognised the other, but they stood as perfect strangers under the clear summer sky. There was a short space of bustle, noise, and confusion, during which the assemblage had been stowed safely on deck, and then the paddles slowly revolved; the steam came forth from the funnel in spasmodic gushes; the theatrical band, who occupied the stern of the boat, produced their instruments, which they had kept ready, and struck up a lively dance tune, as the boat began to move on her course.

"How happy they are!" mused Morrison. "Some may think this pleasure trip, to which I treat my people, a great matter; but it seems very little when I think how zealously they have laboured for me during the past season."

As he spoke, he drew his wife's hand through his arm, and mixed among the groups of happy folks, talking and laughing, and still heightening their pleasure by his kindly presence.

Merrily, and yet more merrily, the boat steamed up the river, cutting the water with its noisy paddles, and making a long wake of swelling waves as it continued to move on its way.

Merrily, merrily, past the town, until wide, open fields and woody landscapes bordered its banks, and the water lost its murky hue, and reflected brokenly, in its thousands of dancing waves, the green trees and rushes on its brink, and the blue sky above it.

Paul, having seen the invalid and his wife comfortably bestowed, had seated himself on a coil of rope, and gathered round him a cluster of children, whom he amused by singing old ballads, and recounting to them marvellous impromptu fairy tales, ever increasing in interest and thrilling sensation.

Merrily onward went the pleasure-boat, with Rachel kneeling on a seat, leaning over the low bulwark, her eyes fixed on the water, as it glanced by.

Once or twice she raised them, as a burst of laughter came from the children, or Paul's deep, mellow voice broke forth in song, and looked at the happy group and their friend; then turned away with the old scornful smile, and once more gazed into the river.

There was a boy of about ten years of age standing by the scene-shifter; a boy with dark curls, and merry, black eyes—a mischievous urchin, who had soiled his face and hands, and torn his jacket, in scrambling about the deck; a boy who brought Paul, the crossing-sweeper, the city Arab, to her mind; and, in spite of herself, made her think of the time she would willingly have forgotten.

She thought of him as she had known him from the first—friendless, poor, abused—the boy her dead mother had sheltered, taught, and fed; then on through the years which had followed, when she had been left an orphan, to the world's charity.

She thought of him as he had stood between her and starvation; the boy who had ever been loving, gentle, and good.

She thought of him as she had last seen him, sitting alone in the dusty road, sad and weeping; unselfishly parting with her, that she might be made happy.

And, oh! with what keen self-reproach, as she remembered the carelessness with which she had learned to regard him—the pride which would render it pain for her to meet with him again.

Then, once more, she turned and looked at the child who had brought these things to her mind. He had thrown his arm over his new friend's shoulder, and had bent his head towards him.

They were much alike.

Paul might be grown into just such a stalwart, handsome fellow as this scene-shifter.

As stalwart and handsome, but was he even as desirable acquaintance as he who sat before her?—the man to whom she would not accord a friendly smile or touch of her hand, because she considered him so far beneath her?

Poor Paul!—poor, loving, humble fellow! Though her sympathy, her gratitude were enlisted on his side, the world was against him, and his cause must go down, defeated by pride and prejudice. No, she must never meet him; or, meeting him, acknowledge his claim on her.

Her mind was made up, and yet, as once more she turned away, the tears sprang to her eyes—tears sacred to the memory of "lost Paul."

"Sentimentalizing, eh, Miss Rachel?" said Richard Bogg, approaching her, while his cold, gray eyes lit up with the nearest approach to tenderness they could assume. "I have been watching you for the last five minutes, wondering of what you were dreaming. Haven't I, Charlie, old fellow?" he added, to Charles Clayton, who was still with him.

"Yes—that is, I suppose so," answered that young gentleman, as he loosed his arm from Richard's, and sauntered on to another part of the deck, where he joined the heavy tragedy man and his blooming spouse.

"Nice fellow, Charlie," said Richard, trying to look into Rachel's face. "He knows when he is one too many."

"It is a pity others are not conscious of it, when such happens to be the case," she said, pointedly, bending her head still lower, to hide the traces of tears on her cheeks.

"Aw! yes!" he stammered, confusedly. "Very good!—prodigiously sharp of you, Miss Rachel! By Jove! what is that fellow staring at?" he continued, savagely, as he, too, turning round, caught Paul's eyes fixed upon them. "It is not the first time, either. I've seen it before, at the theatre."

He tried to frown him down, but finding he could not succeed, wheeled round on his heel, and redoubled his attentions to Rachel.

"I should *like* to know what you are thinking about."

Still no answer. She was slyly trying to wipe those tell-tale eyes with one ungloved hand.

"If I could only hope it was of me!"

He spoke in a low, passionate voice, still trying to look at her face; while Rachel, half angrily, half coquettishly, bent more perseveringly in the opposite direction.

On sped the boat.

The band struck up a dance tune, and soon half a dozen couples were footing it gaily, while the lookers on vehemently applauded. Still, Rachel knelt in her old place, looking over the low bulwark, trailing her kerchief to catch the spray which flew from the paddles.

Still, Richard Bogg whispered his gallantries in her ear, and still, from his place on the coil of ropes, Paul looked on, with a jealous gleam in his eyes.

There was a bend in the river, and as the boat rounded it, a couple of the dancers reeled and struck the kneeling girl.

A cry—a splash—her place was empty; and close by the vessel's side, almost under the paddle-wheels, rose her white face above the cruel water, the curls swept back from it, and her blue eyes upraised in terrified supplication for help.

A universal shriek pealed from the spectators. The face gleamed for a second full in view, then went under, drawn down by the force of the current made by the steamer.

"Stand aside, fool, and let me save her." It was Paul who spoke, as he thrust Richard Bogg roughly away.

He had thrown off his boots and coat, and before any one had recovered from the panic, had sprang overboard and reached Rachel just as she came up again, still closer to the paddle wheels.

A moment more, and his arm was round her clasping her, while his face became radiant with joy.

She had murmured a few words in her bewilderment; words brought forth by the memories she had just before loosed.

"Paul, Paul! help me!"

"Saved, Rachel, my darling!" he whispered, as her head sank upon his shoulder, and her eyelids closed.

He bowed his face, and rested it for one instant against her forehead, his whole being thrilling with joy as he held her in his arms once more, the only shield between her and a destroying fate.

The next moment they were safe on deck again, and Rachel consigned to loving hands, while Paul was hurried away to dry his clothes in the engine-room, amid the plaudits of the excited crowd, who forthwith made him the lion of the day.

And, all the while, Richard Bogg stood moodily looking on, his heart full of anger and jealousy, and muttering to himself the words Paul had used to him in his terror, "Stand aside, fool, and let me save her!"

CHAPTER XXVII.

SAVED from death!

Two days had passed away since the eventful water party, when Paul received a summons from Mr. Morrison to call upon him at his own residence.

It was with a beating heart that he obeyed; and, at the appointed hour, ascended the steps of the house, and timidly rang the bell. The servant who opened the door received him with marked attention, and ushered him at once into the worthy manager's study.

An hour later, he came from the room, with a radiant face, his eyes beaming with joy and hope.

"You must not go yet; you will stay and see Rachel. The fright, and the shock of her involuntary bath, have somewhat unsettled her; but I know she will feel slighted if you do not pay her a visit. Besides, I have purposely delayed sending for you until she was sufficiently recovered to see you."

As he spoke, he led the way to the drawing-room, Paul following, bewildered by the events of the morning, but strangely happy.

On a couch, near the window, Rachel was half-reclining, holding in her hand a handsome gold watch and chain, which she had been swinging lightly to and fro.

She looked up as the pair entered, and, with a slight smile, held out her hand to Paul. But there was no look, no flush of pleasure on her face as she did so.

Predominant in her mind was a feeling of annoyance at the whole occurrence—a sensation of anger that she should have been saved by him; that so lowly a person as a scene-shifter should have any claim upon her.

Morrison was rather chagrined at her coldness of demeanour.

"Rachel has not been quite well since her accident," he said, in a tone of apology; "but I am sure she is glad to see you, and have an opportunity of thanking you for the service you rendered her."

"I am happy to see you, Captain," she said. "Will you accept this as some slight payment for your brave act?"

She tendered the watch as she spoke, expecting that he would grasp it eagerly.

What was he, after all, but a boor—a rough, untutored clown? Surely gold must be the height of his ambition; and by his acceptance of this costly gift, she would escape the irksome debt of gratitude which he had thrust upon her!

To her surprise, he put her hand back, and rejected it.

"I require no payment," he said, lifting his head full as haughtily as her own. "I have only performed my duty in rescuing you; so let it pass."

Morrison looked from one to the other, in surprise. He had not expected such a scene; but he wisely held his peace, and, mortified and angry, Rachel laid down her gift.

"You must call him Captain no longer," he observed, after a pause. "Next season he will join my company as a regular actor, and has chosen the name of Vincent. I expect, some day, our young friend will make a good figure in the theatrical world. He has talent and experience, and the opportunity for their exercise will not be wanting."

He patted Paul kindly on the shoulder, and went on speaking.

"Will you wait for me here for half an hour? I have a business-call to make; after which I will fetch you, and we'll go down to the theatre, where you shall indulge me by rehearsing for my benefit some little dramatic part—say, for instance, *Claude Melnotte*."

He was gone, and the two were left alone.

"I rejoice to hear of your good fortune, Mr. Vincent," said Rachel. "I perceive you will accept a favour from my father, though you reject anything I may offer you."

She looked full at him as she spoke.

Their eyes met.

For a moment they gazed at each other—Rachel with a strange emotion at her heart; Paul with the full tide of his devotion to her rushing over him, and breaking down all the barriers which Time and Circumstance had built between them.

With the impetuosity which marked all his actions, he sprang forward, and knelt by her side.

"Not everything!" he said, in a passionate tone. "Do not offer me such gifts as those. Give me a smile, a kind word, a look of interest or affection, and I should feel repaid, though I risked my life a thousand times to serve you."

Rachel spoke not, moved not; she was bewildered by this sudden burst of emotion, and made no effort to stay him.

"You do not rebuke me," continued Paul. "I may speak, and you will listen to me."

Her head drooped, but she was still silent.

"You do not know all that has been hidden in my heart, or you would not blame me. You would not even wonder when I say that I love you!"

She shrank before his intense gaze, and stretched out her hand to silence him.

"Let me speak!" he pleaded. "I can utter no greater treason than I have already said. I love you, Rachel—I love you! A few months ago, I was a rude, ignorant man, without an aim or a hope in the world. Then you came; and my whole heart bowed in worship of your beauty, your purity, your refinement. I could no longer live the old life—dream the old dreams;—all was changed. I resolved to make myself worthy of you—to win you, if man's devotion could win her he loved. I came to London, I studied, I laboured to raise myself in the estimation of the world, that you might look more kindly upon me."

The tears were in Rachel's eyes, and one hand fell lightly upon his shoulder as she listoned, entranced, in spite of herself, to his story.

"I did not mean to speak yet—I meant to make myself an honourable place among men before I came to you with my suit. But you have forced the truth from me before the time. Do not be angry. I will not ask you to answer me now. Only give me hope—be my friend until I can come to you with fame and with wealth in my possession, and lay them and myself at your feet."

His voice was husky, and Rachel, carried away by his earnestness, bent still lower, listening, but making no reply.

"With hope, I could do and dare everything," he continued. "Ah, Ray—dear little Ray, whom I have loved so faithfully and for so long a time!—I know you will not send me away despairing. Only think of what my life has been! You know it! A lonely, abused child, with but one tie, one love, to cheer him; and the tie was broken—his love robbed of its object. A lonely child, growing up into lonely manhood, until I met you, and loved again, but with a passion different to my boyhood's!"

Her curls brushed his cheek, and the tears fell from her eyes, and dropped upon his clasped hands.

"You have been poor, almost friendless—you know what the suffering I have experienced is —you, who have been a little child, toiling at the crossing——"

The charm with which he had held her was broken. She had been, as it were, in a dream, heeding not Paul's pointed allusions until that one word smote upon her ears.

She sprang up, her cheeks flaming—her eyes sparkling passionately.

"So," she said, in a hard voice, "now the truth is clear! You come here to take advantage of the service you did me to insult me!"

"Rachel!" he cried.

"How dare you speak to me thus?" she continued. "You, a vagrant, a vagabond, whom my father has patronised out of charity —you to make a show of independence, and refuse my golden gift, as though you were a gentleman born! And I for one moment to give you the credit of refinement of spirit! I see — the payment was not great enough! You aimed at a larger proportion of gain —my hand, and Mr. Morrison's wealth, for both go together! See, I will double your reward! Take up the watch, and this." (As she spoke, she threw her purse on the ground beside him.) "It is full," she continued. "But if you think it not enough, ask for more. You shall have it—the money—I promise you; but do not come here to insult me by talking of love! Remember, if I have been poor, I am now your superior, and may, possibly, have as great an anxiety to rise in life, by marriage, as you seem to have, There are my thanks for the life you saved—take them, and consider the matter as settled!"

Pointing to the purse and watch, she slowly left the room, as Morrison's ringing voice sounded in the street beneath the window.

With a stern face, Paul arose from his knees, and, picking up the purse, laid it on the table by the watch.

"Lost for the second time!" he said; "and lost to me for ever, my little Ray!"

CHAPTER XXVIII.

"HAVE you heard the news?" said Charles Clayton, as he walked into Mr. Bogg's office one morning, having made an appointment there with his friend, Richard.

"No; what is it?" said the youth. "Any bank broken, or fresh *company* come to grief?"

He cast a significant glance at his father as he spoke, but the old man was deeply engaged with his paper, and paid no heed to him.

"Oh, nothing of that kind!" said Charles Clayton. "Besides, I should not call that news—it would be known here before I heard of it. No; it is something connected with the theatre—with the trip to Richmond."

"Miss Rachel Morrison has a severe cold, I suppose, and has sent for the doctor to attend her, and a reporter to insert a sensational paragraph concerning her adventure in the daily papers."

"As far out as ever," said Clayton. "It concerns that young scene-shifter, who leaped into the water and rescued the fair lady."

Richard Bogg frowned slightly.

"Well, what of him?" he questioned, sharply. "Is he going to *marry* her, as a reward for his pains."

"I should not wonder if he were to eventually," answered Clayton, somewhat maliciously. "He is a handsome fellow, and now Morrison has taken him in hand, he is in a fair way to make his fortune."

"What *do* you mean?" said Richard. "Cannot you speak out at once, without beating about the bush for an hour first?"

"Well, I'll take pity on you, and go right on with my story; that is, if my noise will not disturb you, sir," he added, turning to the young man's father.

"Oh, no, no; to be sure not!" said the lawyer. "Talk on; do not mind me."

There was a slight expression of interest in his wrinkled face, as he wheeled his back round to the two young men, and went on, apparently reading his paper.

"Well, the long and the short of it is, that Morrison has raised him from being a scene-shifter to be an actor; he opens with him next season. It seems that he is a wonderfully clever and persevering fellow, and has been studying hard for a long time past with a view to the stage."

"A self-taught genius, I understand," interrupted Richard, with a sneer.

"That he certainly is, if all his manager says is true," said Charles Clayton, warmly. "And so, you see, your first guess concerning him was not so bad a one, after all; for he really, in my opinion, stands a fair chance of making the pretty actress his wife."

"He had better not make too sure," muttered Richard. "If I am not mistaken, the pretty actress, as you call her, has a tolerable amount of pride, and soars high in her ideas of what her future lord and master must be. A title, if possible; if not, a gentleman and a fortune, at the least."

Mr. Bogg had gradually let his paper slip from his hand, and with his head turned, was looking keenly at his son.

Charles Clayton intercepted the glance.

"That is not all," he cried. "I am sure, sir, you will be interested in the next portion of my communication. This hero has turned out to be none other than the boy whom my parents took in, ragged, sick, and exhausted from the road-side, years ago. The boy, who called himself *John*, you know; and who ran away in the night, when he heard that he was to be taken into this office. His erratic nature, I suppose, would not permit him to be bound down to a routine of set, monotonous duties. I can account for it in no other way."

At the beginning of the speech, Mr. Bogg's pale face had flushed, and his whole being had been agitated; but he had curbed his emotion, and sat listening quietly until Clayton had finished speaking.

"Did he give you no reason for his absconding?" he asked.

"Yes, a strange one, I must confess. He said he had been afraid of *you*. Why, he would not tell. However, it must have been a mere childish whim, for he laughed as he confessed it; and even said he should like to see you again. I don't much wonder at it, though, for he knew you were a lawyer, and anything connected with a police-court must at that time have been a terror to his infant mind."

"Very likely—very likely," said Mr. Bogg.

"You would never recognise him, I am sure," rattled on Charles Clayton. "A tall, manly, handsome fellow—one any parents might be proud of; but that, of course, is, for him, quite out of the question."

"Yes, *quite* out of the question," repeated the lawyer. "And how does he style himself now? By what name is he known?"

"That is another strange affair," said Clayton. "When he was with us, he called himself *John*; then he turns up among the Kentish hop-pickers as 'Captain,' by which name, and no other, he has since been known. But *now*, since his rise in the profession, he has adopted the name of 'Vincent,' which I suppose he will stick to; though it is more than doubtful, in my opinion, that he has a right to either appellation. By the way, Vincent is one of our family names; so that, if he ever becomes a shining light in the world, he will reflect glory upon us."

"Ay, ay, lad! he will be sure to do that!" said Mr. Bogg, with a laugh.

"Anyhow, I wish him all success," continued Charles. "Whatever his antecedents may be, it is certain he is a noble fellow, with a true heart, a brave nature, and honest and upright into the bargain. There is not a soul in the whole theatre, high or low, who has not a kind word for him."

"And, pray," said Richard, "how did you learn all this?"

"I met him by the theatre, and took him to my club to dine yesterday evening—though, to be sure, he is rather rough,—where he told me all. Our people at home will be delighted to hear it."

"So am *I*—so am *I!*" said Mr. Bogg; "your visit has given me great pleasure. And now I must ask you to leave me; my business hour is commencing. Call back in a few moments' time, and Dick shall have the rest of the day. I must keep him here now for a consultation."

Richard looked at his father in surprise; but, at a warning glance from him, made no remark, save to wish his friend "*Au revoir!*" and settle himself comfortably in a second easy chair, which had been added to the furniture of the room.

"Now, what's in the wind?" he asked, when

THE LAWYER TEMPTS MAHAH. (See page 67.)

a few minutes of listening had convinced him that Clayton had departed.

"Lock the door, and plug the keyhole," said his father. "I'll give no second clerk an opportunity of listening to my conversation."

Richard obeyed; then returned to his seat.

"Dick, my boy, I have work for you to do," said the lawyer.

"Precious dirty work, I'll be bound it is," answered Richard. "Remember, I'll have nothing to do with your bubble company. I am not going to place myself within the pale of the law."

"Far be it from me to wish you to," said his sire. "No, no, my boy; I'll take all the danger; you shall only reap the reward."

His voice had softened, and he softly patted his son's hand, which rested on the arm of the chair.

"I agree to it willingly," said Richard; "but what is this task?"

"Only to ascertain all you can learn concerning the young man of whom Clayton was speaking; his habits, his means, his residence, and report your information to me."

"If that's all," said his son, "I'll do it; and the more mischief it can work him the better," he added, in an undertone. "But why am I to do this? What is this fellow to you?"

"I cannot tell you, Dick," said his father; "leave me and my work alone. I have no wish to see you implicated in it. But do as I bid you, boy, and do it speedily; *that* cannot harm you."

"You remember the old saying," continued Richard; "'The workman is worthy of his hire?'"

"What; more money, Dick?" said the lawyer, in a tone of displeasure.

"Only twenty pounds," urged Richard. "I'll not ask for more for a couple of months to come."

"Remember, Richard, prudence now, that you may be rich in the future! My scheme prospers, but I dare not infringe on my trust-money. Vincent falls but slowly into the trap, and I must float unsuspected, until my end is gained; then, boy, you shall spend if you will."

"And the twenty?"

His father drew forth his pocket-book, and counted out four five-pound notes, laying them down on the table, with a sigh.

"Hark! here comes Clayton," said Richard, pocketing them, and listening to his friend's voice as he spoke to the clerk in the outer room. "I suppose I may be off?"

"Yes; don't forget your work. Good-bye, Dick, my boy; be careful with your money."

"I'll set about that business at the theatre at once," said his son. "And as for the money, I'll make it last as long as I can. Good-bye! I'll be back in the evening with your news. All right, Charlie," he continued, opening the door; "I'm free at last. Let's be off."

They were gone, and the lawyer was left alone.

He rubbed his hands and chuckled, as he seated himself again in his chair, while his whole face was working with joy, malice, and triumph.

"On the trail once more!" he muttered, between his bursts of glee. "I shall hunt him down at last—at last!"

CHAPTER XXIX.

"You hate him like poison, but not more than I do!"

As Marah spoke, she stamped her foot fiercely on the ground, and looked into Bogg's face, with a species of exultation in her own evilness of nature, which made her seem more witch-like than ever.

They were standing in the kitchen of old Levi's house; the wily lawyer, in spite of the heat of the weather, muffled in a great coat, and wearing his hat low over his eyes, as if for concealment; Marah still clad in her old-fashioned garments, and resting herself on a stick, as she spoke.

"You hate him," she repeated; "but not as I do. He came here a stranger, and stepped between me and the man I have served faithfully for more years than he has lived."

"It's hard to bear, eh, Marah?—very hard to bear. Why, you must have been almost a young woman when you came here first," said the lawyer.

"I *was* young when I first saw him, the year after his wife died. But that's more than thirty years ago!"

"I wonder he did not marry you," continued Mr. Bogg, marking the effect of his words.

Marah's eyes snapped maliciously.

"I'd forgive that," she answered. "It would be no great happiness for a woman to be wedded to Levi Nathans. But he is rich. You know I have told you before of the bag of gold and the jewels, which he keeps in his strong box up-stairs."

"Yes, I know. I have been thinking that a bag like that would hold a great sum of money; whoever gets it, will have quite a fortune."

"That would have been *me*, if he had not come here with his sly ways, creeping round Levi, and weaning him from old friends. Not an evening but they are together, with their books and their pipes, and they jeer and laugh at old Marah. I heard them, when they little thought I was near. And now he will rob me of what is my due—all Levi has to bequeath. It would have been mine if he had not come; for Levi is older than me by nigh ten years, and he has not a relation in the whole world."

"What a pity!" said Beverley. "You would have been quite a rich woman. And, after all, it is your right."

"Yes; it is my right," she answered, setting her stick firmly down. "And you said I should have it. You will not break your word?"

"I have not the slightest intention of doing so," said the lawyer. "See, here is one token of my good faith!"

As he spoke, he held up a key.

"What is that?" asked Marah, eagerly.

"A key for the treasure-chest," he answered. "I had it made from an impression I struck when you showed it to me the last time I was here. With this in your possession, you could open it at your pleasure, and would find it easy enough to obtain this wealth, which should be yours by right, and of which this youngster would rob you."

"True!" said Marah. "But you forget I should be detected. I have no wish to go to prison."

"Suppose you could manage it so that the whole blame would fall upon this young man who calls himself Vincent? Suppose the result was that he went to gaol instead, while you enjoyed your gains?"

"I'd do it, if I knew how," said Marah. "Be plain with me. You came here a month ago, a stranger, and worked your way into my secrets."

"You did me the honour to confide in me," said Mr. Bogg.

"Be plain, I say," she interrupted. "You wormed from me that which I had never yet told to any living creature—my anger against Levi, my dislike of his new friend, my fear that he would leave to another the property I covet. You fanned the sparks of bitterness burning within me until they have broken into a fierce flame, full of mischief and hurt."

"Hush, Marah!" said Bogg, soothingly. "Some one may overhear you."

"There's no fear of that," answered the old woman. "The servant is out; Mr. Vincent, as we are now bid to call him, is away also, and my old dolt of a master is with him; our lodgers are out pleasure-seeking, business-hunting;—there is no one here but ourselves. So, speak out. Do you think I believe you came here moved only by regard for a withered crone like me—by pity for my wrongs, such as they are?"

"Why should I not?" he said, in a cold, unimpassioned voice, strangely at contrast with that of Marah.

"Because you are like the rest of mankind, caring only for yourself. What do you wish the crime you tempt me to commit to lead to? You hate Paul Vicent, and, through me, you would harm him. You see, I understand your motives. So again I say, be plain with me."

"Your penetration is marvellous," he answered. "But let us return to the former subject of our conversation. Be quiet, and I'll tell you a story. There was once a woman who hated a man——"

"*Once!*" she repeated, sarcastically.

"Don't interrupt me, or I shall never get to the end of it," he said, smiling. "She hated him, and would do him an injury. They were both in the same house; and in the dwelling there also lived an old miser, who had a bag of gold and jewels, which the woman coveted. Do you follow me?"

"Yes; I follow," answered Marah.

"By some means, she obtained a key to the miser's strong-box." (He was dangling the duplicate he had shown her on his finger.) "One night, when the house was quiet and lonely, as this is now, she opened the chest, and stole the treasure."

"And was found out, and sent to gaol!" she muttered.

"Not so," he answered. "*She* was a clever woman. She placed a small portion of her booty, with the key, where it would fix the crime upon the man she disliked; and he was suspected, tried, and punished, while she went free!"

"I see—I see!" said Marah. "You would have me follow her example?"

"I merely told you a story," said the wily lawyer. "If you can work it to your profit, well and good. As for this key, it is of no use to me; it may prove useful to you one day. Take it, and, as a mark of my interest in you, accept this also."

As he spoke, he pressed into her hands the key, and a purse, the contents of which jingled musically.

Marah clutched both eagerly.

"Gold!" she said, while an avaricious expression passed over her face. "Gold! and the means to obtain more!"

"Twenty sovereigns!" said Bogg. "And now my business with you is over for the present. It will be your own choice whether we ever meet again. Listen! Should the time ever come when you help to convict your young lodger of a crime, I shall hear of it; and I shall be, on the night after his conviction, when he has been sentenced, waiting at our old meeting-place, from after dark until eleven at night, to thank you. I would even, on such an occasion, present you with eighty more bright, golden sovereigns."

"With the twenty I hold, they would make a hundred?" calculated Marah. "A hundred pounds! Why, you must be a rich man to be able to give away so much! I have scraped and pinched for many a long year, and I have not saved much above half that sum!"

The lawyer smiled.

"Shall I say good-bye *for ever*, Marah?" he asked.

"No; we shall meet again, never fear. I'll do it. I'll not bid you good-bye this time."

She took up the light, and pattered up the stairs before him, then opened the street door, and watched him depart, muttering all the while to herself, in a joyful tone, "I shall see him again—I shall see him again!" and her thin lips writhing into a smile, as she held in one hand, screened by her apron, the key and the purse of money.

As the lawyer turned the corner of the street, she went into the house, closing the door sharply after her.

A draught of wind caught her candle as she entered the kitchen, and blew it out.

She looked around her, and at last discovered the cause. The window, which opened on an area leading to the street, was ajar.

She closed and secured it; then, moved by an impulse of caution, went to the area door, and undid its numerous fastenings of bolts, bar, and chain, and looked out keenly into the darkness.

But quick though she had been, she proved too slow in her movements.

Warned by the rattling noise she made, a man had risen from where he was crouched close against the black wall, under the window, had walked softly and rapidly up the steps through the open gate, and into the street, undiscovered.

As he passed beneath a lamp, the light fell fully upon him, revealing the face and figure of the lawyer's son, Richard Bogg.

CHAPTER XXX.

"WELL, Marah! So you have let the little back room next to mine at last?"

The housekeeper nodded her head in silent assent, and went on darning a pair of Levi's black worsted stockings—never even raising her eyes as he addressed her.

"And what kind of a lodger is he?" continued Levi.

"An old man," said Marah, briefly.

"Respectable? References, of course?" he pursued.

Marah put down her work, and, rising, went to a drawer in a side table, producing therefrom a small parcel, which she opened, displaying two half-sovereigns and some silver. These she placed before Levi.

"A month's rent in advance," she said; then re-seated herself, and went on with her darning.

"The best of all references," said Levi, laughing. "I'll give you a receipt for it to-morrow. Well, well, Marah, as he is an old man——You said he was old?"

"Somewhere about sixty years of age," she replied.

"You must pay him all possible attention—make him comfortable. It is not often we get lodgers who pay a month's rent in advance."

Again Marah nodded silently; and, tired of her uncongenial mood, Levi abruptly left the room.

As he reached the hall, a cab rattled up, and the street-bell rang; and while he lingered curiously, Marah came hastening up the stairs.

"It's the new lodger, I daresay," she said, as she advanced to the door, and opened it.

Her surmise was correct.

The new lodger stood upon the steps, while behind him was the cab-driver, who held upon his shoulder a dingy, brown leathern portmanteau, which he was about to deposit in the hall, when its owner spoke, in a mild, deprecating tone of voice.

"Wait one moment, friend," he said—"that is, if you would earn an extra sixpence by carrying the box to my chamber."

"Stay where you are, Marah," said Levi,

advancing to meet the stranger. "I will lead him to his room myself."

He took the candle from her hand, and, with a still sourer expression on her face, she retired.

"This way," said the Jew, courteously, beckoning the waiting pair to the staircase.

The new lodger took a few steps, then stopped; coughed asthmatically, and again came totteringly forward.

"You seem feeble, sir," said Levi. "Take my arm. I'm old, like yourself; but, unlike you, I am tough; and can, I daresay, assist you to mount the stairs."

"You are very kind—very kind," said the stranger, still in the same low, deprecating voice, at the same time laying his hand, which was covered with a baggy, buff glove, upon Levi's arm, while the cabman, bearing the portmanteau, followed them.

"The new lodger" certainly justified the remark his landlord had made regarding his feebleness; for it was with infinite pains and labour he ascended to his room, his progress being often interrupted by his spasmodic coughing and short breath.

He was a tall old man, with a long face, thin and pale, with gray eyes, gleaming keenly from beneath his bushy eyebrows, with iron-gray beard and whiskers, and a scanty head of grizzled gray hair. His shoulders, which must have been brawny in his youth, were bent; and as he moved, his head and hands shook, as though with a palsy.

"Courage, my dear sir—courage!" said Levi, as they neared the top of the first flight of steps. "We are almost there."

"Ugh! ugh!" coughed the decrepit old man. "Don't mind me—it's only my cough. I'm used to it."

That voice was the most remarkable thing about him—so very near akin to a whisper, and so indicative was it of an amiable, mild, and long-suffering disposition.

Levi's heart warmed towards the owner of it; and he still more stoutly supported him up to the landing, and, across it, to the chamber, which lay at the back of his own; while opposite to it, up a few more steps, and across a second landing, was Paul's.

"You'll have plenty of company, you see," said Levi—"neighbours on either side of you. Myself, here; yonder, a young friend of mine; and both of us will be happy to afford you any help we can, if you need it."

"A young man?—ugh! Hope he is quiet? —ugh!" said the old man. "Put the luggage down in that room," he added to the cabman; " and here's your money—ugh!"

He handed the man half-a-crown, and watched him down, then once more repeated his question to Levi.

"Quiet, I hope? Not one of your young men of the period—all rattle—ugh!—and dissipation; late hours, and come lumbering in half-tipsy—ugh! ugh!—waking honest folks from their first sleep—ugh! ugh! ugh!"— and he went off into a fresh fit of coughing.

"Never a steadier or a quieter lad," said Levi. "And though he is in the theatrical profession, and, as a matter of course, bound to stay out late at night, you'll never hear him return, for he's off with his boots in the hall, and creeps up to his room as quietly as a girl in satin slippers. What's more, too, it's the vacation now, and he won't commence business again for a fortnight; and I'll warrant he will be in bed before half-past ten at night. Ay, he's a steady lad, and one after my own heart, is Mr. Vincent."

"Glad to hear it," said the coughing, wheezing stranger. "I came here because I thought it retired, and out of all noise. I cannot bear a riot. I shall be obliged to leave you if I cannot have peace—ugh! ugh!"

"You'll find the place silent enough," said Levi. "My lodgers are all staid, sedate men of business. And now, sir—Mr.—Mr.——"

"Davis," said the old man—"Jasper Davis."

"Mr. Davis," continued Levi, "I'll leave you. Shall I send you any supper?"

"Supper?—yes. Gruel—water-gruel; it's good for my complaint—ugh! ugh!"

"Water-gruel? Very good," said Levi. "Good night, sir; and I hope you'll sleep well. I'll send up the gruel in a very few minutes."

"Good night—good night!" said Mr. Davis. "I hope I shall sleep—ugh!"

He sat down in a large arm-chair, and rubbed his hands, which looked muscular and strong for so feeble an old man, when the baggy gloves were off, and then drew his coat-cuffs down over them, as though to shield them from the air.

Presently, Marah came into the room with the basin of gruel, and a carefully toasted bit of bread by the side of it.

"Your supper, sir," she said, with a curtsey. "I hope you will find it to your liking."

"Thank you!" exclaimed Mr. Davis, with a faint smile, as he tasted the preparation; "that'll do. Good night—ugh! ugh! ugh!"

He coughed more violently than ever; and holding open the door, politely bowed the worthy housekeeper out, and locked it behind her, leaving the key in the lock in such a position that no one could, by peeping through it from the outside, obtain a single glimpse of the interior of the room.

Then he returned to the little table by the bed, where his supper was still smoking.

He looked at the gruel with anything but a satisfied glance.

"I suppose I must," he muttered; "I dare not throw it away; it would excite suspicion." And so, taking up the bowl, he swallowed a great part of its contents, then set it sharply down, with a shudder.

"If ever I do order it again," he said, "I deserve to live on it all my life long. But it's worth a little inconvenience, for here I am, thanks to my dramatic experience, safe in the citadel. It will be a strange misadventure if I do not succeed in my plans."

A change had passed over Mr. Davis.

He had lost his stoop, and stood upright; brawny shouldered, and broad of chest.

He moved to the looking-glass, and laughed softly as he removed, first, his head of iron-gray hair, then his whiskers and beard, disclosing the dark locks and youthful face of Richard Bogg, now but little disguised by a yellowish hue imparted to his skin by a cunning dye, and by the skilful whitening of his bushy brows.

Then drawing a chair to him, he sat down and contemplated, by turns, his reflection in the looking-glass, the wig, and false beard, and the half-demolished supper of toast and water-gruel, which still stood on the table by his bed-side.

CHAPTER XXXI.

MR. DAVIS proved to be a very quiet lodger; seldom out of his room, and giving but little trouble, as Marah and the servant unanimously reported.

He had been in the house nearly a week before Paul caught even a glimpse of him, and that but an indistinct one, as he moved across the landing to his room, groping his way in the dark, and coughing as he went; and, contrary to Levi's expectations, the old man neither sought his companionship or kindly service, but seemed content to live by himself and for himself, without troubling his fellow-creatures for friendship or sympathy.

But they would all of them, Levi, Marah, and Paul, have been surprised had they discovered the movements of the supposed old man. Had they known how he played the spy upon them, watching them through the keyholes, and from dark corners, when least suspected; and sitting up far into the night, often till the early dawn, vigilant and alert, when they gave him credit for being sound asleep in bed.

Richard Bogg was no idler in carrying out the scheme which had induced him to don a disguise, and become a lodger in Levi's house.

He paid stealthy visits to his two neighbours' rooms when the coast was clear, and possessed himself of a business letter belonging to Paul—a letter relating to his first appearance on the boards, and addressed to "Mr. Vincent."

He had also obtained a key, which fitted Levi's treasure-chest; and one afternoon when Marah had stepped out to the market, when Paul was at the theatre, and Levi had gone out for a stroll, he entered his landlord's room, and took from the box the bag of money and the jewels, on which Marah had set her covetous mind.

Full of exultation, he relocked the chest, and returning to his own apartment, examined the booty.

"One thing is certain," he said, joyfully; "I sha'n't be short of money for some time to come. It was a lucky chance which led me to follow the governor the night he put old Marah up to this trick. Now for the rest of the plan!"

He opened the jewel-case, and selected from it a brooch; then placing the case and the bag of gold in one of his huge under-pockets, went out into Paul's chamber.

After a swift glance round him, he placed the brooch, and the duplicate key, in the pocket of a coat which was over the foot of the bed.

It was the one Paul always wore when he smoked his pipe in the evening, and was placed there ready for use.

This done, he returned to his room, from whence he sallied forth in the gloom of the evening.

After he had walked a little distance from the house, he halted, looked sharply around him, and then slipping into a court-entrance, took off his wig and beard, drew himself up, and went on his way.

He stopped at a small oil and colour shop, and entering, purchased some turpentine, which he had served to him in a porter-bottle, one of a number which belonged to Paul, and which he kept in one of the cupboards in his room. As he waited for the turpentine, he held the letter addressed to Mr. Vincent in his hand, and when paying for his purchase, laid it on the counter, apparently forgetting to pick it up again when he left the place.

"That young chap has forgot his love-letter," said the shopkeeper, picking it up.

"Vincent," he continued, reading the address; "No. 1, —— Street. Well, that's not far off, and to-morrow I'll step down and return it. Do as yer would be done by, is my motto."

In the meantime, Richard Bogg had reached the court-entrance, and again donned his disguise, after which he retraced his steps homeward—once more the feeble, asthmatic, tottering old man, Jasper Davis.

As he neared the house, he saw Paul, quite alone, ascend the steps.

"Good!" he said laughing. "He will find it all the more difficult to prove his innocence by an *alibi*."

CHAPTER XXXII.

IT was midnight when the door of Richard Bogg's room was gently opened, and the lawyer's son stepped out upon the landing.

He stood a moment, and listened.

All was still in the old house, for the landlord and the other inmates, with the exception of Paul, who was visiting one of the theatres, had retired to rest; and, with a smile of security, he moved towards a closet which stood between his own and Levi's chamber.

The door was simply fastened with a wooden button, and opened readily beneath his hand, revealing the interior, which apparently served as a depositing place for old clothes, musty papers, and discarded band-boxes.

After one more cautious glance around him, Richard busied himself with the heterogeneous mass; picking from it a quantity of light, inflammable substances, and piling them together in a heap in a clear space upon the floor.

He looked strangely enough, as he bent over his task, with the light from his candle shining full upon him.

He still wore his disguise, but had thrown over his street dress a voluminous dressing-gown of faded scarlet hue; while, surmounting his grizzled, gray locks, was a white cotton night-cap, the tassel of which dangled down upon his forehead.

His face, yellowed by art, gleamed with a ghastly hue, and his eyes shone with excitement and the mingled feelings of triumph and malice which held possession of him.

In a few moments he had collected his heap; and, drawing from his coat-pocket the bottle of turpentine, he poured a portion of the contents upon it.

The light rubbish absorbed the spirit greedily; and, with a pleased look, he placed around it a quantity of woollen rags, so as to form a slight barrier between the dangerous mound and the rest of the lumber.

Then, setting the half-emptied bottle in a conspicuous nook, he arose, closed the cupboard, and returned to his room.

"So far safe," he said, with a sigh of relief, as he sank into an easy-chair, and once more listened intently; while his hands ever and anon stole to the pockets, in which he had concealed his ill-gotten booty.

Half-an-hour lagged slowly by, and still he sat there, sleepless and vigilant, watching and listening, with a perseverance worthy of a better cause.

Presently the street-door opened.

"Back again!" said Richard, as the sound reached him. "Poor fool! Well, I'll not envy him his last night of freedom and enjoyment, even though it *has* been spent with *her!*"

He heard Paul cross the hall, and steal quietly up the stairs, where he paused.

A look of fear crossed Richard's face, as he noted the movement.

"He has smelt the turpentine," he muttered, becoming rigid in his agony of suspense.

But his fears were groundless.

Paul had merely remembered Levi, and passed on into the old man's room, to see if he were by any chance awake, and to bid him a friendly good night. There was a rushlight burning in the room, and by its glimmer he could see Levi lying in his bed, sleeping peacefully, with his long, white beard rippling over the coverlid.

Paul moved to his side, and stood looking at him affectionately.

He stirred in his sleep; and, afraid of breaking his rest, Paul softly left the room, and retired to his own chamber.

Another half-hour lagged slowly by, and once again Richard Bogg came out upon the landing-place, gliding swiftly and noiselessly in his shoeless feet to the closet.

He made short work of it this time.

In an instant he had opened the door, and,

LEVI NATHAN RECEIVES HIS NEW LODGER (*See page 69.*)

dropping the lighted candle-end which he held in his hand upon the combustible heap, closed it again, and, returning to his room, blew out his light, and threw himself upon the bed, drawing the coverlid over him.

The rubbish in the cupboard caught fire, and flared up fiercely; clouds of black, thick smoke from the turpentine and the woollen rags filling the place, and, finding an outlet through the cracks of the door, spread over the house.

Richard Bogg lay still and laughed for a few moments, then leaped to his feet, and dashed out to the top of the stairs.

The smoke had grown dense and thick, and a lurid gleam shot through the chinks of the closet.

"Fire! fire!" he cried, in a cracked, strained voice, which awoke Levi and Paul, and brought them upon the scene.

"Fire, fire, fire!" he cried again; rousing the lodgers, and scaring them from their beds.

The smoke grew denser, and the crackling in the cupboard grew louder, as the flames seized upon the woodwork.

"It's here!" said Paul, rushing towards it, and dashing it open.

Short as had been the time which had elapsed since Richard had fired it, the mischief had increased rapidly, and its interior looked like a red, glowing furnace; while the smoke gushed forth in a cloud, that drove everyone back, and the flames, fed by the free air, leaped forth with an exultant bound, and licked the adjacent oak panelling.

The lodgers hurriedly seized their valuables, and fled into the street, raising the awful cry of "Fire, fire!"

Through the windows shone the red glow; and the neighbours, roused by the noise, and alarmed by the sight, looked out of their windows or rushed to the doors, while a crowd began to form around the building.

The fierce element was gaining ground in the old house, greedily lapping and seizing upon the dry wood with which it was embellished.

"Save what you can—ugh, ugh!" coughed Jasper Davis, as the trio—Levi, Paul, and himself—relaxed in despair the efforts they had made to subdue the fire. "I am going to do the same—ugh! ugh!" and he retreated to his room, from whence in a few moments he reappeared, dragging his portmanteau, and wearing his hat over the white cotton nightcap.

"Ugh! ugh!" he coughed, casting a keen glance round, as, with a kick of his foot, he sent his burden rolling down the stairs.

Paul and Levi had taken his advice, and had returned to save their valuables.

In a moment the youth returned, having hurriedly thrown on a few clothes, and wearing the same old coat into which Richard had thrust the stolen brooch, and the duplicate key, while in his hand he carried a bundle.

"Ugh! ugh!" coughed old Jasper Davis, his face relaxing into a grim smile, as he noted how Paul was attired. "Throw your bundle down, boy. Ugh! Where's old Levi? He has no time to waste. See there!"

He pointed to where a thin tongue of fire had crept over the top of the door of his room.

Paul threw his bundle down stairs, and rushed into the apartment.

He heard a rumbling noise, and could dimly discern, through clouds of smoke, the form of Levi bent over his treasure chest, which he was vainly endeavouring to remove.

"For heaven's sake, come!" shouted Paul. "You have no time to lose."

"My box—my box!" said Levi, heedless of danger, and thinking only of his treasure. "My money, my wife's jewels and wedding-dress are there—let me save them!"

The box was so heavy it could scarcely be moved, but still Levi tugged with all his might.

"Help me, boy!" he said, piteously.

"I cannot!" answered Paul. "It is of no use to try. Take out what you want. Three men could not carry away that box in time."

"Cruel—cruel!" screamed the Jew. "I have dropped the key—I cannot find it!"

The flames had crept inside the room.

Paul noted them.

"Then you must leave it to its fate!" he said, resolutely. "Your box is nothing in comparison with life and safety!"

"Never—never!" shrieked Levi. "It is all I have left of poor Leah. I will not—cannot!"

But seizing him in his arms, Paul forced him away, and carried him, struggling, through the burning entrance, through the smoke and flame beyond, and down the stairs.

At the foot of them stood Jasper Davis, guarding the portmanteau and the luggage.

"So you've got him at last?" he said. "Ugh! ugh! Now, sir," he continued, addressing Levi, as he stood outside the hall door, "I give you notice to quit this very night. Ugh! —I'm an old man—ugh!—and I'm not a strong man—ugh! ugh!—I want peace and quiet. I see I'm not likely to get it in your house—ugh!—fires, disturbances—ugh! ugh! —I should soon be in my grave!"

Levi looked at him with a glance of bewildered misery.

An engine had dashed up, and the energetic fire brigade were soon busy on the premises.

"Not so bad, after all, Tom," reported one of his fellows, "though another ten minutes would have made it a hard matter to put out the blaze. Be quick with the hose!"

Soon the water was being thrown upon the burning-rooms in copious jets, and gradually the flames subsided.

Levi, who had been looking on in deep anxiety, breathed freely again, and the lodgers began to congratulate each other.

Old Jasper Davis beckoned a boy from the crowd.

"Fetch me a cab," he said, "and I'll give you twopence."

The lad darted away on the errand.

"I'm going to an hotel—ugh!" said Jasper, again addressing Levi.

"Sir, I beg of you," said his landlord; "the danger is over now——"

"So *you* say—ugh!—so *you* say!" interrupted Jasper. "Do you call it nothing to be awoke from your first sleep by the noise of some one stealing past your door?"

"Past your door? I don't understand!" said Levi.

"Ay, ay! soon before I smelt the fire and smoke—ugh!" continued Jasper. "Sir, I've been in danger enough this night through fright—ugh!—and exposure to the damp air, to upset me for a month to come—ugh! Here is my cab."

It drew up before the house at this juncture.

"Boy, here is your twopence—ugh! Landlord, good night! I am going to see if I can find a quiet place to finish my sleep in—ugh! ugh! Driver, that portmanteau belongs to me; drive on towards Charing Cross. There's a house I know there; I'll show it to you—ugh! ugh!"

He stepped into the vehicle, and was rapidly driven away, leaving Levi staring after him in blank dismay.

"You can go in again if you like," said one of the firemen; "the fire is quite subdued, and not much damage done, after all, considering."

Levi remembered his box.

"My chest!" he exclaimed. "I must see if it is injured."

He hurried in, followed by Paul, and proceeded at once to his room.

After a sharp search, the lost key was discovered in a corner; and kneeling, the old man opened the box eagerly.

Then he uttered a cry of despair.

"They are gone!" he cried,—"the money and the jewels! Some thief has been here and robbed me!"

"There's a strange smell of turpentine here," said a fireman, as he examined the closet; "and here is a bottle in which a few drops still remain. It has been protected against the fury of the flames under an old great-coat, which has fallen upon it, and which is not quite consumed."

As he spoke, he drew from among some half-charred ashes the bottle which Richard Bogg had placed there.

A policeman came up the stairs, and behind him was the oil and colourman.

They overheard what the fireman said, and nodded their heads sagaciously.

"I thought so," said the constable. "There's more in this business than appears at the top. You have found a turpentine-bottle?" he observed to the man. "Let us see it."

He took it, looked at it mysteriously, and then handed it to the oilman. "Stout!" he remarked, smacking his lips at the bare mention of that luxury; "and the very identical bottle in which I served that turpentine to the young man," he added, sniffing at the neck of it.

"Very good!" murmured the policeman. Then he inquired, pompously, "Where is the master of this house?"

"In there," said one of the lodgers, who was looking on. "There's something the matter, I fancy."

"Robbed!—robbed!" sobbed Levi, as the pair entered the chamber. "Don't try to comfort me, Paul; I could bear the loss of the money, but my poor Leah's jewels—it is too cruel!"

"Oh, ho!" cried the constable. "So there has been a robbery as well as a fire, eh? We shall find out something by-and-by. Sir, have you a lodger in your house named Vincent?"

"That is *me!*" answered Paul, stepping forward.

"Young—tall—dark; it's the very man, I'm sure," whispered the colourman.

"Does this letter belong to you?" again queried the constable, holding out the one Richard Bogg had left in the shop.

"Yes," said Paul; "but I cannot imagine how you obtained it."

"I dare say not, young man," remarked the policeman. "But, anyhow, under existing circumstances, I shall have to request you to walk to the station with me."

"What do you mean?" cried Levi. "If you think he has robbed me, you are mistaken. He's an honest boy, is Paul."

"So are all of us till we are found out," chimed in the oilman.

"That's one of his bottles!" shrieked Marah, who had been listening to the whole conversation, with feelings of rage that she had been forestalled in obtaining Levi's wealth. "He had a dozen of 'em in his room, and I can give witness against him if it's needed."

"Thank you, ma'am," said the constable. "I'll take these bottles you spoke of with me. Now, what have you lost?" he questioned of Levi; "money and jewels?"

"Never mind me," said the old man. "What is this about the lad, yonder—about a bottle and letter?"

"Why this?" said the shopkeeper. "That bottle was brought to my place to-night, and I served the man as brought it with turpentine; and when he went away, he, accidental-like, left this letter on the counter. 'Mr. Vincent, No. 1, —— Street,' said I, when I picked it up; 'I'll run down with it in the morning.' But hearing of the fire, I ran out to see it, and found out as 'twere at the very house where the man lived as dropped the letter; and home I goes, and fetches it; an' I tells the officer, here, the story, an' we comes in; an' strange it is that your place has been robbed, an' set on fire with that very turpentine; an' that is the man who fetched it."

"I deny it!" cried Paul. "I know nothing of the story you tell—nothing of the robbery. I am innocent."

"I daresay you are; but it's my duty to take you with me, after I've searched your room," said the constable. "An' you, sir, had better come along with us," he added to Levi.

"Yes; I'll come, of course," said the old man. "Cheer up, boy! It's all a mistake; and we'll come back, and have a night of it, in spite of misfortune."

So Paul's room was searched, and the eleven other bottles packed, and taken possession of by the policeman; and a cab being called, Paul, Levi, the oil and colourman, and constable, were driven to the police-station.

Having arrived there, he was searched.

"What's this?" said the official who performed the duty, holding up the key and brooch.

"Oh, heaven!" cried Levi; "he is guilty! It is one of the missing jewels."

Utterly bewildered, Paul looked around him, in silent amazement, his face fading to an ashen-white hue.

"It's a case of robbery and arson, that's clear," said the policeman who had taken him; "and a deep-laid scheme it is, too."

"Paul guilty?—Paul a thief?" said Levi. "And I loved him, as though he were my own son!"

He moved slowly away; and Paul was left to his own gloomy thoughts—to his solitary, first experience of a prison-cell.

CHAPTER XXXIII.

So much were appearances against Paul, that on the very first hearing he was committed for trial.

Then tried at last, at the Central Criminal Court, and before Judge Vincent, who had returned from abroad, and resumed his labours on the bench.

Paul's was the most important case during the sessions; for there seemed a strange dearth of the more serious crimes, and there was no criminal to rival him in the attention of the court-frequenting public.

There was quite a hum of expectation and interest when, after the disposal of some petty cases, he was brought forward to the prisoners' dock. It was known that he had contemplated making his début in the theatrical world in the ensuing season; and not the least painful portion of his position was his recognition, among the dense crowd of spectators, of many of his professional friends—men with whom he had associated on terms of friendliness and good-fellowship—women who had admired him for his handsome face, his kindly nature, and the halo of romance which hung over his history.

For a moment, he bowed his head in shame as he encountered the sea of eyes, all fixed upon him, and heard the murmur which greeted his entrance; then, with consciousness of innocence, lifted it proudly, and swept a haughty glance around him.

As he did so, a man struggled through the crowd, and holding out his hands, grasped Paul's warmly.

It was Mr. Morrison.

A sound of applause rang round the court. It had burst from the members of the profession, who were touched by this honest display of friendship.

The noise was instantly suppressed by the crier.

"Cheer up, boy!" said Morrison, heartily. "We are here, all of us—the missis, and Ray, and the company—to see you through this. We shall take you home in triumph."

A policeman stepped forward, and, in a kind manner, requested Mr. Morrison to stand aside, and suffer the proceedings of the court to be carried on.

Paul watched him wistfully as he returned to his place.

It was in the front row, among the witnesses; and there were seated Rachel, Mrs. Morrison, and a female, in a dress of sober brown, who was closely veiled.

A swift flush rose to Paul's forehead as he caught Rachel's eyes fixed on him; then he turned away, afraid to trust himself to look upon her.

He dreaded her scorn; but, had he watched her, he would have seen only pity on her fair face, while her bright eyes were rendered brighter still by tears.

Near them, too, were Levi Nathans and Marah, the former quaint-looking as ever—the latter having concealed her old-time costume with a long cloak, while her head was covered with a black satin poke-bonnet of comfortable and respectable proportions.

Levi took no notice as Paul entered the dock, but remained, with his head drooping upon his breast, in an attitude of intense melancholy. Marah, on the contrary, looked up with exultation in her glance, nodded her head in a satisfied manner, and seated herself more comfortably, with an air of determination, prepared to listen attentively to the proceedings.

Beside them was the oil and colourman, looking pompously important, and as though he thought his position one of the most enviable in the world.

But, though Paul looked closely, he could nowhere perceive the old man, Jasper Davis, who had been so active on the night of the fire.

And in the background, near the door, where he could hear all without being perceived, was Richard Bogg; and he too, seemed as though this misfortune of his rival was a joyful event, for he was smiling with delight, and his eyes had a cruel glitter in them, as he noted Paul's agony of anger, pride, and shame, as he stood before the world, in the light of a thief and incendiary.

The trial commenced.

One by one the witnesses were called into the box; old Levi to state how he had befriended him, how he had shown him his treasures, how he had, trusting him implicitly, given him opportunities of accomplishing the theft. Even Paul's efforts to save him from the fire, his refusing to waste the precious moments in the rescue of the chest, told against him, when touched by the subtle skill of the prosecuting counsel.

The listeners began to pity the duped old man, so innocent, kind, and sad, so reluctant to give his accusing evidence, and to look upon Paul as a monster of ingratitude and wickedness.

Then came the shopkeeper's testimony to having sold the turpentine, placed it in the bottle produced in court, and, on the departure of his customer, having found the letter (also produced by the counsel for the prosecution) on the counter, where he had observed him place it while paying for his purchase. He also swore to his conviction that Paul was the person who had bought the turpentine—a fact strongly borne out by the certainty that the letter in question really belonged to him.

Paul's heart sank within him, as he now saw this link in the chain of circumstantial evidence which was fast being bound around him, fettering him to a felon's doom; while Rachel wept, Morrison fumed, and glared at the smiling colourman; and the veiled female in brown sat still as a statue, her hands clasped tightly together, as if in prayer.

As the witness sat down, a moan issued from her lips, and she shuddered as he turned his face, replete with satisfaction, full upon her, and nodded his self-approval for what he had just done.

And yet, hard-hearted as he seemed—false as his testimony had been in its most vital point, the identity of the prisoner with his customer —he was an honest man; and not having noticed the purchaser of the turpentine very closely—having only the recollection that he was a tall young man, brawny, and strong of form, with dark hair—had, in his desire for notoriety, his intense wish to create a sensation by fixing the crime upon somebody, persuaded himself firmly that Paul and the party he had seen were really one and the same person, and had taken oath unhesitatingly to the fact.

Paul could not refute his statement, save by a simple denial of the affair. He had left his friends an hour before, and had rambled on alone, arriving home just about the time which gave most colour of truth to the shopkeeper's evidence.

Last of all came Marah.

Paul wondered what testimony the old woman could have to give against him; but it was soon evident. In some respects, her evidence tallied with that of her master: in the points relating to the prisoner's intimacy with Levi; the approximation of his room to that of the old man; and the opportunities he had of entering the latter at his pleasure, unwatched and unsuspected of any evil intent.

Thus he would have ample time to commit the robbery, and secrete the spoils, which he had seemingly done, as, in spite of the strictest search, the bag of money and the jewels could not be found.

Thus far, Marah spoke glibly enough; then, at the further questioning of the prosecuting counsel, she paused for a moment, and seemed to be gathering her energies together.

There was a momentary shade of indecision on her face, but it passed away; and in a firm, clear voice, with a look of intense hatred at Paul, she answered, "I saw the prisoner at the closet, where the fire began, a short time before the old gentleman lodger had given the alarm."

A murmur ran round the court.

This last piece of evidence seemed to hustle away from the listeners' minds the last persuasion of the prisoner's innocence.

His friends looked disheartened.

Rachel buried her face in her hands, and wept unrestrainedly.

Marah nodded her head triumphantly, and looked with a sneering smile at the man she had just accused.

Paul started forward indignantly, and was about to speak; but was checked by a warning gesture from the lawyer Morrison had engaged for his defence.

From his place by the door, Richard Bogg laughed softly, as though he were thoroughly enjoying the scene.

Judge Vincent wore a look of pity as he looked on the unhappy young man, and thought of his ruined life and blighted fame.

Sharply enough, Paul's counsel cross-questioned the old housekeeper, but failed to shake her evidence. Every fresh attempt to baffle her only seemed to call up new condemnatory facts against his client.

"She was old and wakeful," Marah said. "She had served Levi for years, and the charge of the house was a heavy responsibility on her mind. She slept in a chamber one landing above that of her master.

"On the night in question, she had heard the street door opened with a latch-key a little after midnight; and wishing to be sure all was right, had risen, and, going down a few stairs, had looked over to see who had entered.

"It was Mr. Vincent.

"A short time after, she had heard some one moving on the landing below, and had once more resumed her watch over the stairs.

"She saw the prisoner busy at the cupboard; but not thinking any ill, imagining he was looking for something he had placed there, had felt no alarm; but when he closed the door, returned to her rest.

"Not long after, she had been aroused by the alarm of fire; and on hearing of the robbery, of the brooch and duplicate key found on the young man, had told of what she had seen.

"The bottle, too, she identified as one of a dozen which had been supplied by a well-known firm, to the accused; which assertion was corroborated by a member of the establishment."

"And all this you affirm on your solemn oath?" said the defending counsel, as he gave up his futile efforts to shake the old woman.

Again Marah made a momentary pause. Then raising her hand upward, she said, boldly, "All this I affirm on my solemn oath, before heaven!"

The barrister sat down, perplexed and despondent; himself fully persuaded of his client's guilt, and knowing that he had lost his case.

It was in vain that he called up witnesses to speak as to the previous good character of the accused.

Mr. Morrison, several of his theatrical friends—even the Kentish inn-keeper and his wife, with the proprietor of the hop gardens in which Paul had laboured,—all spoke of his honesty and industry in warm and eloquent terms, without moving one jot of the crushing weight of proofs brought against him.

There was but one further question mooted. "What had become of the old man, Jasper Davis, who had given the alarm of fire?" All search for him had proved useless; he had entirely vanished from the scene.

It was supposed too, that he could have thrown a further light upon the subject, as he had, when he left Levi's house, spoken of being disturbed by some person creeping past his door.

It was, however, concluded, on hearing Marah's and Levi's description of him, his habits, and ill health, that he had purposely withdrawn, to avoid the trouble and excitement of being called as a witness on the trial.

This decided, Paul's lawyer rose to plead. His speech was full of subtle denials of the charges made against his client, and replete with appeals to the sympathies of the public and the jury.

An excellent speech, but, as its utterer felt a complete failure.

One glance at the jury had convinced him their decision would be against him.

Equally vain were Paul's assertions of his innocence. His words were looked upon as subterfuges, and prejudiced unfavourably his cause, so that he, too, relapsed into a despondent silence.

In a short time the actual trial was over. Judge Vincent arose to sum up the facts, and dismiss the jury to consider their verdict.

His speech was brief and sternly impartial, and swept away all hope from the hearts of Paul and his friends.

As he concluded, Richard Bogg stepped quickly from the court, and sped away as if on an errand of life and death.

CHAPTER XXXIV.

RICHARD BOGG, on leaving the court, had hurried on until he neared a street corner, about five minutes' walk from the place.

There he met with his father, who was, apparently, on the look-out for him.

"Well?" said the old man eagerly, as he advanced to meet him.

"If you have anything to do yonder, be quick!" answered Richard, pointing with his thumb over his shoulder. "The jury have retired to consider their verdict."

"And that?" said his father.

"Will be 'Guilty,'" said Richard; "or I am no judge of such matters."

"Then there is, indeed, no time to lose!" continued Mr. Bogg; and he started off at a run, in the direction of the court.

Richard followed, curious to see the end.

They were in time; the jury had not yet re-entered the court.

They were examining the case, carefully and pitifully, compassionating the young man whom their verdict must either restore to liberty or condemn to utter ruin.

And this they did, despite their convictions that their debate must have but one dire conclusion.

People waited in suspense for their reappearance.

Judge Vincent employed himself in looking over the notes he had taken of the proceedings.

The lawyers and clerks conversed with each other.

The audience followed their example.

Levi still retained his despondent attitude; Morrison's round face was drawn down lugubriously; Rachel wept on; and the veiled woman sat rigid, her face turned towards the jury's box.

The oil and colourman stood up, and looked around him, as though he expected to be applauded for what he had done; and old Marah sent her keen gaze, searchingly, into every corner of the place, looking for the man who had visited her so strangely, who had fathomed her secrets—envy and hatred of the youth before her—and had, through her avarice, tempted her into crime.

She had just concluded that he was not there, when there was a bustle at the entrance, and Beverley Bogg, panting and excited, dashed into the court, and elbowed his way towards the judge's bench.

Marah smiled.

"That's him!" she muttered.

Her sharp eyes had detected him, in spite of the mufflers he had worn on his visits to her.

The lawyer's face was pale and agitated; and, as he pressed forward, he held a folded paper in one hand, while in the other was a small note, which, on reaching an official, he passed on to his friend.

The judge took it, and opened it with a wondering look; but, when he had read it, his face faded to a livid hue, and an expression of intense agony glared from his eyes, as he cast them on the prisoner.

The words on the paper had power to shake him to the very centre of his being:—

"I have hastened here at my utmost speed, but I fear I am too late. For your own sake, be merciful in your judgment! The young man, Vincent, on trial for robbery and arson, is your own son! Save him, if there is a loophole of escape!"

"Too late!" said the Judge; and, bowing his head on his hands, he uttered a deep groan.

The woman in brown had risen to her feet and was watching him attentively.

The spectators were roused to intense curiosity by the strange scene.

Had anything occurred to change the aspect of affairs,—to prove the prisoner innocent?

Slowly the judge removed his hands from his face, and looked up.

People looked on him with astonishment.

So white—so stern and set were his features—so deep an agony spread over his countenance.

He turned towards the prisoners' dock, and spoke.

"You have refused to give any real name during this trial. We know you only by the one bestowed upon you by the hop-pickers—your late comrades—that of Captain, and by the name you chose for your theatrical career, that of Vincent."

Paul bowed his head.

"Some years ago you were found on the road-side by a gentleman named Clayton, sick and in distress. You then styled yourself *John?*"

Again Paul bowed an assent.

"Before that period how were you known?" said the judge.

"That I decline to say," replied the young man.

He could not let Rachel know that it was her childhood's friend who stood before her in such an infamous position.

"You cannot hide it from me," said the judge, his voice rising higher in his excitement. "You lived with a man called Jacob Prew?"

Rachel stood looking with an eager face at the pair—at the prisoner and his judge.

"Your name is——"

"Paul!" he cried, desperately, interrupting his questioner.

Rachel's voice echoed the word, and as she sank back helpless, Morrison took her in his arms, and carried her from the court.

Judge Vincent was silent; the veiled woman stood with both hands stretched out towards the unhappy youth.

"How you have learnt this, I know not," continued Paul. "One thing I defy you to say—and that is that any shadow of evil, save that of friendless poverty, rested upon the boy Paul."

Still the judge was silent.

"You might even own that I have the virtue of *gratitude*," he said, bitterly. "Years ago, when I was a ragged child, a mere crossing-sweeper, I met you. The kind words you spoke,

G

the friendly touch of your hand, sank deep into my memory. They were so new and strange to one whose young life had been one long experience of wretchedness and persecution. When I began to rise in the world through honest perseverance (mark me, I say *honest*), through gratitude I adopted your name, resolving, if I prospered, to let you one day know how much you had done for me."

The judge had stretched out his hand: he was leaning towards the speaker, forgetful of the time, the place, and the listening, eager crowd.

More intense grew the excitement of the throng, and they pressed forward in a more compact mass, fearful of losing one syllable of the strange conversation.

"My present position disgraces that name," added Paul. "I ask your pardon, and lay it aside for ever, and take up once more the name with which I commenced life—Paul, the outcast—the vagabond!"

He was standing proudly erect, in his despair and loneliness, defiant of the whole world.

In spite of his crime, people looked upon him with admiration.

There was another stir.

The jury had re-entered their box.

The judge turned to them.

"Gentlemen of the jury, your verdict?"

"Guilty, my lord, on both charges—robbery and arson."

Sterner and more set grew the judge's face.

"Prisoner," he said, slowly, to Paul, measuring his words as though they were forced from him against his will, "you have been fairly tried by a jury of your own countrymen, and found guilty. It is my duty to sentence you——"

A wild scream broke from the woman who had sat veiled through the whole of the proceedings.

With eager hands she tore the covering from her face.

Pale, worn, but still beautiful, Catherine Vincent stood before her husband.

"No, no!" she cried, in a shrill voice of entreaty. "Do not *sentence* him! William—husband—he is your own son!"

She had sprang to the dock, and was clinging to it with a frantic hold.

Paul bent over towards her.

"Mother!" he whispered.

"Yes, your mother! My boy—lost for so many years—your mother, come to save you! Look up, Paul! he cannot—he will not condemn you! He will let you go free, now he knows you are his own son!"

All was silent in the crowded court.

Suddenly the quiet was broken by the judge's voice, deep and hoarse.

"I sentence you, Paul Vincent, to seven years' penal servitude."

Again the mother's scream of agony rose piercingly on the air, while a universal sobbing breath of sympathy throbbed from the lookers-on.

CHAPTER XXXV.

THAT night, Lawyer Bogg stood on a quiet spot by the river-side, waiting for Marah.

An hour had passed, but he seemed by no means impatient; with his eyes fixed on the dark water, indulging in his darker thoughts, he had ceased to regard the flying moments.

"It is done at last!" he said, as if speaking to the river. "After twenty-one years of striving and waiting, I have accomplished the first epitome of my revenge!"

"Swish, swish, gurgle!" went the muddy waves, as though in answer to his musing. "Swish, splash, gurgle!" as though delighted that they had met with something fouler than themselves.

"The first portion," continued the lawyer, "ruin to his pride, his happiness, their love; a blight on the name he boasted had never been soiled!"

"Gurgle, gurgle!" went the water exultingly, with a sound like thick laughter.

"The second, ruin to him in fortune. I will see him a beggar, then I will reveal myself to him in my true colours!"

"Splash, dash!" chorussed the river, as though it applauded the idea. "Gurgle, gurgle!" sounded its weird laughter.

A hand was laid upon the lawyer's arm.

He looked round, with a start.

Marah stood beside him.

"I am come to receive your thanks," she said, in a whisper.

"Meaning the eighty pounds I promised you, if Paul Vincent were convicted through your agency. I have the money ready, but you must first prove that you have earned it."

"Have I not?" said Marah. "Whose testimony was it which completed the evidence brought against him at his trial?"

"I was not in court, Marah," said Bogg.

"It was mine," she continued; "when I swore I had seen him at the closet where the fire commenced. After all, eighty pounds is little enough for what I have done!"

"You forget you have the bag of money, and the jewels," said her companion.

"I have not got them!" she replied, morosely.

"What!" cried the lawyer, in astonishment.

"Ay, you may well be astounded!" said Marah. "There was little enough need to plot against Paul Vincent. He was ready enough, of his own accord, to throw himself into the power of the law!"

"I cannot understand you!" repeated Bogg.

"I mean that he was in reality the thief who robbed Levi," said Marah. "While I was plotting, he was working; and he has taken and hidden the money."

The lawyer saw, from the old woman's manner, that she was speaking the truth; and, in perplexity, once more gazed into the water.

"That story of the shop-keeper was *true*," said Marah. "He fetched turpentine, and fired the house, to hide what he had done. Who else could it have been? The man knew him again."

"True, true!" murmured Bogg.

"He had a duplicate key, too," added Marah. "And plenty of chances were given him to have it made, and to open the chest. He could go into the room when he pleased without question. If you think I am deceiving you, see here. This is the key you gave me. The one he used is detained by the police."

She held out the key.

The lawyer took it, and examined it carefully, and then threw it into the river.

"It is best not to keep such things about one," he explained. "I will not dispute your story; but if all these things are true, you did not do much towards helping on his conviction."

"Did I not?" she answered. "I swore I saw him at the closet where the fire commenced only a little time before the alarm was given. *That* completely convinced people of his guilt, you will own?"

"It was certainly a conclusive proof," said Bogg; "but what of it?"

"Just this," said Marah, sinking her voice to a whisper, and looking around her, fearfully. "That night I never moved from my bed after I had retired to rest, until I heard the cry of fire."

"What!" cried the lawyer.

"I heard Paul Vincent come home, but I never thought of looking to see who it was. I am too used to his ways. I never got up, or peeped over the stairs, as I said I did; I only lay still, and wished he would hurt himself in the dark."

"Then you have committed *perjury!*" he said, in the same low tone.

"Call it what you will," replied Marah. "I heard that Levi had been robbed; I heard the colourman's story; and when the key and brooch were found upon the young man, I knew it was he who had committed the theft, and the mischief, as well as though I had *seen* him do it. What harm was there in saying I had watched him? I only fixed a crime of which he was really guilty, and brought him to a just punishment. It is a small revenge for all he has robbed me of."

"It was *perjury*, Marah!" reiterated the lawyer.

"You would have made me a *thief*," she retorted; "which is worse."

"Pardon me; I only told you a *story*, and gave you a key for which I had no use," he replied.

"We had better not quarrel," said Marah. "I might make it disagreeable for you, Mr. Beverley Bogg. Don't start. You see, I know you. What I say is this. I have helped to send Paul Vincent to the doom you wished for him. Is what I have done worth the eighty guineas you promised me?"

"It is," said Bogg, placing in her hands a roll of notes. "Go your ways, good Marah; you have well earned them."

She grasped them eagerly.

"Now," said the lawyer, "good-bye! I need not bind you to secrecy. For your own sake, you must be silent concerning this transaction. Remember, perjury is punishable by the law."

"Never fear for me," she answered. "My tongue was never known to wag unadvisedly. Good-bye, my generous friend!" And clutching her money tightly, the old woman trudged away.

Soon the river-bank was deserted, and all was silent save the splash, splash of the muddy waves, as they went gurgling on their way.

CHAPTER XXXVI.

A VISITOR awaited Mr. Bogg, on his return home.

It was Judge Vincent.

"You are late, Beverley," he said; "I have waited for more than two hours."

"I was compelled to be abroad," said the lawyer, "much to my regret; for I knew how anxious you would be to see me."

He sat down, and drawing a paper from his breast-pocket, opened and glanced it over.

"This," he said to the judge, who was watching him anxiously, "is what you have come to demand—the proof that the young man, Vincent, is indeed your own son."

The judge made a gesture of assent.

He seemed striving to speak, but his tongue refused to perform its office, and only a few inarticulate sounds issued from his lips.

"This is a deposition from the man Jacob Prew, sentenced to penal servitude, ten years ago, for coining, and imprisoned at Portsmouth."

He spoke deliberately; and his listener's impatience mounted into almost anger, as he caught the slowly-uttered words.

"Three days before the trial of—of the young man, I received a letter from this man, requesting to see me, as he had news of vital importance, concerning the prisoner, to communicate."

"Yes, yes!" said the judge.

Beverley Bogg laughed in his sleeve as he noted his agitation, and remembered how, on knowing Paul was hopelessly in prison, he had gone down to Portsmouth, and had contrived to see Jacob Prew, and by means of a promised sum of money, and an assurance that he would interest himself in the man's behalf, and obtain for him a ticket of leave, influenced him to follow the course of conduct he described in his narration of facts.

"I went, and, in the presence of the chaplain and the governor of the prison, I made the following statement, which I committed to paper, and of which I made a legal document."

"Read it," gasped the judge.

Bogg smoothed the paper with his hand, put on his spectacles, and commenced.

"It was in the winter of the year eighteen hundred and —— that I, Jacob Prew, went to —— Hospital, to visit a woman, the wife of a friend of mine, who was suffering transportation, and whom I had promised I would befriend.

"To make certain of seeing Jenny, the woman, I passed myself off as her brother, and got easy admission to the ward where she lay.

"She was suffering from a broken rib, and I kept on seeing her all the time.

"I had visited her for about a fortnight

when one day, as I sat by her side, I became aware that the next bed was occupied by a new patient, a female, who did not seem right in her mind, for she muttered to herself like a mad woman, though it was all in a gentle sort of a way.

"'Don't she disturb you?' said I, to Jenny.

"'Not she,' says Jenny. 'I rather like it; it is company, when I am wakeful at night, to hear her a-talkin' beside me, and to think how low people is brought in the world, as least expected it.'

"I asked her what she meant.

"Said she, 'Jacob, do you remember, six months ago, how Judge Vincent's lady-wife ran away from him, and never was heard on more?'

"I nodded, for, of course, I knew all about it.

"'That's her,' said Jenny.

"'Nonsense!' said I.

"'You knew her when she was a-riding in her carriage to the court, to listen to the trials,' said she. 'You remember she was there when my poor Bill was tried, and sent beyond the sea. You've seen her scores of times; now look, and tell me, is she not the same woman?'"

Judge Vincent shuddered as he listened, while the lawyer kept on in the same cold voice, which changed not from its hard, metallic sound, during the whole time of their conference.

"I looked, and I remembered her in a moment. She was not a bit changed, for her cheeks were red, and her eyes bright with fever, and her hair, which had not been cut off then, was tossed all over the pillow, in the beautiful curls I remembered so well."

The judge sighed heavily.

"'Don't no one know her?' I asked, in surprise; 'not one of the doctors, or nurses?'—for I thought it strange they did not.

"'Not one,' said Jenny, laughing; 'only you and me; and I am not going to tell. I hate her, for the way in which she swept past me, laughing and talking with her friends, and looking into her husband's face as though she worshipped him, while I sat on a bench breaking my heart about Bill! No, I'll not tell. Let her fight it out alone.'"

"Poor Catherine!" said the judge, in a whisper.

"'She took her baby with her,' I said, 'when she left her husband. What's become of it?'

"'In the workhouse,' said Jenny. 'The nurse told me so.'

"Well, I went away; but all that night I kept thinking over what I had seen and heard.

"I was living a life, even then, as made the law a terror to me; and I had every reason to think that, in time, prison and transportation would be my portion.

"And at last I made out a plan, which, if I was in trouble, I thought would help me. I made up my mind that I would get hold of Judge Vincent's child, and that when I got into trouble I would make a condition with his father that he would not be hard on me, if I'd give him back."

The judge's face was painfully earnest, as he listened.

"So I went to the Union, and after a little trouble, and getting some false certificates of my being a respectable man, and offering to pay down five pounds for the trouble the baby had given, likewise making a present to the person as had to make inquiries, and saying as the mother might have the child again when she was well, if she pleased, I got the boy made over to me; and glad the parish was to get rid of him, I believe.

"They told me his name was Paul, for that was what his mother always called him in her delirium, and so I've styled him ever since. I didn't carry out my first notion about him. He gave me a deal of trouble, which I was not used to, never having had anything to do with infants in my life before; and I began to dislike him, and not to treat him in the best of fashion. I tried to bring him up to my way of living when he got old enough, but he didn't take to it natural, and I got more and more tired of my bargain. At last, Judge Vincent condemned to death a friend of mine. I was obliged to keep in hiding, as the police were after me; and I heard, too, that he had friends who were trying to get a reprieve, or I'd have tried to save him through the boy, Paul.

"But Judge Vincent opposed his sentence being altered—at least, so folks say—and my mate was hung.

"Then I made a vow to be revenged, and I swore I'd make the child a thief, a felon, before I sent him back to his father.

"He resisted, and when I was transported, he was still innocent.

"I lost sight of him for four years; when I came back, he was a crossing-sweeper, and I traced him, and took him into my keeping again.

"He was with me in that coining business, for which I am here; but managed to escape, and since then I have heard nothing of him."

PAUL EXPERIENCES A MOTHER'S LOVE.

The lawyer stopped reading, and passed the document over to the judge.

It was signed by the man Prew, and by the chaplain and governor of the convict prison.

"This is incomplete," said the judge. "How did you trace the connection between the child and—and this young man?"

He spoke calmly, but his face betrayed the suffering he had endured during the reading of the convict's confession.

"I had been interested in the child," said Bogg; "having seen him once or twice with Jacob Prew, who came to me for legal advice concerning a comrade. When I saw him at Clayton's, after the affair of the coiners, I recognised him; he called himself John, which I never contradicted, from pity. I tried hard to save him from his vicious life; offered to employ him in my office."

"Noble, generous friend!" said the judge, clasping his hand with a warm pressure.

"But he ran away one night; and I forgot him, until he came to light once more, through his connection with this theatre. He revealed himself to Charles Clayton, and thus I was enabled to complete his identification."

"Unhappy boy!" said the judge. "Beverley, think you this convict's tale is true?"

"It is, alas! too true," answered the lawyer. "My poor friend, the unfortunate youth now in prison is, beyond any doubt, your lost boy. This he owes to his mother's frailty, as you also owe to her your misery."

"Name her not," said the judge. "I curse the day in which I ever met her, and was won by her false beauty. Name her not; I can think only of my wretched son."

Beverley turned aside to hide a smile, then looked at his friend with an aspect of deep commiseration and sympathy.

"My poor William!" he said. "This is indeed a sore trial!"

"Do not waste your time in pitying me," said the judge. "Tell me, what can I do in this dreadful emergency?"

"You cannot save him from his punishment; he must undergo his sentence."

The wretched father groaned, and pressed his hand to his forehead in despair.

"But you might do something for him afterwards," suggested the lawyer; "something which would cause the world to look upon him with less jaundiced eyes—with a less vivid remembrance of his degradation."

"Anything—anything to reclaim him," said Judge Vincent. "Only point out the way."

"Money!" answered the shrewd lawyer.

"Money, which will work any miracle we wish accomplished in these times. Money, which will throw an halo round the unfortunate boy, that will hide his imperfections and failings, and raise up for him friends, where he would else meet with only enemies and accusers."

He spoke sneeringly, and noted every fleeting expression on the judge's face, as he proceeded with a greedy glance.

"I have an ample fortune," he replied. "It will be his when I die."

"Make it larger," proceeded his adviser. "Leave him, if you can, a millionaire, and folks will soon forget this episode in his history. He will have a chance of working out a honourable and useful life, and redeeming the blotted past."

"Leave him a millionaire!" repeated the Judge. "How?"

"There are many fields open for a man who has wealth, to increase it," continued Mr. Bogg. "Speculation, for instance."

He paused to note the effect he had created.

"Dangerous ground, is it not?" said his listener.

"Not if you obtain an experienced guide," answered the lawyer. "For instance, three months ago, you entrusted me with one thousand pounds to invest in the —— Company, of which I am the manager."

"Yes," said the judge.

"Your money is more than doubled," answered Beverley. "Shares have gone up miraculously, and are still rising. When they have reached a certain climax, I shall sell out my own and your shares in the transaction, realizing a handsome profit on our original capital, a profit which will astonish the oldest speculator in London. You see, in safe hands, speculation may be made a mine of wealth."

Judge Vincent sat for some time in deep thought. "Beverley," he said, at last, "I have known you for years; I trust you implicitly. I know you would not mislead me in this or any other matter."

"Deceive you, William, my dearest friend!"

"Never!" said Beverley; and he passed his hands over his face, as though to hide his emotion.

"You are too cool and clear-headed a man of the world to deceive yourself, either," continued his friend. "I believe you would in all things study my interests, as though they were your own."

"Do I not?" answered the lawyer. "William, they are more my study than aught pertaining to myself."

"Give me a few days for thought," said the judge. "In this matter, I may not act hastily. If I am of the same mind at the end of the time, I will trust my fortune in your hands, resting assured that you will not risk it vainly."

"Your confidence overpowers me," said Beverley, with difficulty suppressing his glee at the result of his labour. "For your sake, for that of your son, I will bend my whole energies to serve you in this matter."

They parted.

Judge Vincent went sadly to his home, dreading, yet wishing for the morrow, when he might visit his child; while the lawyer sat far on into the night, brooding over his nefarious schemes.

CHAPTER XXXVII.

THE morning sun was stealing in a long slanting ray of light into Paul's cell, shining on the rough massive walls, stone floor, and meagre furniture, when the turnkey entered, and announced a visitor.

She had followed the man, and when Paul raised his head, stood inside the door.

It was Catherine Vincent.

"Paul, my boy!" she cried, springing to his side, and throwing her arms round his neck.

The gaoler closed the door, and retired.

For the first time since his babyhood, Paul's head rested on his mother's bosom, while her tears and kisses fell fast upon his forehead.

Paul looked up into her face, so pale, so beautiful, so full of anguish, yet filled with perfect tenderness, as she gazed down on him.

And so they sat for a time, locked in each other's arms.

At last, Catherine spoke.

"Thank heaven, you do not reproach me!" she said.

"Reproach you, mother!" he answered. "Why should I? I am sure you can have done me no wrong."

"The greatest wrong of all," she cried, sobbing. "I took you away with me, when I left your father; I deprived you of the advantages of your birth, of your father's care; and this is the wretched fruit of my madness!"

"You do not believe me guilty?" he said, anxiously.

"No, no! though all the world branded you with crime, I would still cling to you—still keep untouched my faith in your complete innocence!"

Paul drew her head down upon his shoulder, and held her in a close embrace.

"If we could only die now," he whispered, "and escape the terrible future before us!"

"Separation!" she said. "Myself, to wander on alone in the world once more! You, to —to——Ah, no! I cannot say it! Oh, Paul, is there no escape?"

"None!" he said, sadly. "Mother, we must bear as best we can this bitter punishment, that has come upon us for another's crime! Be brave! When this is over—when I come out of prison, we shall be together again!"

Catherine clung closer to him, sobbing.

"I will work for you," he continued, trying to cheer her, "in some place where I am not known; and we shall be happy, in spite of our present sorrows!"

She looked into his face, with a faint smile, which was instantly quenched in tears.

"Seven years—seven years!" she said. "I cannot bear it!"

"They will soon pass," he answered. "I shall be still young when I come out again; and I will devote my whole life to you! They tell me, if I am industrious, I may earn money, even in a prison. If it is so, I shall still have something to toil for—the hope of something to help us along our way, to smooth it for us."

He had no thought of being a pensioner on his father's wealth. In his sturdy independence of nature, it had not entered his mind; and Catherine, realizing this, looked on him with pride mingling with her affection for him.

"How were we separated?" he questioned. "How did you find me again?"

"When you were a baby, I was ill in the hospital, and you were taken to the workhouse. While you were there, a man came and removed you from the care of the parish, saying he wished to adopt you for his own child; and leaving an address where I might reclaim you on my recovery, if such was my wish. You see, Paul, I was poor, friendless, unknown; and the officers thought they were doing me a kindness when they let you go."

"I suppose that man was Jacob Prew," mused Paul. "But I cannot understand why he should burden himself with me."

"When I got well, I hastened to fetch you. That was the story they told me, and they gave me the address of the person who had taken you. You can guess the rest. He was nowhere to be found; he had disappeared with you, and left no clue to his whereabouts."

She clung to him, sobbing, as she recounted her miserable story.

"For years I searched for you," she continued; "but I am poor, and I could not do it as I would. I am now a nurse in the hospital," she added, looking at him wistfully, "though I was born a lady."

He pressed her closer to him.

"I had well-nigh given up my efforts in despair," she continued, stroking his face with one thin, white hand. "I thought I should never see you again."

"I devoted myself to my labours among the afflicted and wretched, trying to find my happiness in works of charity, and I gained the goodwill of my employers. Among them is an old man, a surgeon, who often brings me in a daily newspaper to pass away some of the tedious hours of my night-watching by the beds of the sick. In one he gave me a few days ago was an account of the robbery of the old Jew, and the fire."

"I begin to see how it was," said Paul.

"I read that a young man, named Vincent, was accused of the crime. The name first attracted my attention; and then a sickly hope sprung up in my heart that perhaps you were my lost boy."

She sobbed again, and her voice grew tremulous as she spoke on.

"I heard you had been engaged at the theatre, and I found out the manager, and questioned him concerning you. What he told me of your story, made my hope grow stronger. Touched by my earnestness, he offered to take me with him to the court, where I could see you. I went. You know how my hope was realized."

"Sadly enough, mother," said Paul; "but let us hope that this sorrowful meeting may be the commencement of brighter days."

"Judge Vincent!" said the turnkey, opening the door.

Catherine uttered a cry of terror, and shrank closer to Paul.

"He will take you from me," she said, sadly, as the judge entered the cell.

Once more the three, husband, wife, and child, stood face to face.

Scarcely glancing at Catherine, the judge stepped forward, and held out his hands.

"Paul, my son!" he said; and bowing his head on the youth's shoulder, the strong man wept.

At last, he raised his head, and gazed into Paul's face, stroking back, with a tender, pitiful touch, the dark curls which had fallen over his forehead.

"For years I have prayed that you might be restored to me," he said. "I never dreamt our re-union would be so bitter."

"Father," cried Paul, "I swear by heaven I am innocent of the crime laid to my charge!"

The judge shook his head mournfully.

"I would give all I possess in the world to be able to prove it, my poor boy!"

"This is the hardest trial of all," said Paul. "Father, believe me, I speak the truth. I have never, from my boyhood, committed a dishonest action, or willingly injured my fellow-creatures."

Still the judge shook his head, while an incredulous look rested on his face.

"The proofs!" he murmured. "Oh, heaven! it is a fearful thing to be compelled to doubt my own child!"

Paul sighed despairingly, and sank into gloomy silence.

"Boy, do not fear that my heart will be closed to you. Were you tenfold more guilty, I would still cling to and defend you against the world; for this I know—you have been more sinned against than sinning."

A quick, sharp sob broke from Catherine's lips; but heedless of it, the judge spoke on.

"I am rich, and when you are once more free, my wealth shall ensure you against poverty—against the trials and temptations which have hitherto beset you; shall prove a barrier between you and the world's scorn. Perhaps, in some other land, you will redeem the past, and win an honourable renown, that will cover the blot upon our fair name."

There was deep affection and pathos in his tones, and he still caressed the handsome face turned so eagerly upon him.

"Father," said Paul, "were I guilty of this crime, your kind words would crush me with remorse and sorrow—would leave me no alternative but to confess my misdeed, and crave your forgiveness."

"And it should be accorded willingly," he replied. "You have nothing to fear from my anger."

"But this I cannot do," continued Paul. "How can I, when I am innocent? You have spoken to me of your wealth—have promised to share it with me. This I do not wish. Let me battle with my hard fate alone. But if, in the time to come, I return to you—having won for myself an honourable place in the world,—

will you not reward me by the only gift I prize from you next to your love—your confidence? Will you not say, 'My son, I am proud of you—I believe you were falsely accused of crime?'"

"It cannot be," said his father. "You do not know the world. It will not suffer you to rise again—it will crush you remorselessly. Paul, you must not go forth into it friendless."

"Not friendless," he replied. "I have still one who clings to me—believing me not guilty —loving me with a changeless affection."

He pointed to where Catherine sat, in the darkest corner of the cell, weeping.

"My mother!" he said, gently.

She sprang forward, and knelt beside him.

"You will not cast me from you?" she said, as she clung to his hands.

The judge's face darkened.

"So, woman," he said, "you have come to look upon your work?"

"I have come," she said, "to comfort my child in his misfortune. Oh, William, why are you so pitiless? I have never wronged you. From the first, I have been your true and faithful wife—thinking of you only with love —sorrowing that I ever listened to the promptings of my jealous nature, and left you! You blame me that I took my baby with me. I could not leave him. You forget I am his *mother*, or you do not know what a mother's love for her child is."

"Had *I* no heart to be broken by his loss?" said her husband, sternly. "Oh, woman! your selfish act—your unwifely conduct—has wrought grievous mischief."

"William, have mercy! My whole life since has been one long punishment for my error. Husband, forgive me!"

"I have answered you once, many years ago, when you pleaded for my pardon," he said. "I will forgive you all the sorrow and dishonour you have brought upon me, when you can bring my son to me as free from disgrace and crime as he was when you stole him away."

He smiled bitterly, and drew farther from her.

"Courage, mother!" said Paul. "Have patience and hope. Providence never deserts the innocent, though it may often try them sorely. Be brave; the day may—it *must* come, when even those hard conditions will be fulfilled; when my fame will be cleared, and your husband take you to his heart again."

Even the judge was touched by his earnestness.

"I pray heaven it may!" he said, solemnly.

"Until then, mother, I will be your comforter and helper," said Paul; "and the one beam of hope, which will cheer us on in our toils, shall be the prospect of the thorough reunion of our long-broken family circle. Father," he continued, passing his arms over the judge's shoulders, "you will not say nay to this? Remember, she is but a weak woman pitted against the world. Let me be her shield, remembering that all our hopes and love are turned towards you."

"You forget," he answered. "You are not free. What can you do, shut up in a prison? Be content, and trust her to me; I will settle a yearly sum of money upon her, sufficient to keep her from want."

"Nay, William!" said Catherine, proudly. "I do not need it. I cannot accept from your charity what your love denies me. But if you ever loved me——"

"If I *ever* loved you," he repeated. "You know I did, so deeply, so truly, that seeing you now, hearing you speak, I am tempted to forget all the bitter past, and take you back again. But our boy—this prison—his disgrace, comes ever between us, and thrusts you away."

"You love me!" said Catherine. "Now I am indeed brave! Let us be, husband—let us work our own way from the darkness of suspicion and imputed crime, into the bright day, when all the world will look upon us and our own innocence. Then—then you will not forget your promise. You will take me back again —you will say, 'Catherine, I forgive you!'"

He bent forward, and placed his hand upon her head.

"Catherine——" he began, when, after tapping softly, the gaoler entered.

Catherine arose. Her husband's face once more grew stern and calm.

"Your pardon, sir," said the man, "but a messenger has arrived from the court, where your presence is desired, on important business."

"I will come immediately," he replied. "Paul, I shall be with you again to-day. Madam, I shall not forget my promise."

He clasped Paul's hands warmly, and hurried away, and the mother and son were once more left alone."

"Patience and hope!" whispered Paul to the weeping woman. "After darkness, comes the dawn."

CHAPTER XXXVIII.

It was the day before Paul's removal to Portland, to work out his sentence in the hulks.

He was thinking sadly of the past—of his early life—his struggles—his hopes—his disappointed love and ambition.

"And this," he said, "ends it all. A prison—a convict's fate—life to be commenced again, with the brand of thief fixed upon me."

He bent his head despairingly. It was so hard to keep hope alive in that gloomy cell.

The turnkey entered, bringing his mid-day meal.

"Don't be down-hearted,' he said, consolingly. "I have no doubt you will have a few privileges down yonder as will make your berth easier; and may get a ticket of leave into the bargain, which will shorten your term. Hope for the best; you ain't the first gentleman's son who has been in a scrape; and in a few years, people will forget it, and say it was only sowing your wild oats. Any way, fretting won't mend the matter."

He emptied his basket while he was speaking, and spread its contents on the table.

"You've many advantages," he pursued, consolingly; "your friends are determined you shall not starve. There's a dinner fit for a king, and a bottle of wine as does you good only to look at it. If that isn't enough to raise your spirits, here's something I've kept till the last!"

He held out a small bunch of violets and moss-roses.

Paul took them, and looked at them wonderingly.

"The young lady who brought them is waiting along with the stout gentleman who has been here before to see you," continued the turnkey, somewhat slyly. "And a pretty young lady she is, asking your pardon for being so bold as to mention it."

Paul flushed, then turned pale.

"May I admit them?" said the man, evidently enjoying the effect his communication had created.

Paul bowed his head; and the goaler hastened away, presently returning with Mr. Morrison and Rachel.

"Well, my boy!" said the kindly manager. "You see, I have not forgotten you."

He looked round the place with a dissatisfied glance.

"Every time I come, I grow more certain you never deserved a lodging in this hole!" he said. "Not all the evidence, all the verdicts in the world, could make me believe that a boy who would give up the thing he most desired, and part with his only companion that he might trudge back to London to pay a debt of five shillings which he might easily have avoided, would, when he came to be a man, commit a cowardly theft upon an old fellow like Levi Nathans. Nothing, I say, would make me believe it, or that one who was so kind and gentle to a friendless little girl could do such a cruel and brutal act as fire a house, endangering the lives of a number of his fellow-creatures. And I'm not the only one who is of the same opinion. Here's Rachel, come to tell you the same thing. She would have been here with me before this, but, as I have told you, the silly little thing made herself quite ill, and has not even been able to act. There! come forward, child, and speak for yourself."

He drew Rachel towards Paul as he spoke, and, turning away, took up a book which lay on the table, and busied himself with it.

For a moment, Rachel stood irresolute, then she held out her hands to Paul.

Paul took them, and pressed them to his lips.

"Ray—little Ray!" he said, gazing down on her fair face with the first look of joy which had crossed him during that dreary day.

"Paul," she cried, flinging herself into his arms, with a passionate burst of tears, "can you ever forgive me?"

"Forgive you?" he answered. "That is impossible, since I was never angry with you."

"I hate myself when I think of the past," she continued,—"of the paltry pride which made me ashamed to think of my childhood—which made me dread the thought of meeting with any who had known me—even you, who had been so kind and good to me!"

Morrison looked over the top of his book with a satisfied smile; then again became deeply absorbed in its contents, which must have proved highly interesting, for the smile deepened on his face, and he chuckled audibly.

"Since—since the time you were accused of this dreadful crime," she continued, "I have thought of you with pity—with sorrow; and I longed to comfort you, for never did I believe that one who had proved himself so noble and brave could stoop to such wickedness."

"Bless you, Rachel!" he whispered, looking down fondly upon her. "Neither am I guilty, though the proofs are so strong that even my father condemns me."

"Then he knows nothing of human nature!" muttered Morrison.

"When I discovered in the court that you were Paul—my childish protector and friend—I hated myself more than ever for my scornful unkindness—the ungrateful return I made when you saved my life."

"Do not speak of those things," said Paul, soothingly. "They are past for ever."

"I have no longer any pride in my heart," she said; "nothing but gratitude for your goodness." She was silent for a moment, then spoke on—"Paul, once you said you loved me. If that affection has not died away, if you still care for me, I am here to-day to offer to become your wife."

"Brave little girl!" quoth Morrison, over the top of his book.

"Rachel," said Paul, his voice trembling with surprise and agitation, "you must not tempt me thus. I love you—have loved you my whole life long—but that very love forbids me to drag you down to my level. You forget —I am a felon—a convict!"

"I remember only that you are in sorrow," she said; "that—that——Oh, Paul, I love you! Do not refuse to let me comfort you."

She nestled her head upon his shoulder, and looked timidly into his face.

"Let us be once more, as we were in our childhood," she urged—"everything to each other—making our own happiness, in spite of the world."

"Sir," he said, turning to Mr. Morrison, "take her away! I dare not listen to her pleading! I dare not trust my own heart!"

Morrison put down his book.

"Rachel and myself have talked it all over before we came here," he said. "We both have faith in your innocence, and believe you to be suffering for another person's crime. You will bear your trial none the less bravely for knowing that at the end you will not be left lonely,—that there is a true woman willing to become your wife."

"You will not put me from you?" she pleaded. "You will let me atone for my folly?"

"Rachel, think what you ask of me!" he said.

"To be your wife!" she answered. "To ensure my happiness! Trust me, I shall find it nowhere but with you!"

Paul bent down, and drew her fervently to his heart.

Morrison took up the book, and again became absorbed in its pages.

Truly Paul had spoken when he said, "After the darkness comes the dawn!"

CHAPTER XXXIX.

AT Portland.

Chained down to a dreary round of labour—a wearying, monotonous existence.

What wonder was it that Paul grew depressed and gloomy, while his brawny frame shrunk, and his face assumed a sallow hue?

It was hard to be shut out from the world—from the free air—to toil at uncongenial tasks, dreaming all the while of the green fields, the waving trees, sunlit streams, and the thousand beauties of nature, for which he longed, which had been his inspiration for years, knowing that for seven long years the stone walls of the prison would hold him back from enjoying them.

He chafed under the restraint—under the vile companionship into which he had been thrust—the jeers with which the convicts hailed into their society the gentleman's son, the child of a lawyer in the land.

Harder than all to bear were the sneers and gibes of Jacob Prew, and his associate, Ned the cripple.

"Met again, Paul!" was the daily greeting of the miscreants; while Jacob would congratulate him on the discovery of his parents, and beg him to remember his old friends when he should come into the possession of his fortune.

He began to sicken, and not even the thought of Rachel, of his mother, of the kind hearts turned ever towards him, could comfort him in his exile.

At last came a day when the faces of the keepers grew grave, and even the convicts wore a more subdued expression.

Day after day, one after another were missed from the ranks, and the whisper began to circulate among them that fever had broken out in the prison.

For the first time, Paul's face lighted up with a gleam of interest, and without hesitation he proffered his services as a nurse to the plague-stricken patients, from whose tainted breath the bravest shrank in terror.

But, undaunted by danger, he went on with his work of charity, until, through the length and breadth of the country, the story went forth, and covered the name of Paul the vagabond, the convict, with honour.

* * * * * *

RACHEL CONSOLES PAUL. (See page 52.)

"Water—water! For the love of heaven, bring me water!"

It was night, and Paul was softly crossing the ward, to reach a patient at the other end, when he was arrested by the cry.

He turned.

Stretched on a pallet beside where he stood, was Ned the cripple, tossing and writhing in the agonies of approaching fever.

"Water!" he again cried, fixing his eyes imploringly on the young man. "You won't bear me any malice now, Paul? Bring me drink—I am parched with thirst."

Paul filled a cup with lemonade, and held it to the sick man's lips.

He drained it eagerly.

"You're one of the right sort, arter all," he said, thankfully, "and won't revenge yourself on me, now I'm lying here, sick and helpless? Say you won't."

"Rest easy," said Paul. "I will forget the past, or try to look upon you as an old friend whom it behoves me to be kind to. Now sleep."

He bent down and shook the pillow, placing it more easily under Ned's head; then, having performed his duty to the patient at the other end of the ward, returned, and seated himself by his side.

All night long he watched unweariedly, and all the while Ned grew worse, and tossed restlessly on the bed.

Soon he began to mutter; then the muttering changed to incoherent raving; and before morning the fever was on him in all its strength.

Day after day Paul ministered to the suffering man, mindful only of his helpless condition, thinking nothing of the evil he had endured at his hands.

Day after day, night after night, until Ned began slowly to recover, to look round him, with the light of reason in his eyes.

"So, Paul," he said, one day, as the youth stood by his bedside, "you've been an' done for me what not a soul in the world would have done. You've nursed me like a mother through this 'ere fever. You're a plucky one, you are, and must have a good heart to do so much for me."

"I only perform my duty," answered Paul; "it is not worth talking about."

"So you may say," replied Ned; "but if it ain't much to you, it's a great thing for me. I believe you've saved my life, when not one of my old mates, not even Jacob Prew, has once sent a message or token to show that they care whether I am dead or alive. It would have been as easy for one of them, as it is for you, to be a nurse here, if it were only for the sake of helping an old friend; but the cowards were all afraid of catching the fever, I suppose."

Paul bent over him, trying to stay his vehement speech, but, without heeding him, the cripple went on.

"I am only a poor, weak creature, but I've been of more use to *them* than the strongest man among them. It was my brains, my headpiece, that hatched all their best plans, that led them on safely for so many years; but they have no gratitoode, Paul — no gratitoode."

"How could you expect it from such vile companions?" said Paul. "They care only for themselves."

"You're about right there," said Ned; "I oughtn't to have expected it; and yet it hurts me, somehow, now it has not come."

He spoke in a sad tone, and Paul looked down on his wasted face pityingly.

"You've known me only as a real bad one," he continued; "ready for anything which would bring me in money, no matter much what it was. But it ain't much to be wondered at, considering what my life has been. I've been a cripple ever since I can remember, and was laughed and jeered at, until I began to hate everybody as was strong, and healthy, and straight-limbed."

"Poor fellow!" murmured Paul.

Ned looked up gratefully.

"There was only one in the whole world who spoke kind to me; that was my mother. She loved me, though I was such a misshapen, ugly fellow."

His voice was low and tremulous, and a mist, which looked like tears, had gathered over his eyes.

"Poor woman! she was not over good, and not much of a lady in her ways, but we'll let that pass; she has been dead this many a year, and since then I've never had a friend."

"It was hard to bear," said Paul.

"I fell in love once," continued Ned, "and I really thought the lass had overlooked me ugliness, and felt kindly for me. But when I'd spent all the money I had upon her, she married somebody else, and laughed at me for being such a fool as to fancy she could love me. Since then, I grew to care for no one; I mated with bad characters, worse than I ever had before, and I helped them in all their lawbreaking work; but I never made a friend among them, never felt a soft feeling in my heart towards one of my fellow-creatures, until now."

He paused, smiled at Paul, and spoke on.

"I've not behaved in the most friendly way to you, not even when you was thrown into my hands, a poor little persecuted chap, who had never harmed any one. I've not bin very considerate in this place, but you've done me a good turn; you've risked catching the fever to nurse me, and you've been as gentle as my own mother would have been, when you might easily have paid me for all I ever did to you. You've been kind, I say, and you shall find out I can be grateful, though I'm afraid what I've got to say won't do you much good now."

"What do you mean?" said Paul, in surprise.

"I means all as I am going to say," responded Ned. "It will be no news to tell you that Jacob Prew and myself knowed as you were Judge Vincent's son, years and years ago."

"None," replied Paul.

"But it may be to hear that the whole circumstance of your being separated from your mother, and put into my mate's hands, was the work of an enemy of your parents?"

Paul bent down eagerly.

"I see, you never suspected that," continued Ned.

"I have," said Paul. "Speak on, for mercy's sake!"

"That enemy was no other than a lawyer chap in London, and his name is——"

"Beverley Bogg," interrupted the youth.

"Right you are," said Ned. "The way I came to know it is this. Jacob Prew and I were mates; and when he brought you to my place, the night after he had found you, when he came back on his ticket of leave, more than ten years ago, he told me the whole story of how he had come by you."

"I wonder you never tried to sell the secret," said Paul.

"Honour among thieves, lad," replied Ned. "I promised him I'd never tell the matter. Besides, if I had, he would have been revenged on me; and what can a poor cripple do against a man like him? He might have killed me in his spite; but times is altered now he's safe in the hulks, and I'll break my word out of gratitude to you."

"Speak on, then," said Paul, impatiently.

"Well, the long and short of it is this," continued Ned. "It were about twenty year ago that this here Mister Bogg, who had defended my mate on a charge of robbery, and got him off scot free, engaged him to take the care of a child, for so much money down, and so much a year after so long as the youngster remained with him—one part of the agreement being that it should be treated as rough as my mate liked, and be brought up as a thief."

Paul clenched his fists angrily.

"You may well do that," said Ned, "for that child was your own self. The lawyer owed your father a grudge, and he got your mother to run away from him, and take you with her. The poor thing hadn't much money, or she was robbed—one of the two; for when, soon after, she was took with a fever, there was nothing for her maintenance, and she was sent to an hospital, and her baby put in the union, for nobody knew who she was. It was arranged that Jacob should go to the workhouse and fetch you, which he did, the lawyer giving him false recommendations as an honest man. He got you, by paying a small sum of money; for the guardians, not believing you would ever be claimed again, gave you up, on condition he left an address, where your mother might have you, if she wished it, when she got well. But, in course, that address was all moonshine—for Jacob, he made clear off with you, and there was no finding you, or him either, though she tried it on desperate enough, poor thing! Now, that's the story of how you came to be with Jacob."

"Does my father know of this?" inquired Paul.

"Not he! It's my opinion, he thinks Mister Bogg his very best and truest friend. A day or so after the affair for which you were sent here, the lawyer comes down to this place, disguised, with an order to see Jacob, and the two makes up a story which was told Judge Vincent—a story which hadn't half-a-dozen words of truth in it; and for making the false confession, my mate is promised a ticket of leave and money. So, Paul, the sooner the judge knows the truth, the better; for he's makin' a friend of a man as is only trying to do him all the harm he can; warming a viper in his bosom, as is ready to sting him in return for his kindness."

"And *this* is truth?" said Paul.

"It's just what Jacob told me, and what I'd never have repeated if he'd behaved friendly to me now, or if you hadn't saved my life, and made me anxious to do you a kindness in return. What's more, I believe this affair for which you were condemned only another plot of the lawyer to see you where he always wished to—in a prison. Nothing could persuade me you were ever guilty of theft. I have known you too well for that."

"You are right, Ned," said Paul, thoughtfully; "and if what you have told me now will help me to prove my innocence of the crime which is laid against me, you shall see that I am not ungrateful."

"At any rate, I've showed you I am not," said Ned. "And if you please to fetch witnesses here, you shall have my story in black and white. It may be better for you in the end."

An hour later, the chaplain and governor of the gaol had attested this new and strange version of Paul's history, a copy of which was straightway despatched to Judge Vincent.

CHAPTER XL.

IT was some time after the trial and conviction of Paul that Levi Nathans sat alone in his room, his feet upon the fender, his eyes fixed upon the empty fireplace, with its grim, dead, black bars.

"Ay, ay!" he muttered. "Empty and chill, like my life, from which all warmth and comfort have fled, even as last winter's fires have died away from here! It is worse than it was before *he* came, for then I was content; but now I am for ever regretting the merry times we had over the books and pipes. They were merry times—merry times!"

He sat a little longer, whispering to himself, needless of the golden bright sunshine, which filled the room, and sighing heavily when, at times, he raised his head, and glanced to where, over the doorway, the marks of the fire still lingered.

At length he became restless, and, rising from his seat, walked slowly from the room, and entered first that of Paul, where he stood a moment, looking about him; then, brushing the rising tears from his eyes, leant more heavily on his old stick, and passed out along the little space of landing, and into the room which had been occupied by old Jasper Davis, Levi's asthmatic lodger.

Here, as in his own chamber, the traces of the recent fire remained in the charred woodwork and blackened ceiling of the apartment, which were still unrepaired, and were so damaged as to render it impossible to re-let the apartment until the mischief had been remedied.

There had been but few attempts made to place the room in order, and this only served to make it look more desolate.

The bedding had been removed by the careful hand of Marah, and the empty bedstead stood in the centre of the floor, looking like the gaunt skeleton of departed comfort.

The carpet had likewise been taken away, and the litter which had been swept up from the boards had been thrust under the fireplace, and lay there in a melancholy heap.

Levi sat in an old wooden chair, the only one remaining in the chamber, and once more fell into musing.

Perhaps the deserted-looking place suited his temperament, for he lost his restlessness, and, drooping his chin upon his breast, seemed to forget himself and all around him.

He did not even hear the patter of Marah's feet on the stairs, or that she went to his own room, from whence, meeting no answer to her summons, she turned away, and came directly to the door of the one where he was seated.

Her sharp little rap failed to rouse him, and he started nervously as, pushing open the door, she put her head through the aperture and called him by name.

"Well, well, Marah—what now?" he asked.

"I knew I should find you here," she said. "You always make this your sitting-room now, though why I cannot tell."

"What do you want?" again queried Levi, who seemed impatient at her appearance.

"Yes; speak to me as though I were a dog!" growled Marah. "Is it my fault Paul Vincent abused your kindness, and robbed you? Is it my fault he wished to burn you in your bed? If you had made less of a stranger, and more of those who have been faithful to you for years, this would not have happened."

"Be silent, Marah," said Levi, angrily. "The loss is *my own*. What reason or right have *you* to complain? One would imagine you were jealous of the unhappy boy!"

"That's right, Levi," she retorted. "You had better bid me leave your house at once; it is plain you have wearied of me and my services."

He smiled.

"You have been very faithful, Marah," he replied "and I do not forget it; but I cannot also forget that it was your testimony which fixed the guilt of this robbery and fire upon that poor boy. It angers me; for you need not have given it—nobody asked you for it."

"No, no! Nobody asked—nobody thought Marah knew so much; and, as you say, it was my testimony which finally convicted him."

H

"And I loved him as though he were my own son," said Levi, fretfully. "Go away—go away! Why do you come here?"

"Why do I come here?" she repeated, shrilly. "A pretty plight you would be in, if I took you at your word, and went away. I came to tell you that the man you ordered to repair this room is below, and wants to know whether he shall begin to-morrow."

"Yes, to-morrow—to-morrow!" he replied. "Now go."

Marah closed the door and retreated, and her laugh might have been heard as she passed down the wide old staircase.

Levi was now thoroughly roused from his quietude, and, rising from his chair, went tottering about the room, examining the damages wrought by the fire, and, with a slight return of his shrewdness, calculating their cost.

He stood a moment looking at the heap of rubbish under the grate, then carelessly thrust his stick into it, and scattered it over the hearthstone.

There were pieces of newspaper, which looked as though food had been wrapped in them, and coiled round the end of his stick was a piece of faded narrow blue ribbon.

Levi uttered a cry, and pounced upon it, bearing it to the window.

"It is the same!" he said—"the very same piece she wore in her collar the day she accepted me for her husband!—the piece I have cherished so many years, and it was in the case with her jewels. How came it here?"

He placed the ribbon in his waistcoat pocket, and returning to the rubbish, searched it eagerly.

Putting on his spectacles, he examined every piece of paper, every stray shred of string, as though he expected in them to discover some trace of the missing gems.

At last, he arose from his knees, holding in his hand a torn and crumpled fragment of paper, and carrying it to the light, examined it carefully.

A look of perplexity crossed him as he did so, then cleared away, and with a brightening face he thumped and thumped his stick on the floor, saying, joyfully, "I have it!—I have it at last!"

It was the fragment of a tradesman's bill, the address in full of John James, hairdresser, wigmaker, and perfumer; and the next item of information—the only remaining one, in fact—was, "For making an iron-gray wig, one pound, eleven shillings, and sixpence."

The rest of the paper had been burnt, as though it had been used to light a candle or a pipe.

"There's enough left for me," said Levi, as he deposited the scrap of paper in his pocket-book.

One more careful search was vouchsafed to the rubbish heap and the room; but, finding no further reward for his labours, he took his departure, and shortly afterwards, to Marah's astonishment, left the house, his cheeks wearing such a glow as they had not since the night of the fire.

Proceeding to the Strand, he hailed a passing cab.

"Where to?" questioned the driver, looking curiously at the quaint figure beside his vehicle.

Levi read off the address on the bill-head, and was soon borne away in that direction as fast as the jaded hack could carry him.

It was a long drive, and in the course of it he passed through the busiest and most fashionable quarter of the metropolis, without once evincing sufficient curiosity concerning them to look through the window.

With his eyes fixed on his pocket-book, he remained lost in thought, while occasionally the words "Jasper Davis—iron-gray wig," broke from his lips in his musing.

In the course of an hour he arrived at his destination, a barber's shop, standing in an obscure street, over the door of which was painted, in red letters on a dingy black ground, the name "John James."

"You may wait," said Levi; and, springing from the cab with an alacrity which would not have done discredit to a more youthful man, he entered the shop.

It was a dark little den, capable of allowing one person to stand within it, before a miniature counter, not quite a yard in length, and another to wedge himself behind it, for the purpose of serving any customer for the two-penny and sixpenny jars of bears' grease, the false moustaches, back-combs, side-combs, and chignon pads, with which the window was filled.

Adjoining it was a larger room, from which the shop had been cut and separated by a thin wooden partition, wherein was affixed a solitary pane of glass, against which, as Levi entered at the street-door, the face of a man was flattened for an instant, and as instantly disappeared.

The next moment the owner of the face had opened a small door in the partition, and whisking himself through, stood opposite to

Levi, inquiring, in bland tones, what he required.

"If it's to be shaved," he added, "or your hair cut, why, go through the door beside you, and I'll attend to you directly."

"My business is of another nature," said Levi, "and strictly private. If you are John James, the master of this shop, I must request the privilege of speaking with you alone."

"Walk in—walk in!" said the barber, indicating the door he had just mentioned. "I've only one customer in there, and I shall have finished with him in a moment."

Levi obeyed, and found himself in the room, which had the appearance of half dressing, half sitting room, on a reduced and shabby scale.

In a chair, with a white cloth tied under his chin, enveloping him in its ample folds, sat a burly labouring man, from whose chin the barber seemed to have been mowing a stubbly beard of a week's growth when interrupted by his strange visitor.

The operation completed and paid for, the man departed, leaving John James at leisure to attend to Levi.

"Now, sir!" he said, as he employed himself in stropping the razor he had just used.

"You are a wig-maker, I believe?" commenced Levi.

"I am, sir," answered the barber. Then, imagining that he had divined the old man's reason for calling upon him, he added, "I make every quality and kind of wig. Now, if you want one, I can guarantee that it shall be of real human hair, of any colour and shape you please to select."

"Nonsense!" interrupted Levi. "Do I look like a man who would go about masquerading in dead people's hair? If you will only listen, I will tell you my errand."

The barber was silent, while Levi opened his pocket-book, and produced the fragment of the bill.

"Last July, you made an iron-gray wig?" he questioned.

"An iron-gray wig? Dear me—bless me!" ejaculated John James, making a violent effort to appear as though he had forgotten that particular one, or had difficulty in recognising it from Levi's description among the vast number of wigs he had manufactured since that period.

"Yes, sir," said Levi; "an iron-gray wig; you cannot have forgotten it—the price was one pound, eleven shillings, and sixpence. I have here your account."

John James peeped over Levi's shoulder at the paper, then seemed attacked by a sudden fit of recollection.

"Ah, yes! I remember now. The wig I made for——" He paused, then said, "Why do you question me?"

"Because—well, never mind; perhaps this will do as well as an answer," said Levi.

He drew from his purse half a sovereign, and held it out to the barber, adding, "Believe me, it is for no doubtful or unworthy purpose."

"I believe you, sir!" said the barber, pocketing the money. "Well, I remember making an iron-gray wig for a young gentleman, who came here and ordered it in July, giving no name, but paying a deposit of fifteen shillings when I measured him, and the rest of the money when he fetched the article away."

"Describe him," said Levi, eagerly.

"Let me see," said John James. "He was tall, and very broad in the shoulders."

"So must old Jasper Davis have been, if he had stood upright," murmured Levi.

"He had straight, dark hair, gray eyes, and rather a long face," continued the barber, "I remember; for I cut his hair, and cleanshaved him of moustache, beard, and whiskers, so that he might wear the false ones I supplied with the wig."

"Clean shaved?" repeated Levi.

"Yes; his face was as smooth as a boy's of sixteen, when he left this shop, carrying away his purchases."

"Clean shaved," again muttered Levi. "And Paul had as luxuriant whiskers and moustache as one would wish to see. Oh, I begin to understand now!"

"He was rather a swell," continued the barber. "I fancied he must have been connected with one of the theatres. You see, my customers for such things are mostly in that line; they come to me, because they are recommended by some of the actors, who know me, partly that, and because I am low in my charges; but I make few wigs now-a-days, sir; they are beginning to forget old John James."

"And you can give me no other clue?" enquired Levi, anxiously.

"None!" said the barber. "I'd advise you to follow up the one you have at the theatres. He was not over good-looking, but he wore a diamond ring on his forefinger—a twisted snake, with a brilliant set in its head."

"Could you identify him, if you met him?" asked Levi.

"I flatter myself I could," said the barber; "I have a capital memory for faces."

"And you will give your assistance if it is wanted for that purpose?" asked Levi. "You will not by lose it, if by your aid I track that man."

The barber felt the half-sovereign in his pocket, and cheerfully promised his aid; and Levi, full of hopeful excitement, hurried to his cab.

"To the Strand," he said to the driver; then throwing himself back, began to review the information he had received from John James, the wig-maker.

It was not quite two o'clock when he alighted in the Strand. He was not far from the theatre where Paul had been formerly engaged, and resolved to call upon Mr. Morrison, and seek his advice on how he should act under this new aspect of affairs.

Hoping to find him at business, the old man trudged on to the theatre, which he was fortunate enough to reach during a rehearsal, at which the manager was present.

Being known to the porter, he obtained ready admittance to the stage; and being observed by Mr. Morrison, was soon engaged in laying before the worthy man, in his own private room, the strange facts which had come before him during the course of the day.

Long and serious was the conference between them. When it was concluded, both Morrison and Levi arose with brighter faces than they had worn since Paul had been sentenced.

"Our first care must be to find Jasper Davis," said Mr. Morrison, as Levi drew on his gloves, and prepared to go. "As the wig-maker suggested, it will not be a bad plan to commence with the theatres; the rogue must know some of the trickery of the profession, to make up as he did. Suppose you were to fetch this John James, and bring him behind the scenes during the course of the first piece, and remain here until the close of the evening. If we look for him in the profession, it will be better to commence in my own theatre."

CHAPTER XLI.

It was late that night before Levi returned to the theatre with the wig-maker. The first piece, a drama, in which Rachel played the chief character, had just ended; and the stage was being cleared for the second part of the evening's entertainment. As the pair entered, they were met by Mr. Morrison, who forthwith conducted them to a quiet corner, where they would have an opportunity of observing not only all that passed on the stage, but also all who went to and from the stage-door.

"You are late," he said; "but none of the company have left as yet, so that you will have a fair chance of finding your man, if he is here."

"I should know him again in a moment," said the barber, who was inspired with zeal by the promise of liberal payment for his trouble, and a reward if he could discover and identify the purchaser of the wig. "If he is anywhere on these premises, he won't escape John James."

So saying, he relapsed into silence, and assuming an intellectual and mysterious air, betook himself to a stern and close scrutiny of every individual who chanced to come into their vicinity.

The place where they stood was a little awkward nook, thrown much into the shadow by two huge side-scenes, which shut them in on either side, and screened from the glare of the gas-lights by the interposition of an arbour, through the lattice-work of which they could peep at the persons on the stage unobserved. Presently, the bustle of the scene-shifters subsided, and the actors began to assemble, and prepare themselves for the second rising of the curtain.

The barber looked at them eagerly.

Levi waited breathlessly for him to speak.

"Not there!" said the man. "There's not one of the whole batch tall or muscular enough for my customer."

The play went on, and John James's face lengthened as he watched fruitlessly.

"I begin to think we are in the wrong shop," he whispered to Levi. "Suppose we step round, and speak to the manager? He can tell us whether it is of any use to wait longer."

As they turned to leave their place, the rustling of a silk robe sounded near them, as the wearer placed herself in another nook, next to the one where they stood.

The next moment, the sound of a heavier footstep was heard to enter it, followed by the deep tones of a man's voice.

The barber placed his finger on his lip, and stood still; while Levi leaned against the other screen, every line in his wrinkled face expressive of disappointment.

"You are cruel," said the man in the recess beyond. "How have I angered you, Rachel? —what have I done to make you shun me as you do?"

"You are mistaken," she replied. "I am not angry, neither do I shun you. I am merely indifferent to your presence."

John James turned, and winked knowingly at his companion; then betook himself to his task of listening once more.

"You will drive me mad!" said the man, passionately. "I spare no pains to please you, and yet you will not give me a smile or a kind word. You reject every token of my friendship or goodwill."

"If you allude to the presents you have offered me," she said, "I tell you, as I have before, that you are not treated more cruelly than others. I never accept gifts from strangers or mere acquaintances."

"Rachel, listen to me," said her companion. "I love you—love you devotedly! Let that love plead for me. Let it teach you to regard me as something more than a mere acquaintance—even more than a friend."

"You forget we are in a public place!" she replied, in an angry tone. "Stand aside, if you please, sir, and let me pass, before you have attracted the attention of the whole company!"

"I will not!" he replied. "We are screened from notice, as you see. I would have my answer to-night, even were the eyes of the whole audience in the theatre fixed upon us. I tell you, Rachel, I love you! I ask you to give me a place in your heart!"

"And I answer, that I have none to give," said Rachel, proudly. "That I have no right to listen to such words as you have just spoken but from the lips of one man in all the wide world—the man I have promised to marry."

"Promised to marry! Who?" said her companion, sternly.

There was silence for a moment, then she spoke out clearly,

"Paul Vincent."

"A convict—a thief!" he sneered. "A pretty match, truly! You had better think twice before you refuse an honourable man for such an outcast. I am rich. You shall hold your place with the highest in the land if you will be my wife. See, Rachel; here is a chain I bought for you. Let me place it on your neck, and tell me you will wear it as a gift from your future husband."

His voice had risen in his excitement; but the orchestra was playing, and a burst of applause from the audience had greeted a song from a favourite actor, so that it passed unnoticed.

"I want neither your jewels or your friendship," said Rachel, still answering in a subdued tone. "I have no love but for him you have unjustly called a thief."

There was another thunder of applause as the scene-drop fell; and groups of ballet-girls, in fairy costumes, came running upon the stage, filling every entrance, talking in whispers, and peering everywhere about them, so that the little love-scene between the wings ended, and the voices ceased.

Mr. Morrison, released for a time from his managerial duties, came to Levi in his lurking-place.

"Well?" he said, briefly.

"No success to-night," answered Levi. "But I'll not give over. I'll haunt every theatre in its turn—I'll search all London, no matter how weary the toil may be. I shall know no rest until I have shown the world that my poor boy is innocent."

"Good night, Rachel! In spite of your cruelty, I will not give up all hope."

It was the man who had been standing on the other side of the screen who spoke.

The next moment he had emerged from his place, and in doing so, caught sight of the three men standing in the shadowy nook.

He came towards them unhesitatingly, speaking cordially to Mr. Morrison.

It was Richard Bogg.

"You are leaving us early to-night," said the manager. "Are you not going to stay out the ballet?"

"No. The fact is, I promised the governor I would be home early, and the old man is apt to cut up rather roughly if I disappoint him," he replied, with an insolent laugh.

A couple of scene-shifters removed the mimic arbour, and let the light into the dark little corner.

"Good night, Mr. Morrison; I'm off," said Richard, turning to leave the place.

He was confronted by John James.

"One word, sir," said the man, his face radiant with satisfaction.

"Well, fellow, and what do you want?" queried Richard.

"Perhaps you've not a good memory for faces," answered the man, who was nettled by his manner. "I have; and that makes a difference between us, you see. I am John James, hair-dresser, perfumer, and wig-maker."

A sickly pallor spread over Richard Bogg's face.

Levi and Morrison looked on in silent attention.

"And suppose you are John James, barber, what is that to me?" said the lawyer's son, drawing himself up haughtily, and looking his detainer full in the face.

"Perhaps not much," he answered. "I only wished to ask whether the iron-gray wig, beard, and whiskers I made for you in July, gave satisfaction?"

Still whiter grew the young man's face, but raising his head, he glared defiantly at the speaker.

"You mistake, my good man," he said; "I have never worn a wig in all my life, therefore I could not have employed you to make one for me. I am a private gentleman, as Mr. Morrison will explain to you, and have nothing whatever to do with theatrical matters."

"That may be, sir," said John James; "but I've a good memory for faces; and in spite of all you have said, I must maintain that you are the person for whom I made a gray wig last July, with whiskers and beard to correspond."

"And I tell you that you lie!" said Richard Bogg, losing his self-control.

The barber appealed to Levi.

"Did I not describe him before we came here?" he said. "Look! there is the very ring on his finger, of which I told you—the twisted serpent, with a diamond on its head."

He pointed to Richard Bogg's left hand, on which the snake's head glittered like a spark of fire.

Morrison looked grave; Levi was surveying the form of the youth with keen eyes.

"This grows serious," said the manager. "Are you sure, John James, that you speak the truth—that you have made no mistake in the identity of this person? The gentleman before us is well connected, and has an ample fortune. Think again."

"There's no need to," answered the man. "I've not so many wigs to make as to forget my customers when I meet them again. I say that this is the gentleman for whom I manufactured the things I have described."

"Tall—so was he," said Levi, as though he were taking notes. "Broad-shouldered—so was he, though he stooped. Put the wig and the rest of the disguise on him, and we have the old man to the life."

He moved nearer to Richard Bogg, and peered into his face, with a sharp, inquisitive glance, which made him shudder.

"The same eyes, the same thin lips," he continued. "He baffled us in our search when we wanted him for a witness, but we have found him at last. This is my old lodger, Jasper Davis."

"Will you see me insulted in your own theatre, and make no effort in my behalf?" said the lawyer's son, to Morrison.

"I regret extremely," said the manager, "that such an event should happen here; but it is beyond my power to interfere in the matter."

"Then I will stay no longer," he said. "I have suffered sufficient abuse at the hands of these persons. Let them beware; I shall not pass this over without notice."

"Your pardon, sir," said Levi. "I am sorry to detain you against your will, but you cannot leave this place alone."

"What do you mean?" cried Richard Bogg, casting an anxious look around him.

"That on showing sufficient grounds for the same, I have, this afternoon, obtained a police warrant for the arrest of the person for whom John James made an iron-gray wig and beard in July; having reason to believe him to be Jasper Davis, my former lodger, and having still greater reason to think that Jasper Davis was the man who stole my money and jewels, and set fire to my house."

During this speech, two constables, in plain black dresses, had advanced, and placed themselves one on each side of Richard Bogg.

With a look of intense terror and rage, he endeavoured to elude them; but they laid their hands on his shoulders, and detained him.

"There's no help for it," said one of them. "You had better come quietly. If they have been mistaken, you can easily prove it. In the meantime, you will be wise not to attract more observation than necessary to yourself."

So, escorted by his unwelcome attendants, he left the theatre, followed by Levi and John James. And in her nook, on the other side of the scene, stood Rachel, her cheeks flushed, her eyes bright, her hands clasped, her whole expression beaming with hope.

"If, after all," she murmured, "Paul should be proved innocent!"

Then, leaning her head against the dusty, rough scene, she wept softly, heedless of the gay lights, the merry play, and the music that throbbed through the crowded house.

CHAPTER XLII.

It was on the evening of the same day that Judge Vincent sat in his library, engaged in a serious conference with his friend Bogg.

They were bending over a table strewn with papers, which the lawyer was reading aloud, adding his comments on their contents as he proceeded.

They were documents connected with the company for which he was manager, and they placed the speculation in the most glowing hues of success before the eyes of the world.

The judge listened gravely, giving his whole attention to the matter; and when Beverley's voice ceased, he leant his head on his hand, and, taking up a pen, began to make calculations on a strip of paper which lay before him.

The lawyer watched him anxiously, though he feigned to be deeply engaged in sorting the documents, and placing them in regular order, one upon the other.

At last, the judge laid down his pen.

"Suppose this scheme should not succeed?" he said.

"There is no fear of failure," answered Bogg. "I have invested in it myself to a greater extent than you would, perhaps, credit; and you know I am not a man to lightly risk my money."

"I know it," said the judge. "And you say that you have achieved the great bulk of your fortune by speculation?"

"Even so, William," answered the lawyer.

"It sometimes happens that people are unfortunate," continued the judge.

"Rarely, when they have a cautious and able adviser," said Bogg. "It is your visionary, inexperienced novice, who enters rashly and ignorantly into speculation, that loses."

"This is a great matter for me to decide," continued Judge Vincent. "If I risk my fortune, and lose it, Paul will be little better than a beggar."

"The alternative is a very simple one," said Beverley. "You are not compelled to embark in this affair. Heaven forbid that I should urge you to any act you might hereafter regret. Still, I may say, I, too, am a father, with an only child, whose future depends my success in life."

"True," said his listener, who was deeply touched by the tenderness which made Beverley's voice quiver, as he uttered the last part of his speech. "I might have known you would do nothing inimical to his interests."

"You might have known, too, that I should not advise you, my oldest and dearest friend," said the wily lawyer, "to do aught which would not be for your own advantage and the furtherance of your hopes and wishes. I again repeat, if any man had spirit enough to embark sufficient capital in this affair (say twenty thousand pounds), in less than three weeks' time he would be a millionaire. Who would think again of the dark spot in Paul's life if he were the son of such a man?"

"Say no more, Beverley!" cried the judge, who was carried away by his companion's argument. "I have decided. You shall have the money. I trust you without fear, as I have trusted you nearly my whole life long."

The lawyer's face flushed, and he bent over his papers, to hide his smile of exultation and mockery.

"Time will prove how true my friendship has been," he said, as he stretched his hand across the table. "Let us join hands, to the success of our new enterprise."

A rap came to the door, and a servant entered the room, bearing letters and papers, which he placed before the judge.

Conspicuous among them lay an official-looking document, with the postmark of Portsmouth.

The judge snatched it eagerly.

"It is from my poor boy," he said. "I pray heaven he may yet be in health. Ah, Beverley! even after all that has passed, I feel a thrill of pride when I think of what he is doing in his prison—of his loving self-sacrifice—of the brave heart which prompts him to risk life and strength by the bedsides of the poor fever-stricken convicts!"

He passed his hand across his eyes, and brushed away the rising tears.

"It is a noble act," murmured the lawyer.

"And comes from a noble nature. I have not lost all hope of redeeming my son," said the judge, as he tore open the envelope, and drew from it two papers.

"From the governor of the prison," he muttered. "Can it be ill-tidings of Paul?"

The lawyer watched him as he read.

A look of amazement was gathering in Judge Vincent's face as he laid down the first document and opened the second.

Beverley sat waiting breathlessly, for he knew not what, he only felt that some crisis was near.

An exclamation burst from the reader's lips.

His face was pale and set, and he clutched the paper with a fierce grasp.

"William, my friend, what is it?" said Beverley, in a husky whisper.

"Silence!" replied the judge, flashing one keen look upon the lawyer, then turning to the perusal of the writing.

"Certainly, William; I beg your pardon for the interruption," said Beverley, while a sensation of uneasiness fastened upon him. Then he subsided into silence, and resting his forehead on his hands, returned to watching the judge, as he fumbled amid the prospectuses and other documents relating to his bubble company.

"It cannot be; I will not believe that such baseness could exist."

It was the judge who spoke, as he finished his task.

"What do you mean?" again queried Beverley, striving in vain to look unconcerned. "Is it a new criminal case?"

"Yes, Beverley!" he replied. "A case where one man is accused of the foulest treachery, the deadliest of wrongs, towards another whom he called friend."

At once, the acute mind of the lawyer leaped to the conclusion that some portion of his double-dealing had been discovered.

It came upon him with the force of a blow, staggering him from his self-possession and coolness. He cowered beneath the judge's eye, and shifted uneasily in his seat, while a sallow hue spread over his cheeks, and a white circle gathered round his lips.

"I—I do not catch your meaning, William," he gasped.

"You shall have every chance to do so," replied his friend. "Listen to this."

In a slow, measured tone, he read through the paper he had last perused, ever and anon casting a glance of stern inquiry upon his listener.

But Beverley's face was shaded by his hands. As the judge finished, he dropped them, and looked up.

He had regained his composure.

"I understand this," he said. "Some enemy has invented a story to rob me of your esteem."

"Are you sure it is an invention?" questioned the judge.

"I see," he returned, forcing a sad smile to his pale lips, "I must plead before you as a prisoner would at the bar. And yet I might say you should know me too well to render it necessary."

He looked at the judge, and paused for a moment, then proceeded.

"I see it must be so. Think of our boyhood's days—of how we were friends even then—and let them plead for me! Remember how we have grown up into manhood, side by side, sharing each other's pleasures and sorrows! How I sympathised with you when you first loved, when you married the lady of your choice—how I rejoiced in your happiness as much as though it were my own!"

He again made a pause, suggestive of emotion, then took up the thread of his speech.

"And when trouble came, when the wife you loved and trusted proved untrue, who was so faithful, patient, and devoted as the man you deem guilty of the infamous plot unfolded in that letter? Think it over, William; think of how I stand for honour and honesty before the world; and let my past friendship, my honourable character, plead for me, that you absolve me from the suspicion of this crime!"

"You deny it, then?" asked the judge.

"I deny it," said Bogg. "Will you not believe me, or must I take an oath to prove my innocence?"

"Heaven help me!" said his friend. "I know not in whom or what to believe."

"A lady and gentleman desire to speak with you, sir," said the servant, once more making his appearance.

"I can see no one," said Judge Vincent.

The man bowed, and was about to retire. The refusal, however, was too late; for, as he turned to leave the room, he was gently thrust on one side, and the two persons, who had followed him up the stairs, entered.

They were Catherine Vincent and Beverley Bogg's former clerk, Simkins.

"You will excuse the liberty I have taken, sir," said the little man; "but our business is urgent, and will admit of no delay."

"Do not send me away," said Catherine. "We come to speak of my boy."

Simkins was ever rounder and rosier than he had been in times past, and had a well-to-do air about him which was pleasant to behold; but at the first glimpse of his beaming face, the lawyer gasped with terror and dismay.

"So," he said, "it is to him I owe this! Yet if you are wise, William, you will not listen to one word from that fellow's lips—a clerk whom I discharged from my service for his dishonourable practices, and who hatches a vile slander in revenge."

"I did use you somewhat ill," said Simkins, in a tone of mock apology. "In my early days, I was of a prying disposition, and I own to having listened at your keyhole. You detected me in this, and debarred me from the enjoyment of that pleasure. But I soon consoled myself, for I bored a hole through the wall, just a nice convenient

THE TABLES TURNED. (See page 57.)

height for me, as I sat on my stool before my desk. It was a clever piece of work, for it ended in a crack which ran along the surface inside the room; and the orifice on my side I fitted with a painted plug, which was not easily discernible to a careless observer."

"You see what a creditable person he is!" sneered the lawyer. "Will you trust him before your tried old friend?"

But Judge Vincent answered him never a word.

"I acknowledge it was scarcely fair," continued Simkins; "but that has nothing to do with the matter in hand. Well, for many a month I sat listening at my new-fashioned ear-trumpet when he supposed me to be hard at work, and many a little professional secret did I learn. I was listening the day you visited him, sir—one day, years ago—when you spoke of your sorrows, and begged him to help you find your boy. I listened, and I pitied you, though you did not know it, and I wished you success in your search."

And here the little clerk became redder than before, and blew his nose very hard before he went on with his revelation.

"The next thing I overheard was an interview between Mr. Bogg and a ticket-of-leave man, named Jacob Prew. Then I learned all the villany of the man I served. I learned how he had stolen your child, and given it over to that felon, to train up in sin and wickedness. I learnt how he was paying Jacob Prew for his service of evil; and I heard them decide that when Paul should become an accomplished rogue and vagabond—a felon in the eyes of the law—he should be restored to you. And all this, the man you called friend was plotting, in revenge for some injury you had unconsciously done him."

"It tallies, word for word, with the confession of the cripple," said the judge, in a stern voice. "Beverley, my faith in you is shaken."

"I am a father, sir!" cried Simkins, working himself up into a passion; "I was a father then; and I shed tears—yes, I positively shed tears—in his cold, hard office, dropped them on his dry, musty parchments, as I thought of poor little Paul, abandoned to the mercy of those wretches!"

He was flourishing his fists in Beverley's face, and was nearly purple with anger.

"I made up my mind to risk all the punishment he could inflict upon me, and to let you know the truth; and I called at your house to do so, but you were ill, and I could not see you. When you were better, I wrote a letter, and told you all the dreadful truth."

"A letter?" questioned the judge. "I received none."

"A good reason why!" shouted the irate Simkins; "he intercepted it! I wondered why I heard nothing from you; but when you had gone abroad he made the mystery clear, for he turned me out of my situation, after threatening me with his vengeance for what he called my treachery. I did not suffer so much, though—indeed, it turned out a very good thing for me; for, through the kindness of a gentleman who boards in my family, I obtained a post as clerk in a wine-merchant's warehouse; and, through industry and perseverance, have risen to be head book-keeper. My eldest boy is a junior clerk in the establishment, I have purchased our little cottage, and and I am a happy, contented, and prosperous man."

"What answer do you make to this?" said the judge, turning to Beverley Bogg.

"None," he said, sullenly. "I have told you from the first it is an untruth. It is a scheme of yonder traitor and your false wife."

"That I should ever have listened to his false tongue!" said Catherine. "William, yonder stands the man to whom we owe all our sorrow and separation."

"Another tissue of lies!" sneered Beverley. "I am curious to hear what she will invent."

"Before I married you, William," she said, heedless of the interruption, "he also professed to love me. I refused him, and became your wife; and he has never yet forgiven me for the act."

"Pretty, truly!" said the lawyer. "And pray how did you discover this?"

"I have just left Portsmouth, where I have been living near my child, and I knew of Ned the cripple's confession. The governor of the gaol read it to me. My woman's wit helped me to fathom the cause for your hatred. William, he parted us by his falsehoods," she continued, turning to her husband. "He made me believe you loved another woman. He even showed you to me holding her in your arms. I saw you kiss her as she wept upon your shoulder; and, mad with jealousy, I fled from your home, taking my baby with me. But, husband, I fled alone, save for my child's presence. I never was false to you, even in thought. I was poor; I laboured for my daily bread; and I lived a pure life—I swear it, before heaven!"

Judge Vincent listened with a softening expression as she passionately vindicated her faith and honour.

"There were times when I longed to return to you, to beg you to forgive, and take me back again; but, under the guise of friendly advice, he implored me to wait until my child was found, when he might plead for me. I believed in his protestations of brotherly interest, and I obeyed him. I waited for years, until hope and patience wore out, and I went out alone in the world to seek for Paul. I only found him in the criminal dock."

Beverley Bogg laughed slightly.

"I know what the world says of me," continued Catherine—"I know what you think of my flight; but I can give you every step of my life until now. Go where I have lived, and ask the people who knew me, and they will tell you that no shadow of shame rests upon me."

"I believe you," said the judge. "He made me think you false—poisoned my mind against you — slandered you to the world, the villain!"

Again the lawyer laughed a soft, mocking laugh.

"Tell me," said her husband, "when was it you saw me with this lady?"

"On the night of our last gala—the night I had from you."

"I see all now," he answered. "My poor Catherine, you had nothing to fear from her. She was my cousin, dear to me as a sister—nothing more."

Then, in brief terms, he told her the story of how Constance Clayton had visited him, to plead for her husband; of how he had saved him from the consequences of his folly and sin; and how, in her joy and gratitude, she had wept on his shoulder, as she had often done in the days of their childhood.

And all the while Catherine wept happy tears, while Simkins alternately cried, laughed, and flourished his fists at the detected lawyer.

"There's only one thing more to explain," he said. "I heard of Paul Vincent's trial, and came to the court, anxious to find out if he were the lost boy. There I saw this lady; and, when all was over, I took her to my home, and my wife comforted her, and we became friends. When she heard of this convict's story, and that it had been sent to you, she travelled to my place by express train, and we resolved to come to you. You see, we arrived just in the nick of time."

"And I called this man friend—I loved and trusted him!" said the judge. "Oh, Beverley, I would give all I possess to wake and find your treachery a dream!"

"Rave on," said the lawyer. "A deal of good it will do you. Call me what you will—vile, dishonourable, revengeful,—what do I care? From the beginning, I have been your enemy. You thwarted me in all I attempted; rose above me in wealth and fame; married the woman I loved, and I vowed to have my revenge for the injury. I have parted you two lovers through the bright days of youth—the best years of your lives. I made you distrust and shun each other, while your hearts ached at the separation. True, you have foiled me at last; you have proved each other innocent and true—you may even be reunited; but that will not recall the years wasted in agony and vain regrets."

"Never—never!" sobbed Catherine.

"One thing you cannot overcome. Your son—your heir—the pride of your house—is a convict—a felon; and *that*, too, is my doing. Remedy it—find a balm for the sting it inflicts in your hearts—if you can."

He turned, and, still laughing bitterly and mockingly, fled from the house.

The judge sank back on a couch, and hid his face in uncontrollable agitation.

For a moment there was silence, unbroken save by the muffled sobs of the husband and wife. Suddenly he felt a pair of soft lips pressed for a moment on his forehead, and. bending lower, he wept on.

The silence grew more oppressive.

He raised his head, and held out his arms.

"Catherine—my wife!"

There was no answer—the room was empty. The false friend, friendly stranger, and long-estranged wife,—all were gone.

He was alone; while on the floor, beside him, lay the confession of Ned the cripple.

CHAPTER XLIII.

"ALL lost!—all lost!"

Through the long, weary hours of the night the lawyer sat in his room, with fingers locked together in his agony of despair, rocking himself to and fro, and ever murmuring the words, "Lost—lost! all lost!"

His wife slept on in her chamber, without one thought of him, for theirs had been a marriage of interest, not of affection; and even the tie of parentage had failed to draw them closer to each other.

So she slept while the wretched man sat in

MARAH REVENGES HERSELF ON THE LAWYER. *(See page 100.)*

darkness, listening for his son's step on the stairs—listening vainly.

The night wore on—the darkness deepened, then began to disperse in the gray, sickly dawn of a rainy day.

The watcher had gradually become still.

He was plotting and planning a future for himself and his son.

As the light stole through the Venetian blind which shaded the window, he rose from his crouching attitude, and, moving softly about, hurriedly began to pack some linen and a few other necessaries into a small portmanteau.

Having strapped and locked it, he next opened a ponderous desk, and, taking from it several rolls of money, wrapped in stout paper, hid them about his person.

"This for immediate need!" he muttered, as he drew from a drawer a packet of papers—securities on a foreign bank, drawn up in a new name. And these he eyed with great satisfaction.

"They will never trace me!" he said. "Who will recognise in Mr. Henry Wilson, the London lawyer, Beverley Bogg?"

Having hidden the papers, he opened another drawer, and drew out a small casket, which, when opened, revealed a shining hoard of unset diamonds and precious stones.

"A fortune in itself!" he remarked, as he closed the case, and deposited it in a secret pocket. "If all else fails, these will save us from poverty—will keep us in ease and luxury. It was a lucky thought made me invest in this ware."

His preparations now seemed to be complete, for he buttoned his coat tightly over his treasures, and deliberately piling the remainder of the contents of his desk into the fireplace, lit a match, and dropped it into their midst.

The fire seized on them, and the flame went roaring up the chimney, while its reflection filled the room with a cheerful glow.

Beverley's spirits rose as he stood before it, catching the heat, and watching the red blaze.

He smiled, and stretched out his hands towards the bright hearth.

The flames leaped merrily up, then sank, flickering feebly.

They died away, and nothing remained in the grate but a pile of red ashes, which soon deadened into a crisp black heap, inexpressibly dreary to look upon.

The lawyer returned to his watching: drawing an easy chair to the window, he pulled up the blind, and sat looking out into the street.

A solitary policeman walked up and down, clattering his heavy boots on the pavement, as if for companionship. Once, a cab rattled by, bearing some reveller to his home, after a night of excess.

Save these, all was still.

Beverley's eyes grew heavy; his brain was weary with the strain put upon it during the day; his limbs ached, and became cramped.

He stretched himself out more easily.

"I am growing old," he muttered. "It's high time I retired from the cares of business. I wish Dick would come home."

He threw his head back against the velvet cushion of his chair, and, tired out, he slept.

His scanty gray hair straggled over the rich crimson of his resting place; his cruel mouth relaxed; the plotting brain was at rest; and Beverley Bogg, with all his sins upon him, slept as calmly as Hodge the labourer, who had no further crime upon his conscience than his weekly libation to Bacchus, at the village inn.

Deeper grew his slumbers, while the light brightened in his chamber, and the noises of the city grew louder in the streets.

A market cart, heavily laden, rumbled by.

He only smiled, and turning his head a little, spoke in his dreams.

"Dick, my dear boy!"

A man passed by to his daily toil, singing a merry song, with the whole strength of his lungs. He could not disturb the sleeper.

"How fast the ship flies!" he muttered. "How the waves rush from beneath us!"

Then again, as another sound came beating against the window panes, he whispered, with the old smile of tenderness curving his thin lips, "My boy—my dear, dear Dick!"

There was a hurried footstep on the stairs; some one tried the door.

It was locked.

The person seeking admittance rattled the lock noisily.

Beverley awoke.

He rubbed his eyes, and looked stupidly round him, as though he were trying to remember how he came to be lying there in the early morning.

His eyes fell upon the portmanteau, and recalled him to himself.

Again the door was rattled, and a pair of knuckles, applied to the panel, sounded a sharp rataplan.

"It's Dick at last!" said Beverley, springing up, and undoing the fastenings.

But it was not Dick who stood without. It

was a servant, with a scared, white face, and behind him stood a group of four persons. Levi Nathans, Mr. Morrison, old Marah, and a police officer.

CHAPTER XLIV.

WITHOUT waiting for an invitation, the police-officer and his companions entered the lawyer's apartment.

Beverley stood staring at them, with a terrified gaze.

"What does it mean?" he gasped.

Marah eagerly stepped forward, and stood before him.

"It means," she cried, while her eyes twinkled maliciously,—"it means *retribution!*"

The lawyer shrank from the crone, and looked appealingly at the others.

"Be quiet, woman," said the policeman. "Who gave you leave to speak?"

Marah laughed harshly.

"You will be glad enough to hear me by-and-by," she replied. "I can afford to wait my turn."

"We are come to speak of Paul Vincent," said Mr. Morrison. "His innocence of the crime for which he is now suffering is at last made apparent."

"How—how can that be?" said Beverley.

"The real culprit has been discovered," answered the manager. "He is now in prison."

"Do you hear?" said Marah. "He is now in prison, and Paul Vincent will be set free."

The old woman leered at him viciously.

Beverley's face had grown dark and lowering, and he compressed his lips until they looked like thin white cords, in his efforts to repress the storm of baffled hatred and impotent rage rising within him.

"And who *is* the guilty person?" he inquired, in his hard, metallic voice.

The little group looked at one another, three of them with pity in their eyes, the fourth with a smile of malignant expectation.

The constable saw it, and he grasped Marah by the shoulder, saying, in a low tone, "Be silent, woman, or I'll gag you."

"I'll be quiet enough," she replied. "I can wait my turn."

Then Levi spoke.

"He is my old lodger, Jasper Davis."

Then again the three looked at each other, holding a mute consultation with their eyes.

"Jasper Davis," said Marah, taking advantage of the pause,—"Jasper Davis, who was not Jasper Davis, or an old man, after all."

The policeman quieted her again.

"The old woman is right," he said, taking up the story where Marah had dropped it. "Jasper Davis was a young fellow in the disguise of an old man, who had entered the house as a lodger, with the express intention of committing the robbery."

The man stopped for a moment, as though to allow the lawyer to clearly comprehend the facts as they were laid before him.

He was listening with a wondering stare, but without the slightest inkling of the real truth.

"It was a cleverly planned affair," continued the officer. "The disguise was perfect in its way, for the young man had a slight knowledge of theatrical matters, and knew how to set about his work."

For the first time, the lawyer looked startled. Then he shook himself angrily, muttering, "It is impossible—impossible!" and once more listened intently.

"It was well carried out, as you know," said the constable. "The culprit got clear off with the booty, and Paul Vincent was taken in his stead. You know how cleverly he fixed the theft and arson upon the judge's son, so it won't be necessary to go over that again."

Beverley nodded, and bit his lips to moisten them.

"But like all criminals, he outwitted himself, or rather made a slip, which proved fatal to him. In opening the casket in his own room, he let fall from it unperceived a piece of blue ribbon, which Mr. Nathans kept there as a kind of keepsake—a remembrance of his dead wife. But that was not all: he had a bill for his wig, false beard, and whiskers; and instead of destroying it at once, he kept it about him, then carelessly twisted it up for a cigar light, and threw it, not quite destroyed, into the empty fire-place. He thought it would finish burning, but the flame went out, and enough remained to give the address of the wig-maker, and the clue to the disguise. The trail was followed up by Levi Nathans, and it ended in the detection and identification of the real criminal. His guilt is beyond any dispute, for the missing jewels were found stitched into a band, which he wore round his waist; and on searching his chambers last night we found there the portmanteau used by Jasper Davis, and in it was the whole of the disguise, also the leathern bag in which Mr. Nathans had kept the money of which he had been robbed!"

The officer ceased speaking, and Beverley

stood looking at him, not daring to ask the question which trembled on his lips.

At length he forced himself to speak "The real criminal. Who is he?"

Levi turned away.

"Heaven help you!" said Morrison. "He is—he is your own son."

"Retribution!" cried Marah. "'He that digged a pit for his neighbour, hath himself fallen into it.'"

Beverley made no reply. He was glaring stonily at the police officer.

"Now it is my turn," continued Marah. "Perhaps I, too, can throw a fresh light on the subject. I've been Levi's servant ever since I was a young woman; my mother served him before me. There was a time when I thought Levi would marry me—would put me in the place of his dead wife. I do not mind speaking of it now. I am an old woman, and my youth is so far back, it seems like talking about another person. I was disappointed in my hopes, and I was bitter enough over it at first, but it wore away as time passed on. I began to console myself with the thought that Levi would remember me when he died; that he would leave me his property, for he has no other relations. I saw him careful and saving, and I followed his example, for I thought all his money would be for me. I lived in the hope for years, and I reckoned on being almost a lady in my old age. But Paul Vincent came, and all was changed. He won Levi from me, and I grew jealous and envious, and took to spying at key-holes, and listening, and plotting to get him away."

Levi withdrew from her, and stood resting on Mr. Morrison's arm.

The police officer was making notes of what she said.

"One night I peeped through the key-hole of my master's room, and I saw him show Paul the money and the jewels, and tell him they should all belong to him some day. I was so angry, I could have killed them both, especially when they laughed at and spoke slightingly of me, as a crabbed old woman."

"And so you are, if ever one lived," remarked the policeman.

"I nursed my wrath, for I felt as though Levi were robbing me, in leaving his property to a stranger, and I dreamed of the money and the glittering jewels every night, until I was wretched."

"Don't wonder at it," murmured the policeman.

"I was wretched, but I was not *wicked*, as I am now, until I met with that man, Beverley Bogg. He came sneaking round the house, questioning me of Paul Vincent, and he came again and again, always in the dark night, and found out all my secret disappointment, and envy and hatred. He worked upon them, until I was ready to do anything for money and revenge."

"I'll believe that, too," said the policeman.

"At last he proposed to me to rob Levi, and told me how to act, so that Paul should be deemed the thief. He even gave me a key he had made to fit the chest—for I let him into your room one day, and he took off an impression of the lock.

"What's coming next, I wonder?" said the officer. "Well, this *is* a case, and no mistake about it!"

"He gave me money, and promised me more, if by my means Paul Vincent was sent to prison, and I promised to do his bidding, tempted by the money and the bitterness of my own nature. But while I waited my chance, old Jasper Davis came, and forestalled me. You all know how he did it. I felt mad to think how I had lost my chance, and I remembered how he had promised me a reward if I could help send Paul to prison. I made up my mind, and when the trial came on, I swore falsely that I had seen Paul Vincent set fire to the house."

"Perjury!" said the policeman, with a low whistle. "Old lady, you've got yourself into a scrape."

"*He* said it was perjury when he met me by appointment, to pay me the wages of my sin. He told me I should be imprisoned if I was not for ever silent concerning it. What do I care for punishment? I was silent, for I believed Paul Vincent to be the thief, and I was glad my false witness helped to convict him. But I've found out the truth now. He set his own son to rob Levi because he grudged me so much wealth, and he thought to satisfy me, to tie my tongue, by giving me a paltry hundred pounds out of the booty, which I suppose they shared. But I've disappointed him; I have my revenge, you see; and I have hidden the gold, so I shall have it when I am released from punishment."

"You're a knowing one," said the officer; "but you've made a mistake. The lawyer had nothing to do with his son robbing the house."

"My son did not do it," cried Beverley, fiercely. "It was yon old hag; she confesses to having contemplated the act. My boy is innocent! Oh, gentlemen, he *is* innocent!"

"He has confessed his guilt," said Morrison. "He told me the whole story of how he accomplished his design, without reservation."

Beverley threw up his hands with a despairing cry. "Why was I not near him?" he said. "He should not have spoken! Oh, fool! fool! he is lost! Why do you stand here? Let me go to my boy!"

"Yes we will *all* go," said Marah. "To think that his own son should have forestalled me!"

"You'll have to come for certain, old lady," said the constable. "I'd advise your master to look out for another housekeeper, for there's no knowing when you will get out again."

"We go on to Judge Vincent's," said Mr. Morrison; "and then to Portland, to see Paul."

"And we go to the prison!" said Marah. "It's *retribution*—'He who diggeth a pit for his neighbour, shall fall into it himself.'"

CHAPTER XLV.

IN the prison.

They stood face to face, the father and son.

"Oh, Dick! Dick! my poor boy!" said Beverley, as he stretched out his arms imploringly.

"Cease your whining, father," said the young man, sulkily, as he threw himself upon the only seat in the cell. "You have no one to blame for this but yourself."

"Spare me!" entreated the lawyer; "I have been loving and kind to you."

"You have been an evil spirit to me," answered his son. "What chance had I of growing up honest, pure, and good, with your hateful example before me, from my earliest days?"

The father clasped his hands imploringly, but without noticing the agony on his face, Richard went on.

"I saw you worldly, and hard of nature; grinding down the poor, oppressing your neighbours; grasping, lying, cheating; doing anything mean and dishonourable, that you might scrape up money."

"For you, Dick—for you!" murmured Beverley. "Spare me—spare me!"

"What wonder is it that I should grow up hard, worldly, selfish, unloving, unamiable, without one right principle to guide me in my course?" continued Richard, bitterly.

"I was an indulgent parent—I loved you —I denied you nothing," answered Beverley. "I let you squander my wealth—disperse it like dust before the wind."

"You fostered my evil passions with your weak pampering of my desires," said Richard. "I do not thank you for your liberality. Had you been less so, I should not have grown extravagant, gay, pleasure-seeking, as I am now. I spent recklessly, gambled, drank, picked up vile companions, and mingled the evil of their natures with my own. That is what I bought with your gold—that is the result of your generosity."

"Oh, cruel! cruel!" moaned Beverley. "He has no pity for me."

"Why should I?" said Richard. "You have been cruel to me my whole life long. You unfolded your dishonest plans to me—gave me glimpses of your revengeful nature, of your plots and wickedness. I profited by the lessons—I learnt them by *heart*. You cherished enmity against Judge Vincent for years—destroyed his happiness, ruined his peace, and suffered your hatred to recoil on his son, who had never harmed you. You planned to rob your friend of his fortune, his son of his honour, and I knew it all. What wonder I followed so worthy an example?"

"I shall go mad!" cried his father. "I love you, boy—I love you! and you are harder than flint towards me!"

"I loved Rachel, the actress," continued Richard; "I wished to marry her; but Paul Vincent stepped between us, and I began to practise your lesson of hatred and envy towards him. I wanted money for my revels, and you denied me, and I carried out your teaching of dishonesty. Still, I should never have committed this crime had it not been for *you*."

"For me—for me?" repeated his father.

"I felt interested in your motives for inquiring about the youth, when Clayton brought him to your memory. I played the spy on you, and one night followed you to the Jew's house. It was the night you told Marah how to rob her master. I was listening at the open window. I heard all about the money and jewels, and how to fix the guilt on Paul."

"For pity's sake, stay!" cried Beverley, in agony.

"I saw my way to a new supply of money, and to revenge on my rival. I made my plan, carried it out, and it has ended thus. I thank *you* for it, my *father!*"

He spoke the word scornfully, and thrust away the old man, who had drawn close to him.

"Come near me no more," he said, bitterly. "You have ruined me—you have dragged me into evil. I might have been honoured and respected this day, had I been a good man's son; now I suffer the doom you planned for an innocent boy. I shall be a convict, a felon, and abhorred by all the world: while he will rise to honour—will marry the woman I love."

"Oh, heaven! This indeed is retribution!" cried Beverley, as he fell forward on his face.

When they raised him, he was speechless—paralyzed—and was borne from the prison a pitiable sight, with a drawn, pinched face, glazed eyes, and helpless frame, to live through many weary years — a drivelling, imbecile, miserable old man.

Truly Marah had spoken, when she said, "He that diggeth a pit for his neighbour, shall himself fall into it."

CHAPTER XLVI.

PAUL'S innocence of the crime for which he had been condemned had been fully proved, and his discharge obtained from Portland.

It was a day of bustle and excitement at the judge's house.

The long-lost heir was coming to his home again—not branded with guilt, but having, through poverty, trial, persecution, and unmerited punishment, proved himself a true and honourable man.

Judge Vincent's face was radiant with happiness; he seemed to have lost twenty years of his age, and smiled, and jested, and spoke with the kindly graciousness of manner which had been his in the time of his youthful happiness, before sorrow had set its heavy hand on him.

So, as we have said before, there was a merry household in the once gloomy mansion that day; the rooms were decorated with flowers; in the hall the servants had erected a species of triumphal arch of green boughs; and in the great dining-room a feast was spread out, whose splendours formed a theme for conversation for many a long day afterwards in the domestic department of the family. Everybody was up with the first gleam of morning light, and everybody found something to do, something important in their eyes; and a subdued yet animated bustle of happiness pervaded the place.

Busiest of all was Mrs. Bentley, the worthy old housekeeper, who rustled among the merry labourers in a new satin gown, a present from her master, and wearing on her head a marvellous and imposing cap, decorated with white satin ribbons and the pinkest of roses, which cap was evidently the crowning pinnacle of her innocent vanity and delight.

It was her great boast on this auspicious day that she had believed in the goodness of her mistress against all the evil wagging of bitter tongues; that she had been her friend when all the world looked coldly upon her; and if ever woman was justified in her glorying, Mrs. Bentley was, for it was full of loyal devotion to those she had served faithfully since the days of her youth.

But of all the worthy soul's labours, her most assiduous ones were confined to the room which had been the judge's and Catherine's in their early wedded days.

"Nothing had been touched or changed," she said, as she glanced around it proudly on this morning. "Nothing touched or changed, save by the hand of Time. Everything remains as it was more than twenty years ago, when Mrs. Vincent came here a young, blooming bride. And here I am determined their first meeting shall take place."

So, when the judge made his appearance, and peeped into the little chamber to rally her on her zeal and industry, the old lady boldly preferred her request.

"You deserve something for your devotion," he answered. "And though, by right, I should welcome my wife and child on the threshold of their home, I yield to your request. Here let our reunion take place."

Mrs. Bentley smiled and then cried, and smiled again, as she thanked him.

"After all, Master William," she said, "it's only the matter of waiting a few moments longer before you see them. For my part, I wonder much you did not fetch the boy home from that horrible place."

"I stayed away by his own request," said the judge. "He wrote and asked me to wait for him here. I did not refuse, for I think I know his reason."

"A good one it will sure to be," cried the housekeeper, enthusiastically. "He's a noble lad, and he will be a blessing to you yet. Ay, ay," she continued, "he will—though I don't see how he *could* be otherwise. He comes of a good stock, and it was against all reason that he should disgrace and bring it to shame."

The judge smiled sadly; for, in truth, the worthy dame's argument was none of the most logical. It was one of affection and pride, rather than worldly reason.

"I can remember him as he lay in that cradle, a bonny, laughing, bright-eyed baby, that the wind was not allowed to blow on too roughly; and to think of all the misery he has endured—all the sorrow and suffering of his life till now! It makes my heart bleed—ay, and it makes my blood boil with rage against that dastardly lawyer—the smooth-tongued hypocrite, who worked all the mischief!"

"Hush, hush, Mrs. Bentley!" said the judge, while a look of pain crossed his face. "I cannot forget that he was once my friend--& at I loved him as a brother."

"Which makes his wickedness the blacker," said the irate dame.

"His judgment has fallen heavily upon him," returned her master. "It has stricken him to the very dust. Let us be silent about him."

"And willingly, too," cried Mrs. Bentley; "it brings a shadow upon even this happy day to remember that man."

She stood looking at the cradle reflectively.

"Master Paul will be somewhat changed to what he was when he lay there," she said. "He is a tall, fine fellow, now; and he will be bringing home a wife soon, I dare say."

"That is most probable," answered her master.

"And that cradle shall be saved for your grandchildren," she resumed. "And the coral and bells, which he never wore out, will be their toy. It's almost too much happiness to bear." And stooping, she tenderly touched the coral, which lay in its old place on the rug.

As she spoke, the noise of wheels was heard rattling up to the door, and a ringing cheer broke up from the hall, where the servants had stationed themselves to greet their master's son.

The judge turned pale, and stood trembling in the centre of the room, and looking anxiously towards the door.

"It's the young master," said Mrs. Bentley; and smoothing down her apron, she ran from the room, and hastily descending the stairs, saw Paul and his mother standing in the hall. And in her enthusiasm and joy, the good old dame almost hugged him, and wept copiously as she beckoned the pair upstairs to the room where Judge Vincent was awaiting them.

He was still standing where she had left him, his eyes beaming wistfully, his whole attitude full of impatience, as though he could scarcely restrain himself sufficiently to await their arrival. As they entered, the housekeeper drew back; and covering her face with her black silk apron, tottered across the passage, and, seating herself on the top stair, rocked to and fro in her exuberant joy and thanksgiving.

Catherine drew Paul forward, and stood with him before her husband.

"William," she said, softly, "your conditions are fulfilled. I have brought back our boy with a stainless name, as pure and good of heart as when I took him from yonder cradle, and fled from my home. And now I ask you to forgive me—to take me to your heart again, as in the days of our youth, when we were all in the wide world to each other."

"We have both much to forgive," said the judge. "If you have been doubtful of my love, I have been cruel and pitiless to you in your distress. Let the past be buried; let us glean what happiness remains for us in the future. Catherine, my own true wife!"

He held out his arms, and she nestled to his bosom, as in the old days, before their false friend had crept between them, sowing in their minds the seeds of jealousy and mistrust.

Paul stepped to the window, and drew his hand across his eyes, wiping away a mist of joyful tears.

Even his claim, sacred as it was, seemed for the moment forgotten, in the reunion of the long-parted husband and wife.

"Paul!"

It was his father who spoke. He still held Catherine on his arm, and as the youth turned, he gathered them closely to him.

"Heaven bless you both!" he said—"my own precious wife!—my noble boy! and restore to us in the coming years some portion of the happiness we have missed during our separation."

He kissed them; and just then Mrs. Bentley put her head into the room.

"If you please, Mr. William, the company are below stairs," she said. "And they are looking for you; and—and——"

"Come, in, Mrs. Bentley," said the judge, kindly; "and have your wish fulfilled—that of seeing those you have served so well, happy once more in your cherished old room."

"And a goodly sight it is!" said the housekeeper, advancing. "Mr. William, so bright and happy; Mrs. Vincent, so young and blooming still; and the baby, who used to lie and crow in my face in yonder cradle, a young man—and a handsome one, too, though I say it to his face. And, Mr. Paul, if I may make so bold," she added, going to the rug, and picking up the coral, "here is something you dropped in this room more than twenty years ago. It won't be of much use to you now; but they do say, you are going to be married to a charming young lady; and—and—I'm the happiest old woman in the world!"

And regardless of the cherished gloss on her silk apron, she rubbed her eyes diligently therewith; then with a fervent "Heaven bless us all!" ran from the room; and they heard her laughing and sobbing outside as she went down stairs.

A short time afterwards, the judge led the way to the room where the guests were assembled—a merry, jovial party.

His learned brethren of the bench, and a few eminent lawyers, with their wives and daughters; Mrs. Clayton and her family, and a goodly company of other friends.

As the judge, with his wife and son, came forward, a buzz of joy ran among them; and at last, led by a staid old magistrate, who looked incapable of action, they, too, burst into a hearty cheer, which rang through the old house, and was caught up by the servants without.

"Thanks, friends," said Judge Vincent. "Your kindly sympathy renders this bright day still brighter. I would make a speech if I could. As it is, I can only bid you welcome in the name of my wife and son, and hope that for each person here life may hold as much happiness as it promises to me from this day."

And then what hand-shakings, what congratulations were poured upon the two by the guests! They were tumultuous, infectious—everybody joined in them; and when they had poured them upon their host and his family, lavished them on each other; and if ever there was a merry party in England, that party was assembled in Judge Vincent's drawing-room.

Constance Clayton was introduced to Mrs. Vincent, and was warmly received by that lady, who now understood the scene through which the wily lawyer had worked upon her jealous nature, and driven her forth from her home.

"Your husband befriended me in the greatest sorrow of my life," said Constance. "I little thought my gratitude would have brought upon him such a trial. I can never repay the debt I owe him."

"You have done so already," said Catherine, smiling, and pressing her hand. "You comforted and saved my child in his misery and desolation. Henceforward I shall hold you dear to me as a sister."

But there were other claimants on the attention of Paul and his parents.

A little group whom every one regarded with honour and interest—not because they were wealthy, or of high birth, but because, through the dark passages of Paul's life, they had shone out as his faithful and loving friends. These were Mr. and Mrs. Morrison, old Levi Nathans, the Jew, and, last but not least, Rachel, who attracted universal admiration by her rare beauty.

A flash of joy passed over Paul's face as he saw them; and, hurrying across the room, he greeted them warmly, and glowingly led them towards the place were his parents were standing.

The judge kissed Rachel on the forehead, and Catherine enfolded her in a warm embrace, and spoke loving words, which called up smiles and blushes into the girl's fair and animated face, and made Paul still more radiant with delight.

"I always said he was something out of the common," said Morrison. "I've had a respect for him from the time when he told me his story, and, poor, helpless boy as he was, acted in a way which showed the true gentleman—the gentleman, not by accident of money or birth, but by nature. I'm proud I've known him; proud I have been associated with him in our noble histrionic profession; and I say, sir, in all true sincerity, in him you have a greater treasure than in all your wealth and just renown."

And having so delivered his sentiments, the worthy manager looked round him, and smiled on everybody benevolently.

"He was my pupil," said Levi Nathans; "and apt and clever he was. Such a head for learning!—he took to it as naturally as a duck to water. Oh, oh, Paul! we were through with the alphabet, and into Mavor's spelling-book in no time, and from there to *Claude Melnotte* was a swift step. Some day he will completely outrival his old master. But I don't think he will ever forget the pipes and the merry evenings we have enjoyed together."

"Never!" said Paul, patting him kindly on the shoulder. "I look forward to as many more."

"And now," said the judge, looking cheerfully around, "we will go in to breakfast; and marshalling his friends, he led the way to the banquet-room.

Paul took Rachel down, and proudly seated her by his father's side; while Catherine once more took her position as mistress of the household.

It was no stiff, formal feast; but a good, old-fashioned meeting, where every one so auspiciously assembled seemed determined to enjoy themselves.

There were toasts and speeches, and bright faces, and people seemed to vie with each other as to who should be brightest on the pleasant day. But of all the toasts that were drunk, none was so heartily drunk as that proposed by the judge himself, as he looked lovingly on Paul and Rachel, and filled a bumper to the health and happiness of his son's future bride.

CHAPTER XLVII.
FINALE.

THE autumn leaves were falling, and even the sunshine had a frosty glow, when a wedding-party drew near to the church.

As the carriages drew up before the portals of the sacred edifice, and the smiling, blushing bride stepped forth, followed by her train of fair young bridesmaids, and leaning on the arm of Judge Vincent, the crowd outside sent up a ringing cheer, and the crowd inside turned in their seats, and rustled their dresses, and whispered impatiently, as they looked for the procession.

In fact, the public excitement had reached its climax; for it was the wedding-day of the judge's son, Paul—the hero, who had endured so much unjust persecution—who had risked his life in nursing the stricken convicts in his prison.

And as the service proceeded, and the youth took to himself for wife the maiden he had loved through all the changes and vicissitudes of life, there was not a heart in all the vast crowd which did not breathe a blessing upon him, and wish the young pair joy.

Very beautiful Rachel looked, as, the ceremony over, she passed down the aisle, leaning on Paul's arm, and wearing the jewels which had shone on Levi's wife on her bridal day; and proudly Morrison and the old man moved among the guests, each wearing a huge white favour, and lauding his particular *protégé* to the skies.

"Mine now, for ever!" said Paul, as they entered the carriage. "I can scarcely believe in my happiness, after all the misery I have suffered."

She bent her bright head upon his shoulder, and nestled into the hand which wore the wedding ring.

"I am thinking of Ned the cripple," she said. "I wonder if he knows it is your wedding-day."

"Yes," said Paul. "I had a letter from the governor of the gaol to-day, in which Ned sends us his good wishes. The governor tells me he is to be retained to help watch the sick in the hospital, to do light duties there, according to his ability, and this by his own request. When his sentence expires, I shall make him my own particular care."

They were silent again for a time, but Paul's arm was clasped tightly round Rachel.

As they dashed round one corner, he whispered, "You remember this place? It is our old crossing. What a host of memories it brings to my mind! Our childish struggles; our parting; the time when I came back to London, and sat in the court, waiting for the apple-woman, and watching a solitary star twinkle in the sky. Ah, Rachel! times are altered now. I am rich, honoured, beloved; and my heart leaps up in thankfulness to the Power who has tenderly and lovingly watched over and guarded the life of even a vagabond."

THE END.

www.ingramcontent.com/pod-product-compliance
Lightning Source LLC
Chambersburg PA
CBHW031325160426
43196CB00007B/664